ARTFUL LIVES

# ARTFUL LIVES

## THE FRANCIS WATTS LEE FAMILY AND THEIR TIMES

PATRICIA J. FANNING

UNIVERSITY OF MASSACHUSETTS PRESS
*Amherst and Boston*

Printed in the United States of America

ISBN 978-1-62534-207-2 (pbk), 206-5 (hardcover)

Designed by Sally Nichols
Set in Adobe Jenson Pro and Gill Sans
Printed and bound by Sheridan Books, Inc.

Library of Congress Cataloging-in-Publication Data

Names: Fanning, Patricia J., author.
Title: Artful lives : the Francis Watts Lee family and their times / Patricia J. Fanning.
Description: Amherst : University of Massachusetts Press, 2016. | Includes bibliographical references and index.
Identifiers: LCCN 2016004216| ISBN 9781625342072 (pbk. : alk. paper) | ISBN 9781625342065 (hardcover : alk. paper)
Subjects: LCSH: Lee, Francis Watts. | Lee family. | Photographers—United States—Biography. | Printers—United States—Biography. | United States—Social life and customs—19th century.
Classification: LCC TR140.W3785 F36 2016 | DDC 770.92—dc23
LC record available at http://lccn.loc.gov/2016004216

British Library Cataloguing in Publication Data
A catalogue record for this book is available from the British Library.

Unless otherwise credited all photographs are from the
Library of Congress, Prints and Photographs Division,
Francis Watts Lee Collection,
Gift of the Francis Lincoln Lee Family.

*For D,*

*who, too, spent his life in the civil service*

# CONTENTS

# ILLUSTRATIONS

GALLERY (all by Francis Watts Lee)

# ARTFUL LIVES

# INTRODUCTION

This book is a biography of a man, a family, and, in many respects, an age. It begins with a haunting portrait, Gertrude Käsebier's *Blessed Art Thou among Women,* a photograph taken in 1899. A small girl, dressed in a spotless dark dress with crisp white collar and cuffs, dark leggings and shoes, has pulled herself up to her full height and stares boldly into the camera. Only the tenseness of her hands reveals a hesitancy or distraction. Her mother in a floor-length gown drapes one arm around the girl and, with head turned away from the viewer, leans in to offer either words of encouragement or caution. There is something indescribably moving about the tableau, which somehow encompasses the joy and the sorrow of motherhood while simultaneously capturing the anticipation and yet trepidation of the child. The image assumes a more symbolic status when one recognizes the print that hangs on the wall behind the figures as a representation of the Annunciation, the biblical event that gives the image its title. Furthermore, scholars have created layers of meaning from the fact that within months of this photograph's being made the young girl had died, leaving this poignant mother-daughter moment frozen in time. But what do we know about the husband and father, or the rest of the family missing from the picture? What of the life they were living in the room only glimpsed through the doorway? What happened to them?

The two models were contemporaneously identified as Agnes Rand Lee, a Boston poet, and her daughter, Peggy. But later twentieth-century scholars, having only second- and third-hand sources to follow, drew erroneous conclusions. They posited that Peggy's death was due to an infectious disease which also deafened her younger sister, Alice; that the devoutly Christian father, Francis Watts Lee, believed this dual tragedy had been visited upon his children because he had not entered the religious life; that the Lees' marriage ended because of his guilt. The truth was in many ways more mundane, yet situated the family within the religious, cultural, artistic, and medical contexts of the age. Individually and as a family, the struggles, triumphs, and failures of the Lees intersected with the widespread social changes wrought by industrialization, technological advancement, economic realities, and cultural attitudes at the turn of the century. Through an examination of this one family, it is possible to explore the ideals of Christian Socialism, Aestheticism, and the Arts and Crafts movement, as well as America's changing definitions of family, gender roles, childhood, medicine, deaf education, and even mourning. Together the Francis Watts Lee family provides detailed depth and context only hinted at by the image.

Each member of the intimate nuclear family of Francis Watts Lee has a standalone chapter to ensure that their personal biographies are told while the narrative moves forward in a chiefly chronological manner. Francis Watts Lee has two chapters, the first and the last, as the story begins and ends with him. Chapter 1 focuses on Lee's early life. Born in 1867, raised and educated in Boston, by the 1890s Lee was part of a group of ambitious, artistic young people. One of the most versatile members of this sparkling coterie, Lee was an accomplished printer and a talented photographer, skilled in both the workings of the hand-operated fine art press and the machinery of large-scale industrial printing. Married in 1890 to Agnes Rand and by the end of 1893 the father of two, when the panic of 1893 hit Lee accepted a position in the cataloguing department at the Boston Public Library. A little over a year later, when the library's Copley Square building was completed, he was appointed chief of the printing department.

In the late 1890s Lee turned to photography, where he worked alongside his friend Fred Holland Day and became acquainted with Alfred Stieglitz and, of course, Gertrude Käsebier, who eventually immortalized his wife and daughter. Lee was artistically gifted; his images, which often had the appearance of etchings, were praised by critics for their "simple elegance" and "grave reticence."[1] And it was his technological expertise that was largely responsible for introducing the distinctive soft-focus lens to American pictorialists. He exhibited his work to predominantly positive reviews beginning in 1898 and continuing until 1902, when he ceased participation in photographic salons and circles. Lee was a devout Episcopalian, a Christian Socialist, and founder, along with Ralph Adams Cram, of Boston's Church of the Carpenter. Lee was also an officer in the Church Association for the Advancement of the Interests of Labor and he was a lifelong advocate for the working class.

Lee married twice. His first wife, Martha Agnes Rand, is the subject of chapter 2. Five years his senior and the daughter of Chicagoan William H. Rand, cofounder of the printing and publishing firm Rand, McNally & Company, Agnes had traveled extensively, lived abroad, and was educated in Europe. She undoubtedly had expectations of an upper-middle-class lifestyle that included servants, travel, and many social engagements. Lee, whose own father had been a successful banker before his death when the boy was twelve, may have had some difficulty maintaining such affluence. Still, the family bought a large house in Jamaica Plain on the outer edges of the city of Boston and delighted in their two daughters. Agnes wrote poetry and children's verse. Her children's book *The Round Rabbit* was among her publisher's most successful offerings. Agnes became a frequent model for her husband and his pictorialist colleagues, and, like Francis, she was a supporter of the Arts and Crafts movement. Most especially, Agnes was devoted to her two children.

Harriet Templeton ("Peggy") Lee (chapter 3) was the couple's first child. Born at a time when notions about childhood were evolving, Peggy was a cherished daughter, encouraged to participate in contemporary play and school activities by an affectionate mother and doting father. Beautiful, photogenic, and comfortable in front of the camera, she became a favorite subject for pictorialist photographers and family friends F. Holland Day and Gertrude Käsebier. Her angelic countenance graced photographic salons and journals before she was five; she was only seven when she died of juvenile diabetes. As sudden and devastating as it was, Peggy's death left her grieving parents to cope in a transitioning landscape of mourning. The Victorian Age was coming to a close and the commonly accepted bereavement rituals and accompanying consolations were no longer embraced by modern families. It was after Peggy's death that the Lee's marriage faltered; they divorced in 1910.

While Peggy's illness had brought Agnes and Francis unwillingly into contact with medical limits, death, and grief, their second daughter, Alice Stephana (chapter 7), who lost her hearing in infancy, introduced the family to the ongoing debate over deaf education. For cultural as well as educational reasons, advocates of speech and lipreading had challenged the manualist tradition of sign since shortly after the Civil War. By the 1890s, when the Lees were considering the available options for their daughter's education, oralism had surpassed sign language in popularity. As a toddler, therefore, Alice was enrolled at the Chicago Kindergarten Home for the Deaf, following which she spent twelve years at the Clarke School for the Deaf in Northampton, Massachusetts, one of the first oralist schools in the nation. Alice Stephana thrived at Clarke. Eventually she studied wood carving and sculpture in Boston, Chicago, and Florence, Italy and became a working craftswoman.

A few months after their divorce was finalized, both Agnes Rand Lee and Francis Watts Lee married again. Returning to the city of her youth, Agnes wed the well known and respected Chicago surgeon Otto T. Freer and settled comfortably into the literary and social circles of Chicago. Although Alice Stephana continued to visit the East Coast during summer months, she resided chiefly with her mother and stepfather, taking classes at the Art Institute and participating in the activities of the Chicago League for the Hard of Hearing.

For his part, Francis Watts Lee married Marion Lewis Chamberlain, a widow with her own tragic story, which is told in chapter 8. Born in 1874, the eldest child of a working-class family, Marion Lewis graduated from MIT in 1896 with a degree in architecture, one of only a handful of women to do so at that time. She married fellow architect Herbert Chamberlain but was widowed within the year and returned to the fine arts department of the Boston Public Library, a position she had accepted right out of college. She continued in library work for more than a decade with the exception of a short, disappointing few months in the Chicago studio of Frank Lloyd Wright. Marion and Francis had two children, Lucy and Francis. Marion suffered from anxiety and depression and, despite her efforts to understand her illness, she was plagued by unhappiness and instability for the rest of her life.

Meanwhile, Francis Watts Lee remained at the Boston Public Library. Chapter 9 brings his and the family's story to a close by examining his nearly fifty years in printing. As the first head of the printing department at the Boston Public Library, Lee installed and ran the linotype machine and various presses needed to produce the library's publications. He worked long hours, six days a week and, as the years passed, he lost touch with the idealistic, ambitious, fin-de-siècle colleagues of his youth. In the end, it seems, he was a frustrated, disgruntled employee, complaining in annual reports about too much work and too little help. In 1937 he retired. Lee had begun work at the BPL during the depression of the 1890s and ended his career there in the Great Depression of the 1930s.

In contrast to these biographical accounts, the three middle chapters have photographs as their primary focus. *Blessed Art Thou among Women* (chapter 4) and *The Heritage of Motherhood* (chapter 6) are iconic images in the canon of American photography. Here they are discussed not simply as exquisite examples of the work of the famed pictorialist Gertrude Käsebier but as symbolic portraits of the Lee family within the larger historical, social, and cultural context. These two chapters plus chapter 5, "The Daughters of Francis Watts Lee," are also vehicles for the exploration of the ideals of the Arts and Crafts movement, pictorialism, society's attitudes toward art, and the evolving definitions of childhood, family, and bereavement.

Photographs have long been utilized in historical and social science research to learn about the people and material culture they depict. In their evaluations of each image scholars consider not only the process and presentation of a photograph but also what social scientist John Scott calls its "social biography."[2] By exploring the intentions and decisions of the photographer as well as the intended viewers, the researcher can begin to understand how the practice of making the picture is connected to its purpose and audience.[3] Visual sociology has often been employed to study photographs as mediations understanding, as Douglas Harper puts it; that "all images . . . are socially and technically constructed" and thus reflective of the assumptions, purposes, and aesthetics of the photographer.[4] Sociologists are keenly aware of the deliberative nature of any photograph and are, for example, quick to question the work of photographic documentarians who purport to be objective yet use and, in some instances, manipulate their images to advance specific social causes.[5] As the historian Alan Trachtenberg notes, "American photographs are not simple depictions. . . . [T]he history they show is inseparable from the history they enact: a history of photographers employing their medium to make sense of their society."[6] This is particularly true of the pictorialists, whose images were carefully mounted, purposive tableaux with, in the words of the art historian George Dimock, "social implications and symbolic connotations" of their own.[7] For this reason, I have here described and interpreted the "art" of F. Holland Day, Gertrude Käsebier, and Francis Watts Lee with an eye for the texture, light, symbolism, and spatial organizations these artists were known to use.

At the same time, applying the tools and insights of the historian and the social scientist adds a biographical element to this image work. As Susan Sontag wrote, "Photography is an elegiac art. . . . To take a photograph is to participate in another person's . . . mortality, vulnerability, mutability."[8] The "exposure" of the photographic plate simultaneously "exposes" the subject to interpretation, first by the artist and then by others who bring cultural considerations, motives, and attitudes of their own to the viewing. The historical and autobiographical detail uncovered by archival research allows Agnes, Peggy, Alice, and Marion each to have a voice in her own pictorial narrative. Finally, by utilizing C. Wright Mills's "sociological imagination," a study of wider social trends, movements, and realities provides an overarching framework and links each individual's personal biography to the larger cultural history. In this way the book becomes both a biography and a social history.[9]

Two final notes concerning the use of photographs as primary source material are pertinent. First, the era being examined was one in which the production and use of images underwent a dramatic transformation. By the 1920s, "camera work" was accessible to most people and the ubiquitous family snapshot had taken the place of formal portraits. At the same time, these newly minted photo enthusiasts were capturing the increasing informality of twentieth-century life. These parallel changes are especially noticeable when the maternal photographs of nineteenth-century Agnes Rand Lee are viewed alongside those of the twentieth-century mother Marion Chamberlain Lee. The contrast is striking and is representative not only of technological advancement but also of cultural shifts.

Second, the issue of archival and digital photographic resources must be addressed. Online archives of images are increasing. Two important repositories, the Thanatos archive of early postmortem and mourning photography (http://thanatos.net) and the Burns archive of historical and medical images (www.burnsarchive.com) along with significant pictorialist collections found at Photoseed (http://photoseed.com) and Corbis (www.corbisimages.com) are but four examples of collections that are available to researchers worldwide. Other extensive collections can be found in the digital and physical archives of the Library of Congress (www.loc.gov) and other institutional repositories.[10] All of these sources and more can deepen and widen any scholar's understanding of life, culture, and society through visual reproductions. Whether images are housed in a virtual or a physical archive, however, often, Peggy Tinkler has observed, "the original photographic meanings are lost as photos are relocated . . . from their original contexts and uses."[11] While these vast digital archives have their place in the exploration of subjects and cultural trends—as, for example, the Thanatos website and archive, which provides a wealth of information about mourning pictures and practices in historical context—they do not help explain the specialized elements of the photographer's decisions, as Trachtenberg notes, about "where to place the edge of the picture, what to exclude, from what point of view to show the relations among included details."[12] Images (particularly images as artifacts) are most affecting when encountered in a private collection within the context of relationships and attachments. Although their content remains intact, these selected, classified, cataloged, and captioned "photo-objects," as Tinkler terms them, are very different from the powerful prints retained for familial viewing and sharing. "It is important that you factor the archive in to your analysis," Tinkler cautions. "You need to be wary of the archive's impression of innocence and reflect on what kinds of histories are preserved, reworked or obscured by it."[13] Although now housed at the Library of Congress, the majority of photographs in this book were located and initially encountered in family collections, where their emotional impact and authenticity were at their most immediate.

The narrative that follows, then, was inspired by a single work of art, Gertrude Käsebier's *Blessed Art Thou among Women.* My curiosity was piqued by the portrait and I wanted to know more about the woman, child, and family behind the image. I wanted to discover, as the historian Shawn Michelle Smith puts it, "What resides at the literal and metaphorical edge of the photograph? What remains just outside the frame?"[14] My intention, following Alan Trachtenberg's phrase, was to "make sense" of the family of Francis Watts Lee and their society not simply by consulting and assembling the available archival and historical documents but by looking carefully at the photographic evidence—to peer behind the figures in the doorway, into the room, and into the lives beyond.

## *Chapter 1*
# FRANCIS WATTS LEE

For an adolescent like Francis Watts Lee, attracted to learning, art, and questions of faith, there could be no better place to come of age than Boston's Back Bay in the 1880s.[1] Beginning two decades earlier with the Massachusetts Institute of Technology (MIT) and its neighbor the Boston Society of Natural History, a remarkable number of educational institutions were located adjacent to or near Copley Square.[2] Twenty years later as MIT—where Alexander Graham Bell gave his first public demonstration of his telephonic speech machine in 1876—expanded to numerous sites all over the neighborhood, the area had become home to Harvard Medical School, the Massachusetts Normal Art School, the Horace Mann School for the Deaf, Boston University, and Northeastern University, which began in upstairs rooms belonging to the Copley Square Young Men's Christian Association (YMCA). Thomas J. Lee, a successful banker, moved his family to Marlborough Street in the Back Bay in the late 1870s, where Francis spent his teenage years surrounded by the intellectual atmosphere and scientific synergy these institutions created.[3]

FIGURE 1. Allen and Rowell, Francis Watts Lee, 1877, albumen silver print. (PR13 CN2015.052.565)

Little is known about Lee's early childhood or primary schooling, but two portraits of the boy at age four and ten show a handsome, curly-haired child of some affluence; in each he is fashionably outfitted and in the latter he exudes a solemn confidence, his left arm propped casually on a large book (figure 1). By 1882, three years following the death of his father, he was a student at Chauncy

Hall, a liberal preparatory school then located in a Gothic Revival building at the corner of Boylston and Dartmouth Streets within sight of Copley Square. Chauncy Hall provided the perfect environment for an astute, inquisitive, multitalented youth. The curriculum was steeped in the classics, including Latin and Greek, augmented by mathematics and science. French, Italian, Spanish, and German classes formed whenever four or more pupils expressed interest. Advanced offerings included music, drawing, and the study of art, not unexpected considering Chauncy Hall's proximity to the Normal Art School, the Boston Art Club, the St. Botolph Club and its gallery, and the recently opened Museum of Fine Arts (1870), located across the square.[4] As Lewis Mumford wrote, "It was in the Back Bay that Boston first established itself as one of the centers of world culture in the arts and sciences."[5] Here, only a few blocks from home, Lee came to know other young people similarly captivated by the ongoing cultural transformation around them. Among his classmates were Hermann Dudley Murphy, later a master craftsman, frame maker, and landscape painter, and Fred Holland Day, who shared Lee's enthusiasm for both photography and the print arts.

The proliferation of these educational and artistic organizations in the Copley Square neighborhood was not a haphazard occurrence; it was the result of an attempt by Boston's urban elites to differentiate their own high culture and refined tastes from the culture and tastes of the working class and burgeoning immigrant populations. Before the Civil War, there had been few attempts to separate art and entertainment. For example, according to one scholar, "Moses Kemball's Boston Museum exhibited works by such painters as [Thomas] Sully and [Charles Wilson] Peale alongside Chinese curiosities, stuffed animals, mermaids and dwarves," while the museum's associated theater combined high and low art by alternating "gymnasts and contortionists with leading actors of the American and British stage presenting the work of [Charles] Dickens and [William] Shakespeare." By the 1870s, however, the city's upper class had not only consolidated their economic power but had also "united in an aesthetic ideology that distinguished sharply between the nobility of art and the vulgarity of mere entertainment."[6] Boston's Brahmin families, another historian notes, together founded a "network of institutions . . . so effectively in their private control—beyond popular or governmental intervention—that the link between culture and class was reinforced."[7] The Back Bay, a newly created land mass, provided the perfect blank canvas for this elite to populate and to establish or expand its cultural organizations, all just outside Francis Watts Lee's door—and he took advantage of all they offered.

Lee was especially drawn to spiritual matters and early on forged a deep relationship with the Episcopal Church, possibly following the example of his maternal grandfather, Francis O. Watts. Born in Maine in 1803, Watts arrived in Boston in 1818, graduated from Harvard and became a respected lawyer. In 1852 he was selected to be the founding president of the city's YMCA, the first in the country, a position he held until debilitated by illness. According to his 1860 obituary, "Mr. Watts was a devout member of the Episcopal Church, which rejoiced in such a treasure as she found in his wisdom, experience and zeal."[8] His grandson and namesake, Francis Watts Lee, came to the church at a time when, as the cultural historian T. J. Jackson Lears notes, many believers had turned away from a stern Calvinist doctrine, "blunted all the sharp edges in Protestant tradition and produced a bland relation of reassurance." More significant, as Lears demonstrates, clergy and parishioners alike avoided discussions of social conflict and inequality and instead "promoted a vision of progress and harmony that sanctioned status quo social arrangements . . . reinforcing the cultural dominance of their own class."[9]

The result, Lears continues, was twofold. First, "Protestant churches steadily lost influence over a restive urban proletariat as influential clergy tended to their affluent flocks [and] dismissed the complaints of the underpaid and jobless." Thus immigrants and workers felt that religion failed to embrace their concerns or reality. Second, as the clergy led their parishioners away from evangelicalism and its need for an intense conversion experience, religion's vitality and emotional vigor vanished. Lee, along with many of his contemporaries, was dissatisfied with this "spiritual blandness." They yearned for a passionate spirituality, one that embraced social activism and reclaimed the power and majesty of belief. While the Protestant urban elite "sought to exorcise the last vestiges of shadow and magic from their creeds," this younger generation tried to bolster the mysterious while at the same time advocating for social change and individual experience.[10] Deeply affected by this debate, after his graduation from Chauncy Hall, Lee traveled the European continent where, like others of his acquaintance, including Ralph Adams Cram and Fred Holland Day, he was inspired by an exposure to European cathedrals, sacred art, liturgies, ritual, and "supernatural verities."[11] They returned to the United States with a desire to combine an Anglo-Catholicism, an outlook that emphasized the Roman Catholic rather than Protestant heritage, with social reform and creative work, sensing that to unite all three would ensure a meaningful and devotional life experience. In his later autobiography Cram recalled "the tentative motions made toward creative action, and the workings of that spiritual influence that seemed to be implicit in the air we breathed."[12]

Cram, a native of New Hampshire and son of a Unitarian minister, came to Boston as an architectural apprentice in 1881. His own 1886 European journey resulted in a conversion experience; upon his return to the United States, he embraced Anglo-Catholic theology. In spite of his own later assurances that "fundamentally we had, I think, a genuine seriousness both of outlook and purpose," the young architect was also responsible for a good deal of camaraderie and entertainment. He organized a men-only dining club, the Association of the Pewter Mugs, open to all "provided he did, or tried to do, something constructive along any line, was companionable with his fellows, enjoyed a certain Elizabethan tang in the social proceedings and had a sound taste in malt liquors." Members at various times included "Bliss Carman, Bertram Goodhue, Fred Bullard, George Hallowell, Richard Hovey, Fred Day, Thomas Meteyard, Herbert Copeland, Herbert Small, Herbert Stone, Ingalls Kimball, and Frank Lee." A smaller, more select group, self-identified as "the Visionists," described by Cram as "the madder and more fantastic members of the Pewter Mugs," gathered in third-floor rooms off Boston's Province Court, a dilapidated commercial neighborhood populated primarily by tradesmen, where they engaged in costumed rituals, fiery debate, and good-humored, rather adolescent antics.[13]

Francis Watts Lee was invited to join the Visionists in November 1892 by Fred Day. Somewhat intrigued, Lee wanted to learn more about the group. "I feel as if I know little of its nature and purposes," he explained, then went on to note, half in jest, "They tell me I am visionary in some ways, but I do not know that I am therefore a Visionist. Who are the rest?"[14] Unlike most of his contemporaries, the intense, serious-minded Lee, although only twenty-five, had a wife and child to support, and the naive trappings and somewhat juvenile posturing of these young Bohemians may not have appealed to him, but he shared their passion, idealism, and commitment to art and beauty. Beginning in 1892, the group produced two short-lived periodicals, *The Mahogany Tree* and

*The Knight Errant*, the latter of which Lee printed at his own Elzevir Press. Lee contributed an article concerned with the print arts to *The Knight Errant* and his wife, Agnes, published a poem in the journal.[15] In many ways, Lee's beliefs reflected the fin-de-siècle aestheticism of the Visionists, who believed, in Lears's words, that "modern culture had narrowed the range and diffused the intensity of human experience." Together they called for a "regeneration" of occupational intensity in an age of rampant industrialism and particularly advocated fulfillment "through preindustrial craftsmanship and a pastoral 'simple life.'"[16] Still, within a decade most of these young idealists inevitably followed their individual paths into conventional professions and mainstream lifestyles. Lee continued to combine his political activism and religious fervor, however, and found like-minded advocates within the American Episcopal Church.

As Lears points out in his analysis of this period, Anglo-Catholicism was often considered "a more self-conscious form of Episcopalian elitism," yet there were theological and instrumental differences. "Anglo-Catholics," Lears contends, "led in developing an Episcopal social gospel." In Lee's case this inspired a firm commitment to Christian Socialism, an activist strand of Episcopalianism that sought to apply Christian beliefs to social and economic inequalities.[17] Lee was a parishioner of the Society of St. John the Evangelist, an Anglican monastic order known as the Cowley Fathers, who, under the leadership of Arthur C. A. Hall and Charles Neale Field, ministered to the poor on the side streets and alleyways surrounding their Bowdoin Street church. Hall was also behind St. Augustine's, a mission church for blacks on Beacon Hill. For these activities and others, Oliver Wendell Holmes noted of St. John's that it was "a church with open doors, with seats for all classes and all colors alike."[18] Although he was involved in these ministries, Lee sought affiliations with groups that had even stronger socialist leanings as well. Along with Ralph Adams Cram, he became a founding member of the Church of the Carpenter, a congregation led by Rev. William Dwight Porter Bliss, then recognized as "one of the most prominent spokesmen for the left wing of the Social Gospel."[19]

Born in Turkey, Bliss was educated at Phillips Academy, Amherst College, and Hartford Theological Seminary. He was ordained a Congregationalist minister but joined the Episcopal Church because of his belief in the Christian Socialist doctrine advocated by Anglican leaders. The clergyman's critique of the prevailing social system focused on "unbearably long hours of labor, unjust division of profits, land monopolies, [and] the inequitable protection of manufacturers rather than laborers," in the words of the historian Arthur Mann.[20] Aiming to put an end to distinctions and divisions between all classes within society, Bliss founded the Society of Christian Socialists in 1889, edited its periodical *The Dawn* (even financing it after 1890) and played an important role in the Church Association for the Advancement of the Interests of Labor (CAIL).[21] His unconventional Church of the Carpenter held services in various storefronts and halls throughout Boston. Believing there had been an "increasing degradation of the proletariat since the advent of capitalism," Bliss hoped his church would attract liberals of the middle and upper classes as well as the working poor. He kept his definitions of "Christian" and "Socialism" broad, saying only that Protestantism had "carried individualism too far" and that Christian Socialism meant "the sacrifice of the individual, the sacrifice of self for the good of all."[22]

Francis Watts Lee too was concerned by the class distinctions he saw around him. In his *Knight Errant* article he criticized exquisitely produced "pretentious volumes" he called "badges of class distinction" which were created "*for* the luxurious" consumer. "They are helping to raise ever higher and higher the wall of separation behind which an increasing class strive to take their ease while thanking God that they are not as other men are."[23] Sincerely embracing Christian Socialist ideals, he acted as committee member for the Mission of the Carpenter and was associate editor of *The Dawn*. He also contributed a monthly column to the journal titled "Notes on the Social Teaching of the Christian Year" in which he explained the associations he saw between the Christian calendar, scripture, and contemporary social problems. During this same time period, Lee was also a frequent contributor to *St. Andrews Cross* and the *Boston Evening Transcript* on matters of faith, political economy, and morality. Following the serious economic depression of 1893, Bliss's CAIL merged with the Christian Social Union to form the Church Social Union. Lee became secretary of the new organization, among whose objectives were "to study in common how to apply the moral truths and principles of Christianity to the social and economic difficulties of the present time."[24]

One month earlier, on April 14, Lee had asked his friend Fred Holland Day, then traveling in England, to "buy any new book on the relation of Socialism to the Prayer Book or The Church which you may hear of or see," noting, "By 'socialism' I mean any phase of the social problem." Along with this request, he sought "The Church Reformer . . . vols. 1 & 2 to complete my set" and "all published sermons, whether books, pamphlets, or in papers" by the Reverend Thomas Hancock. Hancock's sermons in particular, he wrote, "will be apt to be of great help to me in what I am doing."[25] As a champion of labor and a working man himself—he was by this time employed at the Boston Public Library—Lee was a supporter of the Pullman strike of 1894. When the Church Social Union published a pamphlet on the railroad strike, it included a "Bibliography compiled by Mr. Francis Watts Lee, of the Boston Public Library, which contained numerous references as to the more notable contemporaneous newspaper and periodical comment on the strike." That year and the next Lee produced two other socialist tracts: *A Proposed Constitution for the Church Social Union* (1894) and *Suggestions for Reading on Social Reform* (1895). A few years earlier Lee had edited a selection of writings by William Morris, who, Lee wrote, "has devoted his splendid gifts to the service of the Socialist cause."[26]

Through his involvement in CAIL and his position as secretary of the Church Social Union, Lee became acquainted with another priest of the Episcopal Church, Rev. James Otis Sargent Huntington. Born in Roxbury, Massachusetts, Huntington went to Harvard and St. Andrew's Divinity School in Syracuse, New York, entering the priesthood in 1880. He was initially associated with the Society of St. John the Evangelist and its church on Bowdoin Street in Boston as well as the Church of the Advent. Finding his mission working among the poor, Huntington was a tireless union and land-tax advocate and a founding member of both CAIL and the Church Social Union. In 1884, along with two other priests, he founded the Order of the Holy Cross, a Benedictine Anglican monastic order for men.[27]

Lee, a man of many talents and nearly indefatigable energy, was able to use his relationship with Huntington to expand his artistic endeavors into the field photography. Already a well-regarded printer whose production of the Visionist's journal *The Knight Errant* had been highly praised, Lee may well have taken up photography as a further creative outlet in the 1890s after he closed his Elzevir Press and went to work at the Boston Public Library. Traditional studio portraits of four clergymen, including Huntington, clothed in the black cassock and cross emblematic of their life vows in the Order of the Holy Cross, were among Lee's earliest photographic

FIGURE 2. Francis Watts Lee, Rev. William H. van Allen, c. 1899, platinum print. (PR13 CN2015.052.38)

efforts.[28] Rev. William H. van Allen (figure 2), later rector of the Church of the Advent, posed for formal portraits by Lee as well, a fact attested to by mutual friend Louise Imogen Guiney, who wrote to van Allen in 1897 about a visit to the Lee household where she "found, on the library mantel, your effigy, and also Fr. Huntington's."[29]

Guiney was much admired by those who called themselves Visionists. To Cram's mind she was "the most vital and creative personal influence in the lives of all of us who gathered together at this time."[30] Although only a few years their senior, she was already an accomplished poet and essayist. As a devout Roman Catholic with an ecumenical spirit, she seemed to be living, in Lears's words, "the authentic occupational, spiritual, and emotional experience" these young Bostonians were striving to achieve.[31] Full of courage, good humor, and love of life in the face of financial instability and hardship, Guiney was a generous and unwavering friend to many, including Francis Watts Lee. Although well acquainted with van Allen, Guiney had not met Huntington but recognized him at once: "In fact," she wrote to van Allen, "I walked over to [Huntington's portrait] and addressed it instantly by its own name."[32] Lee's ability to capture Huntington's personal magnetism in his portraiture may account for Guiney's immediate identification, for soon enough Lee joined the circle of Boston photographers then embracing pictorialism.

Inspired by the photographer Peter Henry Emerson, who declared in 1886 that "in capable hands, a finished photograph is a work of Art," a generation of photographers sought to prove the aesthetic value of their craft by emphasizing the artistic rather than the documentary aspects of the medium.[33] Pictorialists, as they came to be known, achieved images that often had the appearance of lithographs or etchings, and they used subjects, settings, and poses that were explicitly reminiscent of the canvas. In fact, one critic commented that some of Lee's portraits had "the qualities of a soft pencil drawing."[34] As a means of creative expression, photography appealed to Francis Watts Lee in several ways. His expertise with printing, particularly the hand press and its relation to other graphic arts, made photography a natural extension of his interests and talents. As a follower of William Morris, Lee believed that all work, including printing and photography, had an artistic as well as a utilitarian purpose, and thus the photographer's creative experience mirrored the engaged emotional intensity that he and the Visionists were seeking. Furthermore, Lee's friendship with F. Holland Day and his circle put him in touch with those craftsmen working at the forefront of the movement. In fact, he and his family became noteworthy subjects among these early practitioners of the art of the camera. Day and the New York photographer Gertrude Käsebier both frequently photographed Lee's wife, Agnes Rand Lee, and the couple's two daughters, Peggy and Alice.

Lee was the subject of works by Käsebier as well. In a well-known portrait, he is seated at a work table, dressed in a well-cut suit, bearded and professional, gazing forthrightly into the camera. In a second image, taken at about the same time, the once again professionally attired Lee seems very self-assured and confident seated in an elaborately carved wooden arm chair. His left leg is

FIGURE 3. Gertrude Käsebier, Francis Watts Lee with pipe, c. 1899, platinum print. (PR13 CN2015.052.552)

crossed over his right, and one hand rests on his lap as he sits back comfortably holding an impressively long smoking pipe to his mouth (figure 3). Louise Guiney believed that Lee's serious countenance and charisma should earn him a part in F. Holland Day's photographic series on the crucifixion. She wrote to Day suggesting that "Lee would be an admirable figure for the Christ; he has the true enthusiast look." She added a cautionary note, however, fearing Lee's political views and fervor might become too apparent: "You must be careful not to let him be fierce; and William—Morris—Socialistic instead of divinely democratic."[35]

There is no written record of Lee's initial artistic photographs, the evolution of his style, or his aesthetic aims and intentions. By 1898, however, Day, who had been inducted into England's famed Linked Ring Brotherhood of artistic photographers in 1895, introduced Lee to the London photographic community. Francis James Mortimer, writing in *Photograms of the Year 1898*, noted that Lee had "produced half a dozen thoroughly good portrait studies," three of which "fall into a class by themselves."[36] Lee exhibited four of his prints at the Linked Ring's Sixth Photographic Salon that same year and one of these was reproduced in the *Photograms of the Year.* Mortimer found the image *Theodora*, the portrait of a young woman in an intricately laced gown, elaborate headpiece and veil, "most satisfactory. The white background, white drapery, and subdued detail, throw the face into strong relief." Lee allowed the model's light costume to recede into the even lighter backdrop using a technique called "vignetting." "The style is not new," Mortimer commented, "but Mr. Lee has worked it at least as well as the few who have gone before him, and this is saying much."[37]

Lee employed the same effect a year later to critical acclaim at the Second Philadelphia Photographic Salon of 1899. Titled *The Vision*, "the portrait of a woman so delicately rendered that it faded away almost imperceptibly into the white background," as the critic Joseph T. Keiley described it in *Camera Notes*, the piece left viewers wondering if Lee had captured an apparition (plate 1). Keiley declared the work a success: "The face was of a spirituelle type, full of delicate refinement and feeling, and the wide-open eyes, which look squarely out at the observer, were so soft with some strange, sacred sadness, that they haunted me long after and made me feel that there are depths in the heart of a woman that man can never know."[38] Lee again seemed to reflect the soul of his sitter and impressed the critics in his *Portrait of Miss E. H.* (plate 2), a work he exhibited often. For this portrait of their family friend Emily Hallowell, daughter of the Civil War hero Edward Needles Hallowell, he depended entirely on the interplay of light and shadow to set off her profile against her dark clothing and even darker background. Keiley, again writing for *Camera Notes* declared that the *Portrait of Miss E. H.*, "the head of a woman of middle age shown in profile, is really an exquisite piece of work, treated with a simple elegance that is almost classic. Of its kind it was the most perfect thing that I have ever seen."[39]

For the most part Lee refrained from including theatrical, architectural, or decorative elements in his photographs, and background scenery was nearly nonexistent, but he was able to reveal the character and mood of his sitters, particularly women, in his straightforward, unadorned compositions. In February

1900, the Boston Camera Club, in an effort to increase its public image and attract new members, mounted an exhibition of Massachusetts photographers who had displayed their work at recent photographic salons. Lee's group of fourteen prints was second in number only to that of F. Holland Day. In his discussion of the exhibit, the critic William Howe Downes called Lee's ability to capture "the psychological moment" in his portraiture "extraordinary," commenting that "it is a difficult matter to define in set terms the intimate charm of this sort of work, apparently so easy and simple, yet really so subtile [*sic*] and thoughtful." Downes also drew attention to the sitters themselves: "Mr. Lee's people look like members of the mental aristocracy. . . . His ideal appears to be the expression of character and of cerebral vitality, rather than that of any conventional material or physical type of perfection."[40]

Lee continued to submit his small body of work to various exhibitions and salons, including the Third Philadelphia Photographic Salon in 1900, where Keiley commented that "the four pictures shown by Francis Watts Lee do not rank with the work exhibited by him last year." Yet the critic understood the reasons for this deficiency. Lee spent long hours at his job at the Boston Public Library and remained involved in his social reform activities. He also had shouldered increased familial responsibilities when his sister's health began to deteriorate and his in-laws came to live with his family. "It would be difficult for a far less busy man than Mr. Lee to keep up to the exceptionally high standard . . . set by him," Keiley assured his readers, a standard "which so suddenly advanced him to the ranks of the most advanced workers."[41]

F. Holland Day included nine of Lee's prints in his *New School of American Photography* mounted in London and Paris beginning in 1900. This exhibition was particularly well received in France, where the critic Robert Demachy may have had Lee's work in mind when he wrote his positive assessment of the American style of photography and its reliance on "the expression of the eyes and mouth to give the effect of life and thought."[42] Lee seemed to specialize in the contemplative image, studies often infused with what one writer called a "grave reticence." Day too noted the distinctive quality of Lee's portraits. Comparing him with two other pictorialists, Sarah C. Sears and William Dyer, Day concluded, "Mr. Lee's work is more 'photographic' than that of either of the others, but it has as well a feeling of greater calm and perhaps spirituality."[43]

Another of Lee's portraits won particular praise from Alvin Langdon

Coburn. *A New England Saint,* a three-quarter-length portrait of a woman in profile dressed in a dark, fitted coat and hat, head bowed slightly over what appears to be a choral book, captured a quiet, still moment in time. It was similar in its emotional tone and character to Day's *Hannah,* which Keiley had called "a pronounced piece of realism" focusing on "an unmistakable type of a New England woman." Likening Day's image to "a whole novel of Miss Wilkins," one critic placed Day's work squarely within the realm of New England local-color literature, a then-popular women-dominated genre of realistic writing. Mary E. Wilkins (later Freeman) was a leader of the local color school. *A New England Saint* too depicted the quintessentially American stereotype embraced by local colorists, the simple, self-sacrificing female head of household. "In this picture," Coburn wrote, "Mr. Lee has given us a character sketch of an individual often seen in country church choirs, but seldom if ever rendered with such fidelity photographically," concluding, "This is surely one of the most successful pictures in the exhibition."[44] Lee's portraits of men effectively focused on personality and moments of vitality. The models for *Portrait of Mr. H.* and *Portrait of Mr. B.* (plate 3) both seemingly strain against the stillness of their poses and yearn for movement. Each is a study in black. One writer called *Portrait: Mr. B.* "splendid in colour and tone," and the critic for *Photographic Times* commented that "Mr. Lee's work shows virility," but, for the most part, his photographs of men received less attention than his character studies of women.[45]

Sophisticated equally in mechanical and artistic processes, Lee developed his own prints and experimented with various techniques. Of the eleven portraits he lent to the Second Exhibition of the Arts and Crafts Society, Boston, in 1899, two were labeled "Mercury developed platinum" prints, one was a "Cold mercury developed platinum," and two others were "Manipulated print[s]."[46] Lee also developed or at least assisted Day in producing his prints for a time. "If tomorrow is fine," he wrote to Day, "I'm going to devote the day to printing for your benefit since it is my off day."[47]

Lee's technical curiosity and aptitude extended to photographic equipment as well as the chemical development of prints. His search for ways to create diffusion and control focus led Lee to a British lens manufacturer and an eventual collaboration with Henry Smith from the Pinkham & Smith Company, prescription opticians and photographic suppliers in Boston. With the resultant lens, a generation of American artists created the diffused and atmospheric images that came to define pictorialism. Many credited F. Holland Day with commissioning this first-ever soft-focus lens made for pictorial photographers in the United States.[48] By his own account, however, Day was not the initiator of the lens's manufacture. "The original honor," Day wrote in 1921, "lies at the door of Francis Watts Lee, of Boston—not mine."[49] According to Day, among serious amateur photographers then working in Boston, Lee was known as "a crack-brained enthusiast" and "the only one of us who had any knowledge of optics, or much of any relating to technical photography."[50] As such, Lee had been "preaching Dahlmeyer [*sic*] for years"—a lens made by the Dallmeyer-Bergheim Company of London—"but had never been able to put hands on a real piece in the flesh." When Day arranged to take his *New School of American Photography* exhibition to London in 1900, Lee encouraged him to purchase a lens while there. Day did, and found that "the work of this lens was a revelation to myself and some half-dozen American photographers who were in Europe at the time." After Day returned to the United States, Lee "begged unceasingly to have the lens put into his hand to show to a friend of his, a lens maker, one Smith," who, in turn, took the lens apart to study it. The result, recalled Day, "was in short the uncorrected Smith lens" and American pictorial photographic history. Lee received the very first lens made by Smith in 1901.[51]

Francis Watts Lee may have used this lens to create three photographs he exhibited at the Fourth Philadelphia Photographic Salon in 1901. *The Cloister Door, The Low Lying Sun of October,* and *Moonlight in the Courtyard,* each depicting the central atrium of the Boston Public Library, were a departure from his customary work. These images, which focused on architectural elements as well as light and shade, evoked the timelessness of sacred space; one critic even noted the prints gave "the impression of convent walls."[52] Lee was invited to hang these photographs in Philadelphia *hors concours* (without going before the jury), and several critics commented on their effectiveness. "Mr. Lee has also made some interesting studies of light in the colonnade of the inner court of the Boston Public Library," Charles Caffin wrote. *Moonlight in the Courtyard,* for which Lee utilized only natural moonlight and artificial light reflected through the library's windows, was a striking image of texture and depth. *The Low Lying Sun of October* (plate 4) featured a single corridor adjacent to the courtyard. This print, developed in an exotic "foreign color," made the observer nearly feel the baking sun. Finally, *The Cloister Door* (plate 5) was a portrait of Father

James Huntington standing in the courtyard colonnade just outside one of the library doors. The windows, door, and large stone pillars conveyed the aura of monastic solitude and a remote locale. This image found favor with the *Photo Era* critic, who wrote, "Mr. Francis Watts Lee has some views in the cloisters of the Boston Public Library, where he has posed a well-known Boston clergyman in his robes, with such effect that the modern pile reminds us strongly of some old Spanish mission."[53] Of the six images Lee sent to the Second San Francisco Photographic Salon in January 1902, three were portraits of Father Huntington (plate 6). He sent two prints to the Linked Ring's Tenth Photographic Salon in London in the fall of 1902 and never exhibited his work again.[54]

As the new century arrived, Lee and his wife confronted tragedy. Agnes Lee was in many respects the perfect partner, sharing her husband's Christian outlook and aesthetic sensibilities. She was also the model for several of his most highly praised images, including *A New England Saint* and *The Vision*, whose "strange, sacred sadness" had haunted Joseph Keiley.[55] The portrait and the critic's response to it may well have been a harbinger of the couple's future.

# *Chapter 2*

## AGNES RAND LEE

In the estimation of one of her closest colleagues, Martha Agnes Rand Lee, who preferred to be called Agnes, "belonged to a literary period and society of which she did not wholly approve,"[1] and yet she strove to craft a life and create a body of work full of grace and sensitivity. Born in Chicago, she was the third child and second daughter of William Henry Rand and his wife Harriet Robinson Rand. William Rand was an adventurer and entrepreneur who had sailed around Cape Horn, mined for gold in California, founded the *Los Angeles Star* newspaper, and moved to Chicago, where he printed and became part owner of the *Chicago Tribune,* all before he turned thirty. Shortly after the Civil War, Rand sold his interest in the *Tribune* and, along with Andrew McNally, formed the printing and publishing firm of Rand, McNally & Company. Owing to serious health concerns, in the 1870s he relocated his family to Europe for half a decade, where Agnes was educated in Switzerland and France.[2] After the family's return to the United States, Rand's five children dispersed across the country. The eldest, Charles Edwin Rand, called "an unlucky son" by one acquaintance, traveled to California, while Susan, the youngest, remained in Chicago. Mary

Robinson Rand eventually settled in New Canaan, Connecticut, and Agnes moved to Boston after her marriage. Finally, William Jr., the younger brother whom Agnes "adored," graduated from Harvard College and Law School and eventually served as Judge Advocate of the Army during World War I, earning a Distinguished Service Medal. He settled in Rye, New York. The siblings all remained close, visiting one another often. During the summer months, the family gathered on Martha's Vineyard where their parents maintained a home.[3]

An "extremely reserved" woman according to friends, Agnes was "invariably charming and warm," likely the perfect counterpoint to Francis Watts Lee's more intense temperament.[4] In addition, while many of her poems contain references to biblical characters and events and thus have a strong Christian component, her religiosity "appears to have been less public than her husband's," as one scholar noted, and certainly less fervently evangelical.[5] Agnes Rand married Francis Lee on December 23, 1890, in Chicago, at the Rand home, decorated for the occasion with Christmas greens, palms, ferns, and various types of roses. The bride wore a classical gown of "heavy white satin with a full sweeping train and sleeves to the elbow and a tulle veil fastened with orange blossoms." She carried "a large bouquet of white roses." According to a newspaper account, after an informal reception and wedding supper, the couple boarded a late train for a brief wedding journey on their way to Boston. There they began married life at 499 Beacon Street in the heart of the city.[6]

While her husband became immersed in his career and varied interests, Agnes began to make a name for herself as a poet. She had been composing verse before her marriage. Her first book, *The Legend of a Thought,* was published in 1889 by Rand, McNally, her father's firm. Poems on places such as Berlin, Lake Geneva, and Munich suggest it was in part a reminiscence of the Rand family's European travels. Other lyrics indicate that her interests coincided with those of the young Bohemian Bostonians she became acquainted with through her husband. Fred Holland Day and Louise Imogen Guiney in particular would have appreciated her odes to both Keats and Haydn. Agnes worked steadily at her craft, and Boston proved to be fertile ground for her literary ambitions. Among the coterie of young people she came into contact with were aspiring poets and others intent on setting new standards in imaginative and attractive publishing. Bliss Carman and Richard Hovey each wrote poetry, including the collaborative and exceedingly popular *Songs from Vagabondia* and *More Songs from Vagabondia,* published by the firm of Copeland & Day, headed by their close friend Fred Day and his colleague Herbert Copeland. Herbert Stone and Ingalls Kimball, Harvard undergraduates and members of the Visionists, made names for themselves as publishers of *The Chap-Book,* a "little magazine" that played a large part in Chicago's intellectual and cultural life. In addition to these literary friendships, Agnes benefited from her relationships with two outstanding advocates of American poetry, Harriet Monroe in Chicago and William Stanley Braithwaite in Boston, both of whom sought to bring poetry to a wider audience through their periodicals and compendiums. Soon Agnes's verse appeared regularly in the *Boston Evening Transcript* and in journals such as *The Independent, Scribner's,* and *Godey's.* She also published her work in religious periodicals including *Holy Cross* magazine, *The Churchman,* and *The Dawn.*[7]

Agnes was not a consistently effective poet. Still, she was among those nineteenth-century women authors who found a niche in popular journals and anthologies. Although later critics believed their work was too sentimental to be held in high esteem, many of these writers had a considerable following in their time.[8] Unlike several other female poets, who focused on domestic topics, Lee drew much inspiration from a broad range of sources. "Agnes Lee's poems are rarely personal, in the narrow sense applicable to many women lyricists," Harriet Monroe wrote in a comment on Lee's lifetime of work which appeared in *Poetry* in 1932. Instead, Monroe observed, she drew from "some historical episode . . . a chance item in a newspaper, . . . mathematical laws, . . . or odd little human episodes" more often than she mined her own life experiences. "Numbers" captured her reaction to an account published in *The Spectator* that numbers are inextricably linked to nature as well as to all human actions and undertakings; "Having Read Lenatre" focused on the French Revolution; and "The Idol" concerned the biblical tale of Maachah, the mother of Asa.[9]

Her friend and fellow poet Louise Imogen Guiney was an unfailing supporter of Lee's work. She sometimes enclosed copies of Agnes's "very sweet verse" in her correspondence to others and once wrote admiringly, "She thinks she only writes poetry, but she is a poet."[10] Like Guiney, Lee often used brief iambic lines and tight stanzaic structure to "express fragile emotions," literary devices that often became restrictive.[11] But while Guiney was sometimes cited for her action-oriented verse that celebrated primarily male heroism and gallantry, Lee's poems were "freighted with memories and a measured sadness," according to one critic.[12] With "A Lonely Man," for example, she conveyed the isolation of an aging solitary individual:

> It must be good to come back to a house,
> And hear the joy, the welcoming shout of it.
> It must be good to have anyone care
> If you come into a house and go out of it.

A similar tone of melancholy is found in "Black Flowers and White," which begins:

> Down to centuries of dark,
> After one short spell of light,
> Sink in Time black flowers and white.
> For with never why nor whether
> Good and bad go down together.[13]

Again unlike Guiney, Lee often composed narrative poems or verse plays, lengthier works that could easily be dramatized. *The Silent House, Eastland Waters,* and *The Sharing* were all of this type, and contemporaries found them worth putting on the stage. *The Asphodel,* one of her most poignant dialogues, recounted the story of a Hawaiian mother whose small son was stricken with leprosy. Rather than allow the authorities to exile the terrified child to a dreaded leper colony, the mother has him drink a poisonous draught of Asphodel, then "Cuddle close" as she sings him to his final sleep. As the poet Eunice Tietjens wrote of Lee, "She had a feeling for the music of words, for the balanced thought and the subtle mood, a tenderness for all small and helpless things whether child, bird, or flower."[14]

Although he felt that Agnes "was not in the usual sense an intellectual poet, and . . . had small critical understanding of philosophy or of history," which he thought "weakened" her work, the critic Yvor Winters praised Lee's poetic gifts. "Her power was a power of personal character united to an extraordinary grasp of certain poetic conventions. When the character, the convention, and the subject were happily met, the result was magnificent." Winters felt Lee's greatest poems were "Her Going," "Black Flowers and White," and "A Statue in the Garden," which he singled out as "the best piece of Parnassian poetry in English."[15] The Parnassian poets of nineteenth-century France, who were influenced by Theophile Gautier and his "art for art's sake" dictum, emphasized objectivity and precision in verse while rejecting excessive sentimentality and less disciplined romanticism, a quality Ezra Pound later referred to as "emotional slither."[16] Winters attributed Lee's attraction to Parnassian poetry to her time spent in Europe and the education she received there. He asserted that Lee's writing was "impersonal and absolute" and sharply realistic when most successful, concluding that when she was at her best, "no American poet of her generation except [Edwin Arlington] Robinson is comparable to her."[17] "A Statue in the Garden"[18]—which closed with the lines

> The souls of all the flowers afar have rallied.
> The trees, gaunt, appalling,
> Attest the gloom, and on my shoulder pallid
> The dead leaves are falling.

—was an often-anthologized poem and had, according to Winters, "an unyielding grandeur," a characteristic he felt distinguished her verse "from all the women poets of our time whether good or bad. . . . Among American writers, regardless of medium," he continued, "her spiritual quality seems to me closest to that of Mrs. [Edith] Wharton."[19]

Upon her return to Chicago in the early twentieth century, Agnes Lee found the city less appealing. Perhaps agreeing with Pound, who stated that "no good poetry is ever written in a manner twenty years old," she found little to admire in the poetry being written in the Midwest. "Here literature seems too faddish," she wrote to Josephine Preston Peabody. "It is going through phases which we discussed and dropped ten years ago—in Boston and New York."[20] Lee's later publications were primarily collections of earlier verse, sometimes reworked, often not. She continued to receive critical praise and popularity during her lifetime, and was awarded the Guarantor's Prize by *Poetry* magazine in 1926. Previous winners had included Robert Frost and Edna St. Vincent Millay. Still, Lee's verse appears dated to a more modern audience.

Lee was at her best when she focused her vision to capture the joy, comfort, and emotion found within a diminished or limited environment, such as in the last stanza from "A Nesting Linnet":

She was so shy with every human
Before she nested in our tree.
Now she forgets the wilder wood,
Glad to be small and understood.[21]

These lines may well be a metaphor for Lee's own personality. Petite and delicate, Agnes had a "fragile appearance" and a shyness, which may have been exacerbated by a speech impediment, that prompted her friends to be quite protective of her. "She seemed always an anomaly in Chicago," Tietjens wrote of her. "In this brash, hopeful, struggling city Agnes Lee lived as one might live in some remote corner of an old-world garden. It was, truth to tell, a gracious and endearing garden, this world of hers. . . . Even the flowers in their formal beds were not quite of today, but were somehow sad and gently beautiful."[22] Agnes's generous nature and kind regard for others allowed her to make friends easily and maintain them for decades, even without direct contact. For example, Yvor Winters considered her one of his "best friends" although the two had met in person only twice. According to the critic, she was a refined, gentle woman, "a great lady [who] would have been at home in the court of Louis XIV." Eunice Tietjens too wrote of Agnes's "gentle liveliness and unfailing loyalty."[23]

The circle of artists, writers, and architects Agnes Lee met in Boston embraced her with equal regard and affection. From the outset, letters between Agnes and Fred Day, whom she usually addressed as "Dear D," and Louise Guiney, centered on shared dinner parties, afternoon visits, symphony concerts, and summer travel to Maine, Rhode Island, and Martha's Vineyard. Perhaps because of her upbringing in the bustle of Chicago's elite, Agnes maintained a busy social schedule, one that Guiney commented on to Day. "If it doesn't rain I'll be pleased as Punch to meet you at Lee's . . . on Thursday. I suppose All Creation will be there before we end." Guiney found at least one dinner memorable enough to write about it to Rev. William van Allen. "The Chinese dinner came off. The company was capital, and the menu exciting to the last degree," she recounted, "so exciting that conversation languished, and that both Lees and I, for example, smiled incessantly at one another across an inlaid table, and turned it into a monosyllabic evening. We had music, after, from Chong Fu, on the weirdest of xylophone-like instruments."[24]

Following the births of her two daughters in 1892 and 1893, Agnes's poetic eye and ear turned more easily to verse of motherhood and childhood. She soon found a home for her lyrics in children's journals such as *St. Nicholas Magazine*, *Baby's Corner*, and *Babyhood*.[25] In 1898 she wrote *The Round Rabbit*, a book of verse for children that revealed her keen awareness of the fantasies embraced by the very young. The opening lines of the title poem established her sensitivity to the imagination of children:

> Oh, where is my rabbit, my little round rabbit?
> The flowers tell not, nor the trees,
> He had such a sweet, such a queer little habit
> Of nibbling about in the breeze.[26]

This book was also emblematic of the friendships Agnes had developed. *The Round Rabbit* was published by Copeland & Day, and the fact that it was the publishers' final commercial offering suggests the charming little book may have been brought out as a personal gesture. It featured a cover design by Olive Lothrop Grover, a Boston artist who participated in Arts and Crafts exhibitions in Boston and who also designed a bookplate for Agnes's brother Charles Edwin Rand. The frontispiece and several illustrations were the work of Rose O'Neill Latham, another acquaintance who later was better known as the creator of the Kewpie doll. When Copeland & Day closed its doors, Small, Maynard & Company acquired the work and reissued it in 1901. For that edition, the publisher added endpapers by Ethel Reed, another member of the talented group of artists who often worked in concert in 1890s Boston.[27]

Throughout the decade Louise Guiney kept a careful eye on Agnes, particularly after the Lees' second daughter, Alice Stephana, lost her hearing in infancy and the couple made the difficult decision to enroll the child in the Chicago Kindergarten Home for the Deaf. "I get a sight of our Lees, now and then," Guiney wrote to van Allen. "Agnes looks very tired, since she left Chicago and her dear baby." A few months later, a worried Guiney hinted at a deeper problem: "I am awfully concerned about Agnes," she wrote to Day. "I never heard of 'nerves' being cured in a week before."[28]

While Francis kept busy with his work, photography, and social reform activities, Agnes had her poetry, friendships, social obligations, and elder daughter, Peggy, to fill her time. Still, her friends felt she was suffering silently, judging by their frequent references to her and their attempts to engage her in various activities. Acknowledging that Agnes "has certainly had a lot to bear of late years," Guiney hoped to lure her friend to Maine for a respite. "I'll see Francis tomorrow," she wrote in May of 1899, "and broach Five Islands for Agnes in June." The invitation was apparently declined, however, because, as Guiney noted, Agnes "is too busy socially, I think," and she likewise had little luck trying to persuade Agnes to accompany her to "the gymnasium." Still, Guiney's affection for the entire family was obvious. "They're three dear, dears, said Lees," she once commented to Fred Day after visiting Francis, Agnes, and Peggy in Boston.[29]

Gertrude Käsebier may have perceived the same sadness surrounding Agnes and tried to bring some joy to the family. When she rented Longmeadow, a "cottage" in Newport, Rhode Island, during the summer of 1899, Käsebier encouraged Day to come for a visit and to "please bring Mrs. Lee down for an hour of perfect rest."[30] When Day and the Lee family visited Longmeadow, described as "like the palace in the sleeping beauty story," they had time for the favorite pastimes of both Lees.[31] Hosted by Käsebier, the little party engaged in photography experiments and poetry readings as well as hours of relaxation on the shore. In fact, one evening Day read poetry until "all his listeners melted away but Lee's wife," according to a subsequent account of the visit.[32] Well aware of Käsebier's enjoyment of beer, Day, Agnes, and Francis shipped a case of the beverage along with candy and cigarettes to thank her for her hospitality. The shipment was addressed to play on the pronunciation of Käsebier's name. She, in turn, acknowledged the gift in the same spirit with her own bit of witty poetry:

> Dear family Lee, dear Mr. Day
> What can we do, what can we say,
> Your spiritual message to repay?
> 'One case of beer to another,' tho' an atrocious pun,
> Made, from expressman down, no end of fun.[33]

That same year, the photographer visited the Lees at their home. They had moved to a freestanding home with land in Jamaica Plain, a more suburban location within metropolitan Boston. There she took photographs of the entire family, several of which she later exhibited. Käsebier found all the Lees, but especially Agnes, to be pleasing and willing models. She was not alone. In fact, when Day mounted his groundbreaking *New School of American Photography* exhibition in 1900, Agnes's image was well represented. Käsebier, Day, and Francis Watts Lee each exhibited photographs of her.[34]

As early as December 1892, before Day even began serious work as an artistic photographer, he sent Agnes a photo he had taken of her, perhaps as a Christmas gift. "Thank you so much for sending the picture so nicely mounted," Agnes wrote to Day. "Mr. Lee, and, in fact, everyone who has seen it, seemed to consider it an exceedingly good likeness, as well as a cleverly arranged picture."[35] Her handsome angular features, high forehead, and luxurious hair made Agnes a versatile and effective model. Photographed in profile, as in Francis Watts Lee's *A New England Saint* and Gertrude Käsebier's *Blessed Art Thou among Women*, her identity was hidden within the staged tableau. In *A New England Saint* Agnes depicted the stereotypical, devout, long-suffering New England matron, while in Käsebier's picture she epitomized the Progressive Era's modern mother. In each, although she represented a tangible type of woman, Agnes was virtually unrecognizable. At other times, for example, in *The Vision* by her husband, Agnes gazed straight into the camera, producing an elegantly moving portrait. Two images of Agnes seated at a piano in an almost identical pose, one by Day, the other by Käsebier, demonstrated both the differing artistic vision of the photographers and Agnes's range as a sitter.

In Day's portrait (figure 4), the seated figure is a study in concentration. Stiffly upright in profile with hands splayed on the piano keys, she has her head tilted up as she focuses on the music in front of her, seemingly unaware of the viewer or the photographer. She wears a heavy, fitted dress with long sleeves, a bustle, and train, her lower body engulfed in multiple folds of cloth. The dress is belted tightly at the waist, and a dense fur collar encircles her shoulders and falls to the front. Her hair is swept up and pinned at the nape of the neck, and her unruly bangs are visible. The soft, curved lines of the head, dress, and fur piece contrast with the sharp edges of the sheet music, picture frame behind her on the left, and the paned-glass window situated awkwardly high on the wall on the upper right. Another piece of framed art is just visible under the window ledge; one candlestick and candle set on the piano exactly traces the middle window mullion. A study in light and shade, curve and straight edge, there is a sense of cool reserve, solitude, and formality to the composition.

FIGURE 4. F. Holland Day, Agnes Rand Lee at the piano, c. 1898, platinum print. (PR13 CN2015.052.521)

FIGURE 5. Gertrude Käsebier, *Untitled (woman at a piano)*, c. 1900, gum bichromate print. Spencer Museum of Art, University of Kansas, Gift of Mrs. Hermine M. Turner (1973.0025).

Käsebier posed Agnes in the same room, at the same piano, but with different results (figure 5). This time the camera is located closer to the model, eliminating the window; only one candlestick remains in view, as does only the barest tip of the picture frame in the upper left corner. Käsebier's gum bichromate photo-development process has made the room and walls appear softer, the setting less stark, as does Agnes's attire and appearance. For this photograph, which Käsebier exhibited as *Portrait of Mrs. L* at the Philadelphia Photographic Salon of 1900,[36] Agnes wears a loose-fitting dress. Though still voluminous, the cut of the fabric and the casually pushed back sleeves result in a less formal feeling, a sense that is further enhanced by Agnes's more relaxed posture. She has literally let her hair down; it is loose and full, almost unkempt, and frames her face as she turns her head to the camera. Although her hands remain on the keyboard, it is as if she has been interrupted at ease, at home, perhaps while playing a favorite piece of music.

The less constraining, smocklike garment seen in Käsebier's portrait was in keeping with the clothing reform movement then being embraced by Arts and Crafts advocates like Agnes Lee. Both Agnes and her husband were greatly influenced by the ideals first expressed by the Pre-Raphaelite Brotherhood, a group of artists and writers working in England in the mid-nineteenth century known for their devotion to nature and their aim to re-create nature's beauty in their art.[37] The Brotherhood revered the poet John Keats, whom Fred Holland Day and Louise Imogen Guiney adored. Their shared enthusiasm culminated in the first memorial to the poet ever erected, unveiled at Hampstead Parish Church in July 1894.[38] The Lees, meanwhile, had a deep affection for the artist Dante Gabriel Rossetti, a founder of the Pre-Raphaelites. It was a devotion well known to their friends. In 1892 Francis acknowledged receipt of a gift from Day: "Mr. Cram handed me at lunch today the photograph of Rossetti's last resting place which you were so kind as to send me. I shall place it in my library and esteem it a treasure as the last connecting link with the human side of one of whom both Mrs. Lee and I are wonderfully fond."[39] For her part, in a poem titled "Rossetti's Wife," Agnes commemorated the disinterment of Elizabeth Siddal Rossetti to reclaim an early manuscript the poet had buried with his wife. Agnes wrote the verse in Elizabeth's voice:

> The little book is winged to outer land.
> The book is gone, which was myself, more fair,
> Myself being buried twice, when my love's hand
> Laid it between my pillow and my hair.
> Ceiled by the earth, it lingered long with me;
> Till in my grave one night a ray was cast,
> And life's own throbbing fingers set it free,
> The blinded songs have seen the light, at last!

Agnes makes it clear that Elizabeth encouraged her husband from the grave to retrieve the lyrics: "I bade my poet. He could not refuse, / Feeling me urging upward from the clay. / . . . Rescue the songs which were my diadem."[40]

Inspired by the work of the Pre-Raphaelites, the Aesthetic movement gained popularity in America in the latter quarter of the century; it found a vital platform at the U.S. Centennial Exposition of 1876. Emphasizing the artistic potential in the production of household items such as furniture, textiles, wallpaper, and decorative accessories, Aestheticism, explains one scholar, emerged from the "utopian belief" of British reformers and designers who held that "a more artful environment could be morally uplifting." John Ruskin and William Morris, whom Francis Watts Lee idolized, argued that society as a whole would benefit if art was made an integral part of everyday life.[41]

Evolving from this ideology, the Arts and Crafts movement sought an alternative to the existing factory system that had eliminated the artistic elements of production while degrading its laborers, artists, intellectuals, and social activists in Boston strove to restore creativity, beauty, and fulfillment to the workplace.[42] Certainly the Visionists were part of this movement, advocating active participation in the struggle to bring beauty to life and work. Through their writing, architectural design, publishing, printing, photography, and music, they sought to bring an aesthetic sensibility into the factory and the home. Aligning with the wider issues of beauty, nature, and healthfulness in work, civic, and domestic life, Arts and Crafts advocates were encouraged to embrace the natural world, conserve natural resources, follow healthy diets, and surround themselves with attractive and wholesome environments. Social inequality remained even within the movement, however. T. J. Jackson Lears points out that "Arts and Crafts ideology was entwined with the class and racial anxieties common among affluent Americans at the end of the nineteenth century," as elite members, many with little hands-on knowledge of crafts, became spokespersons for the movement.[43] Another scholar notes that "many of the leaders of the Arts and Crafts movement were anti-union and used the encouragement of skilled crafts to dampen labor unrest and uphold the existing social structure."[44] Francis Watts Lee, and through him, Agnes, had a unique place in this movement. Although he was skilled in both printing and photography, with his employment at the Boston Public Library, Lee experienced industrial and bureaucratic transformations from the worker's perspective. Unlike many of his contemporaries in the movement, he remained staunchly pro-union and an activist for workers' rights.[45]

This reform spirit pervaded all dimensions of life, from public spaces to the workplace, the home, and even the individual.[46] Inevitably, the gospel of Arts and Crafts became associated with dress reform, among other aspects of everyday life. Dress reform activists began to gain proponents in Boston in the 1870s, when women's clubs, speakers, etiquette books, and even physicians took issue with long skirts, corsets that constricted the ribs and spinal column, and the weight of garments that placed inordinate stress on a woman's hips and lower back. Although writings about "hygienic, rational, and artistic dress" were widely published beginning in that decade, the cause languished until it gained momentum with the inception of the Arts and Crafts movement at the end of the century.[47] The self-expression and independence proclaimed essential for artists was similarly deemed appropriate for women's clothing choices as the movement embraced back-to-nature ideals. Natural, washable textiles such as linen and cotton were promoted, as were simple, flowing designs, patterns, and colors. Tea gowns and smocks that draped loosely from the shoulder increased in popularity.[48] In addition, as one scholar notes, "kimono styles [which] were an identification with artistic attitudes and the Pre-Raphaelites" became more commonplace. Similarly, the idea that even in dress "simplicity is the foundation of all art," a notion expressed by William Morris and Oscar Wilde, among others, gained support.[49] Agnes Rand Lee began to fill her wardrobe with this type of clothing.

When her husband and friends photographed Agnes at home in her own attire, rather than in theatrical costuming, the results were particularly pleasing and emotionally engaging. For example, Lee's image of the young wife and mother reading at a window, Agnes wears a light-colored tea gown with a simple bow and small ruffle (figure 6). It is likely made of cotton and is a dress she wore in several family photos around the time of Peggy's birth. Leaning on the window sill, a book on her lap, she appears relaxed and at ease as she looks gently into the camera. It is an appealing portrait with an openness and immediacy that speaks directly to the simplicity and conscious artfulness of the Arts and Crafts lifestyle.

Gertrude Käsebier created two iconic images of Agnes, *Blessed Art Thou among Women* (1899), and *The Heritage of Motherhood* (1904). In each, Agnes wears her own clothing; she is not so much a photographer's model as she is a woman living her life. In the first she stands in a plainly cut, free-flowing wrapper with a large laced collar and long, loose tie, morning attire clearly worn for comfort yet pleasing to the eye. She wears the same gown for a series of portraits by Francis, one of which he titled *The Vision*. Five years later, on a rocky windswept shore in Maine, Agnes dons another simple, unfettered frock, this time gathering a dark shawl across her shoulders as protection from the elements. In each image Käsebier as photographer is secondary to the vignette unfolding before her camera, the artist merely a witness to a woman whose unconscious gestures and

FIGURE 6. Francis Watts Lee, Agnes Rand Lee by a window with a book, c. 1892, platinum print. (LC-DIG-ppmsca-39442)

expressions convey deep emotions. Eunice Tietjens once wrote of Agnes that although her life was filled with beauty and grace, "one was always conscious of courage, too, in this world of hers, the courage of one who has faced many sorrows and met them quietly and simply."[50] *Blessed Art Thou among Women* and *The Heritage of Motherhood* capture that courage and sorrow. In the former, Agnes is not alone; she is joined by her first-born child, Peggy.

FIGURE 7. Unattributed [F. Holland Day or Francis Watts Lee], Peggy Lee in dining room, c. 1896, platinum print. (PR13 CN2015.052.627)

## *Chapter 3*

# HARRIET TEMPLETON "PEGGY" LEE

"Peggy is adorable!" wrote Louise Imogen Guiney in December 1897 to Rev. William van Allen, curate of Boston's Church of the Advent and a mutual friend of Guiney and the Lees. She had spent an evening playing with the Peggy and her parents.[1] By that Christmas season, Harriet Templeton Lee was five years old. She was a beautiful, round-faced girl with perfect features and fine straight hair cut in a stylish bob with bangs. In an informal photograph taken in the family's dining room, she is seated at the table with milk, cookies, and an open cookie jar before her (figure 7). Immaculately attired in a frilly white dress with starched cap sleeves, she looks like a renaissance angel with tilted head and a beatific half-smile. Her feet are swinging nowhere near the floor. The room is furnished with a substantial wooden dining table and chairs. Behind the girl, a glass-fronted cabinet holds the family's china service and accessories.

Francis and Agnes Lee had moved into their Beacon Street home upon their marriage. A solid row house, it spoke of the couple's urbanity and stood close to St. John the Evangelist Church on Bowdoin Street, where the family regularly attended services. Situated as it was, the residence allowed the Lees to be an integral part of the city. Until the mid-nineteenth century, Boston was a "city of pedestrians" and its architectural style consisted of attached or semi-attached homes built on narrow lots, side by side, with little private recreational land.[2] It was also a bustling, dirty, and, in many ways, unhealthy, dangerous place to bring up children. The city expanded by reclaiming land from the water, the South End and the Back Bay being its two most well known and ambitious projects. While residences in these areas were completed by this time, the historian Sam Bass Warner notes, "only the rich and the prosperous segment of the middle class could afford most of the new houses in these sections."[3] The newly installed street railways, however, enabled Boston to broaden its physical parameters by creating convenient and efficient transportation into and out of the city center. The Lees took advantage of this opportunity to move to Jamaica Plain.

Although it had once been an outer village of the city for those wealthy enough to maintain a second, more rural, residence for leisure and recreation, as the end of the century neared, Jamaica Plain had become a fashionable, moderately priced middle-class residential settlement. Nestled between Jamaica Pond and the Arnold Arboretum, the neighborhood was suburban enough to offer fresh air, trees, and grass-covered yards while the streetcar routes made for an easy daily commute into the city. Jamaica Plain's architecture consisted of detached, wooden, primarily single-family homes erected on generous lots of land. By 1896 the Lees had relocated to a home at 63 Peter Parley Road, an impressive three-story residence with double-hung windows, a large front porch, and the promise of gardens and a play area for their two daughters.[4]

The family's move was also a reflection of their commitment to progressive ideals in lifestyle, politics, and child-rearing. Jamaica Plain would provide their daughters with a childhood unlike their own, for the 1890s had introduced what is often referred to as "the age of the child." A period marked by rapid urbanization, industrialization, an increase in average family incomes, and a decrease in family size, this final decade of the nineteenth century was, as the historian David I. Macleod describes, characterized by the emergence of the "sheltered childhood." Reformers declared that every young person should have ample time for games and amusements, extended and age-appropriate schooling, and a loving domestic setting; a household in which parents and their adult friends, like Louise Guiney, would join in the "play."[5]

Rather than expecting youngsters to contribute to a family's income, parents of even modest means hid the hardships and complexities of life from them. No longer considered miniature adults, boys and girls were expected to behave like the children they were. Manufacturers advertised bows and arrows, stick horses, and skates for boys while girls were encouraged to occupy themselves with mass-produced dolls, tea sets, and miniature appliances. Likewise, publishers promoted "book-length compendiums" of activities for children of all ages.[6]

Memoirs of contemporary childhoods recounted indoor games of tiddlywinks, checkers, and charades, while outdoor activities common to all children included tag, hide-and-seek, and prisoner's base. "During the long summer evenings until our bedtime at eight or eight-thirty," wrote one, "we played with others of the neighborhood in all manner of merry-making."[7] "And always there was reading," wrote another child of the 1890s. "That, after all, was our most treasured indoor pastime." Edna Ferber recalled that "after school, and at noon, and at night . . . I read and read and read."[8] In the Lees' household books would have been especially welcome, as Agnes was a writer and Francis an aficionado of fine hand-bound volumes. In addition, as the scholar Anne Scott MacLeod has noted, there is "plenty of evidence to support the belief that Americans in the late nineteenth century read prodigiously as children, as adults, and as families."[9] Many publishers promoted works aimed at an audience of both children and adults. The author Mary Ellen Chase remembered that her mother "somehow found time for reading to us. [She] chose books which all of us from sixteen to six could enjoy."[10]

This new, chiefly middle-class model of domesticity resulted in the codification of "separate spheres" among women, men, and children. Mothers, judged morally superior to their husbands and capable of much nurturing love and affection, were to bear the brunt of child-rearing and socialization of the younger generation. They were also to supply emotional support to their spouses and children, and remain in the home rather than seek external employment.[11] Fathers, for their part, "would spend long hours in the manly world of work" to provide the comfort and goods that would make their house a home. In addition, fathers were increasingly expected to spend their free time with their families and to entertain and play with their children.[12]

Within this model, families became more child-centered. In households like the Lees' in which liberal Christian theologies were followed, moral nurture and mild disciplinary measures were the rule. As the sociologist Viviana Zelizer explains, children became "economically 'worthless,'" since they no longer could be employed outside the home, "but emotionally 'priceless.'"[13] Scientists too joined the child-rearing discussion. For example, the psychologist G. Stanley Hall's child study movement championed the distinctive period of childhood (and later adolescence), thereby adding the weight of scientific inquiry to the moral teachings of clergy and the commercial aims of toy makers. In many ways these progressive ideas appealed to the two sides of Francis Lee's nature: a deeply felt religious perspective supported by scientific or technological expertise. In this instance, the Christian doctrine that stressed a child's basic goodness and capacity for moral growth was confirmed and enhanced by the scientific theories of psychologists and sociologists.

A well-educated, well-traveled, and liberal-minded woman, Agnes Lee embraced all these beliefs as well. Much of her poetry reflected the mother-child relationship as one of deep affection, sympathy, and unquestioning love. In one of her most anthologized poems, "Motherhood," the mother of Jesus and the mother of Judas, each unaware of the other's identity, share their memories and sorrow of "a child beloved and lost."[14] The affection a mother feels for her children is here recognized as universal, limitless, and profound. What is more, Agnes's career as a poet would have been accepted as entirely appropriate for her station in life. A woman could certainly be both a poet and a doting mother.

There is no question that Peggy was a cherished child. Born in September 1892, she was baptized at St. John the Evangelist Church and brought nothing but joy to her parents. That December Agnes sent greetings to Fred Holland Day: "I trust your Christmas passed as merrily as did that of the Lee trio."[15] Within a few years Peggy was picking cherries with Louise Guiney, planting flowers in her own garden, and being photographed by Day and Gertrude Käsebier, who found the child irresistible as a model.[16] Aside from informal pictures taken of her as a baby in the arms of her parents and Grandmother Lee, perhaps on the occasion of her baptism, the earliest photos are those by Day, then considered one of the leaders of the American pictorialist movement.

Outfitted in another frothy white dress with smocked front, lace at the wrists and shoulders, and a matching cap set on the back of her head (figure 8), Peggy appears completely at ease in Day's Pinckney Street studio. Day had a natural rapport with children, and his young subjects recalled as adults the generosity and kindness he had shown them as youngsters. Many of his photographic

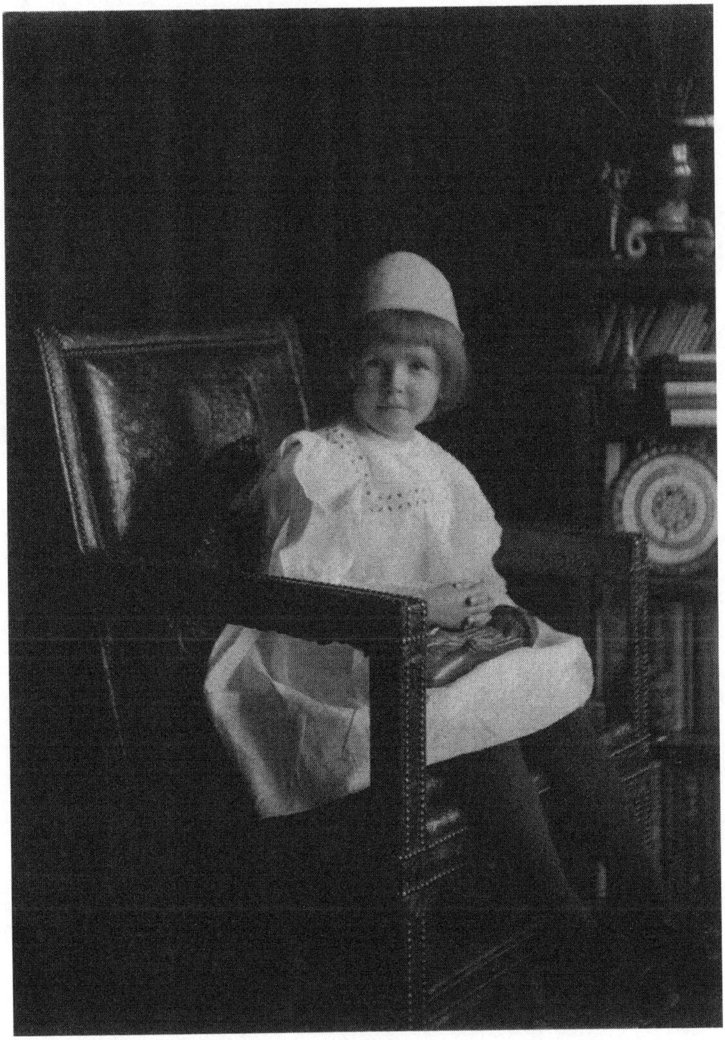

FIGURE 8. F. Holland Day, Harriet Templeton "Peggy" Lee, c. 1896, platinum print. (PR13 CN2015.052.528)

models were the children of friends, and he was always able to put them at ease in front of his camera.[17] A series of photographs captures Peggy perched on and around an oversized leather and hobnail chair surrounded by Day's eclectic collection of doodads and accessories. Among the items are a cast from the Louvre's Princess bust by Francesco Laurana and the metal poppies that grace Day's enigmatic *Beauty Is Truth, Truth Beauty*.[18] In a portrait from this group which appeared in the *Photographic Times* of March 1900, the girl is reading William Nicholson's *Alphabet* book; in others she holds a children's biography of Joan of Arc.[19] Either or both may have been gifts from Day, who often gave "boxes of books" to friends and "liked to give books about famous women to young girls."[20] One photo catches Peggy, her hat removed, bending over a book, pencil in hand, and either writing or more likely coloring the figures on the page. Decades later Agnes rediscovered another in the series, "a perfectly darling picture of Peggy" in which the child holds a "huge doll" and guides its hands along a piano keyboard. "It's absolutely *Peggy*," the mother wrote, "And I bless you, dear D., for having taken it."[21] Gertrude Käsebier captured the photogenic family with portraits of Agnes and Francis, photos of Peggy with her mother and with her grandfather Rand, and Francis with daughter Alice. But Peggy was clearly the enchanting center of the group.[22]

An additional portrayal of the child was included in Agnes's *The Round Rabbit*. It featured delightfully whimsical illustrations of a small, very active little girl in ruffled petticoat and frilly dress.[23] While this girl may have depicted a generic child of the age, one poem at least was written especially for the author's daughter. "Under Peggy's Window" begins with the child talking to the first spring flowers in her garden. Concerned that the warmth of spring has not truly arrived, she asks why the "little violet, / With starry dews all wet," has bloomed "too soon" in the season. The poet's maternal love can be heard in the flower's reply:

> Ah! Peggy dear, forgive,
> And let me near you live,
> And take me to your gentle heart, and love me!
> '*Twas* early, I presume,
> Yet what *could* I do but bloom,
> With Peggy and the sunshine up above me?[24]

The lines seem to imply much about Peggy's precociousness, her irresistible charm, and love of nature.

Peggy may have been encouraged in her nature study by her primary school education. There are no extant records of the child's school years but, once the family moved to Jamaica Plain, they would have found kindred spirits at the neighborhood Margaret Fuller School, a newly opened elementary facility in the Boston Public system.[25] There the school committee adopted a curriculum that would "add to the children's knowledge and interest in the workings and wonder of nature." It also promoted "art education [as] a vital necessity," something Arts and Crafts devotees like the Lees would have embraced. In the primary grades, lessons on shapes, which included clay modeling, paper folding and cutting, and freehand drawing, were augmented by "Picture Days," an activity that required children to select pictures and clippings they thought beautiful in magazines they found at home. They also examined and discussed reproductions of established masterpieces. According to the curriculum manual, such activities "cannot help quickening the mental and spiritual life of the child, strengthening his concept of form, and developing his sense of beauty, imagination, and creative power." The manual itself opened with a quote from the English Arts and Crafts advocate William Morris, whom Francis Watts Lee deeply admired: "What I want to do is to put definitively before you a cause for which to strive. That cause is the democracy of art, the ennobling of daily and common work, which will one day put hope and pleasure in the place of fear and pain as the forces which move men to labor and keep the world a-going."[26]

Thus, a new stage of development was recognized, a time and place appropriately filled with toys, games, and innocence; the joys of reading, nature, and education. Such attitudes took root in the Northeast, where declining birthrates, new policies aimed at the protection of children, progressive educational curricula, and relative prosperity allowed parents to invest more time and energy in child-rearing and family life. And, they were particularly embraced by liberal-minded, progressive parents like the Lees whose children would be steeped in nature, art, and democratic ideals. But this idyllic family circle was torn apart far too soon. On May 12, 1900, Harriet Templeton Lee died.

Despite medical and public health advances and declining infant mortality rates, early death remained a very real possibility in the late nineteenth and early twentieth centuries even among the middle and upper classes. In fact, nearly two out of every ten children died before the age of five.[27] Medicine remained rather rudimentary in the 1890s as physicians had few effective treatments. Some recommended measures even exacerbated an illness or hastened death. Knowing this, parents faced any child's sickness with fear and feelings of helplessness.

The Lees fully comprehended the randomness of illness and the futility of treatment; they had already endured one medical tragedy. Their second daughter, Alice Stephana Lee, born in December 1893, lost her hearing in infancy, most likely as a result of a childhood disease.[28] Elder daughter Peggy did not succumb to an infectious disease, however; the cause of her death was diabetes mellitus, also known as type 1 or juvenile diabetes.[29] At the time, the cause and trajectory of diabetes mellitus were unclear and treatment was in its nascent stages.

Diabetes had confounded medical practitioners for centuries. Although described in written accounts as early as 1550 BC, the disease did not receive its name until the second century AD. It was not until the mid-1800s that the French physician Claude Bernard linked the condition to the pancreas, and another fifty years before Belgium's Jean de Meyer identified the "mysterious substance" that seemed to control "diabetes" and gave it a name—insulin.[30] Even Sir William Osler, the esteemed English medical teacher and scholar, wrote only briefly about the disease in his resource text published in 1892. He and others believed diabetes was a "disorder of nutrition" and that it ran in families.[31] It was not until 1922 that diabetes was sufficiently understood and insulin was isolated, produced, and introduced, along with careful diet, as a life-saving treatment. All of this was too late to help Peggy. In the last decade of the nineteenth century diabetes was, as one physician put it, "a death sentence," carrying with it a prognosis of, at best, "eleven months of suffering followed by death." For most children the outlook was even grimmer. In reality, for a child stricken at this time, diabetes often "proved fatal in a few days."[32]

Peggy's illness would have come on suddenly as her dysfunctional pancreas failed to produce insulin. Her symptoms would have included extreme fatigue, frequent urination, an increased hunger, and an insatiable thirst. Although Osler recommended a diet that "emphasized mostly protein foods combined with severely limited carbohydrate portions," treatment was futile.[33] Within a few decades of Osler's recommendation, Dr. Frederick Allen, an American-born physician and researcher, developed a drastic "starvation treatment" which kept patients alive for a few months, "albeit as living skeletons." But even Allen's work came twenty years too late for Peggy.[34] Ravenous hunger and unquenchable thirst would drive a child, who had been healthy and active only days before, nearly mad. The body acting "as a sieve," dumped all ingested glucose unprocessed and unchecked into the urine, which became sweet, like honey.[35] Dehydration, quickly followed by the hopeless complication of delirium and subsequent coma, would bring an end to the child's acute suffering. According to state records, Peggy was ill for only "a few weeks" before her death. It would have been a chaotic and shockingly swift episode, ending in mind-numbing grief for the small family.[36]

Two years earlier Dr. Elliott P. Joslin, a pioneer medical specialist in diabetes mellitus, opened his practice in internal medicine in Boston. He coupled this practice with his continual investigation of diabetes, its early detection, and treatment. Beginning in 1898 he also published widely on diabetes mellitus, compiled a "diabetic ledger" to record symptoms, treatments, and mortality statistics, and became one of the world's leading experts on the disease. Many of Joslin's earliest recorded cases mirror the sudden onset, excruciating symptoms, rapid decline, and inevitable demise that Peggy experienced. In 1922 Joslin and his associate were "the first physicians in the United States to administer insulin" to their patients. But, when Peggy was stricken and diagnosed in early 1900, "childhood diabetics were a rare entity" and Joslin was a relatively unknown thirty-one-year-old physician just beginning his research. The Lees likely had no knowledge of him. In any event, there is no record of Peggy's case in his ledger.[37]

Harriet Templeton Lee was interred on May 15, 1900, in the shaded, ivy-covered Lee family plot in Mount Auburn Cemetery in Cambridge.[38] Founded in 1831 at the beginning of the public parks movement in the United States, Mount Auburn was the country's first rural cemetery. A contrast to the customary austere and intimidating graveyards of early New England, Mount Auburn was designed to comfort visitors with natural beauty, a tranquil atmosphere, and a newly developed acceptance of death and afterlife. Its hills, ponds, well-kept trees and shrubs, and graveled footpaths made the cemetery a popular attraction for walkers, birdwatchers, and tourists.[39] Gravestones too had evolved from the forbidding death's heads found in Puritan graveyards to cherubic angels, symbols of faith, and mortuary art that included empty beds, grieving pets, and other sentimentalized representations.[40] It is not known whether the family intended to place a piece of statuary at Peggy's grave, but none was erected. Perhaps it was a memorial gesture too painful for either of her parents to face.

Today more is understood about the depths of parental grief. The loss of a child is undeniably a life-shattering event, one that can undermine assumptions about the meaning of life and lead to profound despair. As the poet and undertaker Thomas Lynch writes, when burying infants and children, "we bury the future, unwieldy and unknown, full of promise and possibilities, outcomes punctuated by our rosy hopes. The grief has no borders, no limits, no known ends. . . . Some sadnesses are permanent. Dead babies do not give us memories. They give us dreams." Such was the tragedy of little Peggy Lee's loss and her bereft parents' search for consolation.[41]

Although during much of the Victorian Age etiquette books and customs allowed for, or even encouraged, prolonged periods of mourning and elaborate rituals to support the grief-stricken, by the end of the century such elaborate habits had begun to fade. As family life became more private, life-changing events were expected to be borne in isolation. Memorial albums, scrapbooks, and consolation literature, prevalent in the midcentury when the "cult of mourning" was dominant, became less appealing, particularly to the emerging "modern" sensibility. Demonstrative, public, or long-lasting grief was seen as a sign of self-absorption and self-pity.[42] Such grief was particularly problematic among the progressive middle class who were filled with optimism and focused on the future. As one scholar writes, this age "stirred up choppy waters for the middle class to navigate with regard to commemoration of the dead."[43] Certainly the Lees' circle of friends felt Peggy's loss deeply and were concerned about her seemingly fragile mother. "Agnes is quite as ever," Louise Guiney wrote to Fred Day nine months after the child's death, "but very pathetic to me." A few months later, as the first anniversary of the tragic event approached, Guiney again shared her thoughts with Day: "I suppose you remember Peggy daily about this time, as I do. Dear little heart!"[44]

Agnes Lee memorialized her daughter in the way she knew best, in verse. In doing so, she joined many who worked through their grief in this manner. Since the eighteenth century, elegies for children "had become a common genre in American poetry" aimed especially at women. As scholars have noted, elegiac verse continued to flourish during the mid-nineteenth century, when "maternal grief over infant [and child] death was articulated repeatedly in the prolific work of women writers."[45] Confessional magazines and women's journals such as *Godey's, Peterson's,* and *Graham's* were a rich source of consolation literature.[46] Agnes Lee had previously published poetry in both *Godey's* and *Peterson's* as well as other popular newspapers and magazines and, thus, was well aware of this type of verse. According to Harold K. Bush Jr. in his insightful study of Mark Twain's verses for his daughter, Susy, who died in 1896, these pieces were "notoriously and dismissively referred to as 'graveyard poetry,'" considered maudlin and extravagantly emotional by both contemporary and later critics. Still these compositions allowed mothers (and fathers) to grieve in a public forum as they sought to reconcile themselves to the death of a child and, as Bush notes, can be seen as "tender and moving expressions of loss" on the part of men and women coping with tragedy in a society without an acceptable framework for such profound emotional suffering.[47]

Agnes Lee composed three poems that referred directly to Peggy's death. "Before Sleep" captures the despair of the mother witnessing her child's fight to survive, comprehending its futility and, ultimately, praying for an end to her suffering:

> O child of struggle, here's the night!
> Then rest, then rest.
> Let peace come nestle on your brow.
> Put out the light—
>
> Nor back to the old battle hark.
> Draw down the shades,
> Put out the light. And in your soul
> Put out the dark.[48]

In "Under Peggy's Window" Agnes had celebrated her daughter's magical affect on spring flowers as the violets blossomed early under her spell. Now, in a poignant counterpoint to that image, the poet wrote "In the Spring." The first stanza is a recollection of Peggy in the garden excitedly anticipating the blooming of her carefully planted seeds:

> Joyously planting, a young child said:
> "Seeds, you shall blossom when spring is new,
> And all the garden be gold and red,
> As all my dear little plans come true."

But when the season and the blossoms arrived, the child was no longer there to delight in the unfolding spectacle:

Spring has glided with fond, warm feet.
All the dear little plans came true.
But the sweetest flower that ever was sweet
Is lying lower than seed or dew.[49]

Similarly, the painful reminder of a young life cut short is the subject of another simple but powerful poem, titled "The Diary." In this verse, Agnes recalls the pleasure her daughter took in keeping a record of her innocent childhood thoughts and pastimes.

Deft her young fingers, —
A pleasant thought, a daily note.
"How sweet," she said, "in another year
To see what I wrote!"

But, of course, "another year" was not to be, and the diary entries, like the child's life, had stopped.

And then, the gaps—
Page upon page a blank, nothing to say.
She left the little book at home
When she went away.[50]

According to Wendy Simonds and Barbara Katz Rothman in their study of maternal grief in popular literature, often "a revelation—a voice, a vision, a memory—occurs in the poem which helps a mother resign herself to, or more easily bear, her sorrow."[51] There is little solace or comfort to be found in Agnes's poems, however. There is no reconciliation or mention of an afterlife; there is simply absence, and loss, and the recognition that the beloved child is buried underground, "lying lower than seed or dew." A year later, Agnes sought consolation in the writings of others, as documented in a letter from Louise Guiney to Fred Day. "I hope Agnes will get what she wants out of Mrs. Marriott Watson's poem," Guiney wrote. Rosamund Marriott Watson was a gifted poet and critic then residing in London; but Watson was also a controversial figure who dared two public divorces. Guiney, who would have been scandalized by such behavior, was not convinced that Watson was a kindred spirit or that Agnes would find what she was looking for in Watson's verses. "*She* never lost a child," Guiney wrote, adding caustically, "I can't conceive of her caring a penny if she did."[52]

Mark Twain and his wife Livy found comfort in Alfred Lord Tennyson's consideration of loss and bereavement, *In Memoriam A. H. H.* (1850), perhaps because of its acknowledgment of a continuing bond and relationship between the living and the dead.[53] It was a sentiment that any grieving parent would embrace. In a similar vein, Guiney believed Agnes might find a more sympathetic mind in William Canton, a British writer whose ten-year-old daughter, Winifred Vida, "the W.V. of his sweet books," she observed, had "just died too." Canton had composed a series of books inspired by his children, and, to Guiney's eye, portraits of Winifred had looked "a bit like Peggy's."[54] Certainly Canton had a sensibility closely aligned with Lee's, writing shortly after Winifred's death: "But for us when she died all the clocks of the world seemed to stop, and all the wheels of life to fall still."[55]

The marriage of Francis Watts Lee and Agnes Rand Lee did not survive the death of Peggy. Although divorce was then not as rare as it had been in the past—by one account, "perhaps one marriage in ten contracted in the early 1890s would end in divorce"—they did not dissolve their union quickly or lightly.[56] The couple separated in 1902, attempted reconciliation a few years later, and finalized the divorce in 1910. Each remarried. Still, the memory of their firstborn child never diminished and Peggy's name continued to arise. A faithful correspondent to Fred Day, Agnes wrote in 1919 to request an extra copy of *The Round Rabbit* because she was "anxious to give a Rabbit to a dear little child," a relative of her second husband. She was unable to part with her own copy, however, which was "very precious because thumbed up by darling Peggy," and offered to "pay three times the original price of the book."[57] Day, as always, complied immediately and dispatched a complimentary copy. He received a grateful acknowledgment a week later. "The precious bunnies arrived safely yesterday," Agnes wrote. "If you knew how much I wanted them, you would know how much I thank you!"[58]

A little over a year later, in 1920, Louise Imogen Guiney passed away after a debilitating stroke and several weeks in a semi-coma. "Shocked and grieved" after reading "the bare notice" in the newspaper, Agnes contacted Day and commiserated, "I doubt if any will feel her death more deeply than you and I."[59] Commenting later that "the world doesn't seem quite the same world when one feels that she is not in it," Agnes composed a commemorative poem, "The Death of Louise Imogen Guiney (A Vision)," in which Peggy has a role:

> I think it must have been afternoon,
> So gentle the scene.
> I think it must have been Auburndale,
> The grass was so green.
>
> She walked with me, as often before,
> Through sun-path ways.
> We talked of things we often talked of,
> In the old days.
>
> It was not the glimmering words she said,
> Nor the silences,
> Which brought the great calm into my soul
> At last . . . but this:
>
> That a little child we both had loved
> Drew her from me,
> And led her down a darkened path
> I could not see.[60]

There is a clear shift in tone with this new poetic reference to Peggy. Two decades after the child's death, Agnes has reached reconciliation and found peace. The focus is no longer on the loss and finality of "In the Spring" and "The Diary." With "The Death of Louise Imogen Guiney," she has embraced "A Vision" (as she subtitled the poem) of a reunion in an afterlife, much as Simonds and Rothman would have predicted. As Agnes dreams of a meeting with Louise Guiney, it was not the conversation or camaraderie of the two old friends that "brought the great calm into my soul / At last." It was instead "a little child we both had loved" who appeared to lead Guiney away. Although Agnes "could not see" the two figures as they moved "down a darkened path," she was consoled by her certainty that the path existed and that she would see them both again.

Peggy remained a living force for Francis as well. A devout Christian, who may well have received succor from his faith at the time of his daughter's death, he too mentioned her name decades later in a brief letter to his wife, Marion, who was traveling. He filled much of the note with news of their two children, Lucy and Francis, but, at one point injected a simple, yet moving, sentence: "I went (alone) to High Mass at S. John Evangelist it being the forty-second anniversary of Harriet's baptism in that church."[61]

Even as Agnes and Francis continued privately to hold the memory of their daughter close, one image of her was garnering extraordinary attention in the very public world of American photography.

**FIGURE 9.** Gertrude Käsebier, *Blessed Art Thou among Women*, 1899, platinum print. (PR13 CN2015.052.536)

# Chapter 4
## BLESSED ART THOU AMONG WOMEN

*Blessed Art Thou among Women* (figure 9) is considered by many to be one of Gertrude Käsebier's "most beautiful and most deservedly celebrated images."[1] Universally acclaimed from the beginning, reproduced in photographic journals, and exhibited often, the image is part of major museum collections. By the late twentieth century it had been widely reproduced and made available to the public as a print and poster. The United States Postal Service chose the work as one of twenty photographs in its Masters of American Photography series of stamps. Taken in the Lee family home in Jamaica Plain in 1899, the picture captures Agnes and Peggy posed in a doorway. The child stands upright and regal in a dark dress with starched white collar and cuffs. As the scholar Laura Wexler notes, "She seems eager, confident, yet hesitant, for a moment, before crossing the threshold."[2] Agnes drapes her arm across the girl's shoulder in a timeless maternal gesture, both encouraging her to look and move into the future and simultaneously seemingly attempting to hold onto and protect her, perhaps whispering a comforting word in her ear. In the century since the dual portrait was conceived, it has gained near-iconic status as a comment on the mother-child relationship, a subject with which the artist came to be identified.

Gertrude Käsebier followed an unlikely route to her career in pictorial photography. She was born Gertrude Stanton in 1852 in Iowa.[3] Her father, a saw mill owner and pioneer, brought the family to the loosely organized town of Golden in the Colorado territory. There were few white children, thus Gertrude's early childhood companions were primarily Native American. The Stantons returned to Brooklyn, New York, when Gertrude was twelve. This diversity of places and experiences, which also included time spent with her maternal grandmother in Bethlehem, Pennsylvania, broadened her outlook and, on some level, awakened her artistic sensibilities. At twenty-two she married Eduard Käsebier, an ambitious immigrant educated in both chemistry and business. Eduard became a successful shellac importer and provided well for his family; but, the marriage was not a good one, something Gertrude made clear in a later blunt assessment: "If my husband has gone to Heaven, I want to go to Hell. He was terrible. I could never cook anything he liked. Nothing was ever good enough for him." According to Käsebier's biographer Barbara Michaels, as their children neared adolescence and independence, "by tacit agreement she broke loose from household constraints and, at the age of thirty-seven, began art school," where she found her true calling in photography. Käsebier graduated from Brooklyn's Pratt Institute in 1893 but continued to enroll in classes for the next few years. She also opened a commercial photographic studio in a room of the Woman's Exchange off Fifth Avenue in New York City, where, although "not affiliated with the Exchange, . . . she benefited from its genteel clientele and from the congenial atmosphere among women artists in its studios."[4]

During the final decades of the nineteenth century, photography had become a popular pastime, and, in many instances, a career option for women. As the historian C. Jane Gover observes, "a convergence of technical advances, attitudinal shifts toward women's roles, changing perceptions about the very nature of photography itself, and . . . a burgeoning consciousness of the restrictions present in late Victorian America" resulted in hundreds of women becoming professional photographers. It was thought that photography as an occupation "combined domesticity with a profession" in that empathetic women were considered skilled at coaxing other women, their children, and families into congenial poses.[5] Many of these female photographers not only ran successful commercial businesses but also endeavored to create artistic images which they entered in photographic competitions and salons. Frances Benjamin Johnston positioned herself as a prominent portrait photographer in Washington, DC, capturing images of the political and social elite of that city. In addition, she became known as a photojournalist with her work at the Hampton Normal and Agricultural Institute in Hampton, Virginia, and events such as world's fairs and expositions.[6] Deerfield, Massachusetts, photographers Frances and Mary Allen used subjects, settings, and poses that reminded viewers of Renaissance paintings, and they manipulated negatives and print surfaces to create images with emotional weight. Influenced by the Colonial Revival movement, they created works that idealized the preindustrial colonial past. In Boston, the talent and originality of the photographers Sarah Choate Sears, Mary Devens, and Margaret Russell gained the approval of F. Holland Day and Alfred Stieglitz.[7]

Like these other pioneers, Gertrude Käsebier was interested not only in studio portraiture but in the promotion of photography as an art form. The French artist and critic Robert Demachy believed that Käsebier "exemplified the type of photographer who could produce work for art salons as well as portraits to commission," making her a "double personality as artist and professional."[8] Käsebier first exhibited her photographs at the Boston Camera Club in 1896, at the Pratt Institute in 1897, and at the Photographic Society of Philadelphia in early 1898. Critics immediately compared her photographs to old master paintings. For example, Sadakichi Hartmann wrote, "If I go to her studio to-day, she may make a Holbein of me, to-morrow it would be a Rembrandt, or a Mary Cassatt."[9] Her obvious talent and creativity brought her to the attention of Alfred Stieglitz, the acknowledged leader of American pictorialists, who quickly drew her into his circle. She was selected to exhibit several of her works at the juried first Philadelphia Photographic Salon in the fall of 1898, where she met F. Holland Day, who became a lifelong friend and confidant.

Käsebier refused to use the artificial background scenery or ornate furnishings then commonly found in commercial studios. She was more innovative. In her simple compositions she found the balance between technique and feeling to create masterpieces of, in Ralph Adams Cram's words, "emotional expression" and "intrinsic beauty."[10] A French critic emphasized the unique emotional depths of Käsebier's art: "This incomparable magician of feeling has on more than one occasion violated the rules of aesthetics and photographic technique, but I do not think that she ever produced a single image where we do not feel under her hand the beating of the soul and the heart."[11] In this way, Barbara

Michaels writes, Käsebier brought "studio portraiture out of the overstuffed Victorian era into the age of the Arts and Crafts movement."[12]

In April 1899, Käsebier mounted her work in an exhibition at the Arts and Crafts Society in Boston. When she traveled there to view it, she was quickly embraced by Day's circle. Day, Käsebier, and Francis Watts Lee had more in common than their interest in photographic art, however. Each was associated with and influenced by the artists Arthur Wesley Dow and Ernest F. Fenollosa, both of whom had Massachusetts connections. Dow held a summer school in Ipswich for many years, and Fenollosa was the influential curator of the Oriental Department at the Boston Museum of Fine Arts. Käsebier knew both men as innovative instructors at Pratt.[13] Dow and Fenollosa also contributed essays on Japanese art to *The Knight Errant*.[14] When Gertrude Käsebier arrived in Boston, then, she found not only Day but an extended circle of associates with similar perspectives on art, photography, and the advancement of their ideals. Perhaps because of this shared outlook, Käsebier and the Lees quickly became friends. During this visit or later that same year, Käsebier photographed Agnes and Peggy in the portrait she titled *Blessed Art Thou among Women*, a quintessential expression of her style, composition, and successful implementation of her photographic principles.[15]

In his groundbreaking work on Käsebier, the photographic historian William Innes Homer stressed her "simplicity of design and tone," which "produces an effect of dignity . . . in most of her portraits." He commented too on Käsebier's "ability to select a telling gesture . . . to convey an emotional truth about the personage" whom she was photographing.[16] Arthur Wesley Dow had similarly praised her, observing that Käsebier "looks for some special evidence of personality in her sitter, some line, some silhouette, some expression or movement." Once identifying this distinctive characteristic or gesture in her subject, Dow continued, "she endeavors to give the best presentation" by utilizing the pose, lighting, and developing process to render the "beauty in the sitter" on to the resulting print.[17] Ralph Adams Cram similarly commented that Käsebier's portraits were "vital and personal" and "always adapted to the character of the subject."[18]

H. Snowden Ward, a critic and journalist, witnessed this method in action one afternoon in her studio. After Käsebier had fully acquainted herself with the sitter and set the appropriate lighting, "half-a-dozen exposures were made" all the while explaining her work to the subject until "at last (as Mrs. Käsebier said afterward) the sitter began to lose self-consciousness, and his temperament began to reveal itself." Portraits thus created became, as Ward described them, "'human documents' in which she attempts to penetrate the artificial mask of inscrutability that everyone turns to the world," and eventually reach "some hint of the strength, the patience, and the sweetness that lie behind the mask."[19]

For *Blessed Art Thou among Women* the camera appears to be surreptitiously recording a private moment, a fleeting physical expression of instinct and reaction. Of course, the cumbersome equipment and intricate lighting requirements of the time made the unplanned creation of such a photograph impossible. According to Käsebier, however, she "simulated spontaneity by asking the mother and daughter to hold an actual pose she had seen."[20] The image is a dynamic one. Agnes appears to be relaxed and comfortable, one hand braced on the door frame, the other resting on her daughter's shoulder, her head turned away from the camera. The child, meanwhile, stands awkwardly straight. Drawn to her full height, heels together, hands at her side, staring past the viewer as if at attention, Peggy strains to hold the pose, her taut fingers an indication of her impatience.

It is a flawless composition in color, tone, and shape. First, it is, as one scholar notes, "a study in shades of white" with Agnes's billowing gown and Peggy's brightly starched collar and cuffs offset by the light tones of the background wall and painted door frame.[21] Second, the textures of the varied fabrics—the ethereal yet voluminous dress of the mother contrasted with the depth and solidity of the girl's attire—and the rounded forms of the figures in counterpoint to the rectilinear doorway and artwork on the back wall, enhanced by the elongated cropping of the image itself, result in an eloquent balance of pattern and shape. More significant, Käsebier has sympathetically captured the distinct personalities of both individuals as well as the discrete bond they have with each other. "I have longed unceasingly to make pictures of people, not maps of faces, but pictures of real men and women as they know themselves," Käsebier explained, "to make likenesses that are biographies."[22] Käsebier has, in fact, preserved both the solicitous nurturing yet somewhat anxious mother *and* the eager, self-assured, but fleetingly hesitant child about to cross the threshold of the room, and life.

Käsebier believed her own experiences as a wife, mother, and grandmother enabled her to recognize and reproduce "the essential personality" of her sitters, their "temperament, soul, humanity." In her view "it is impossible to understand people unless you understand life. You see through experience. You cannot read faces, the joy and sorrow in them, unless you have suffered and enjoyed."[23] She drew on her own acquaintance with these emotions and her artistic gifts to elevate the mother and daughter's singular reenactment into a spiritual moment and the depiction of a universal truth. Käsebier accomplished this through both the image and the title she gave the work, a title taken from the piece of art hanging in the background of the mother-daughter tableau.

The print is a portrayal of the Annunciation created by the devoutly religious English Arts and Crafts artist Selwyn Image (figure 10). Many within Käsebier's contemporary audience would have recognized the image. Often the subject of Christian art, the Annunciation marks the angel Gabriel's appearance before Mary, and his announcement that she will become the mother of the son of God. Most master artists, including Botticelli, Leonardo, and Caravaggio, particularly those working in the Middle Ages and the Renaissance, created depictions of the event. Compositions of the scene generally include two figures, the angel usually on the left in full or near-profile, and the Virgin facing the viewer. Most show Mary seated or kneeling in some enclosed area; Image's composition, however, has both figures standing in an outdoor garden setting. Here, Mary also appears completely composed, displaying none of the alarm or reluctance which was often the focus in other depictions. Thus, this poster-sized chromolithograph was an unusual yet reverent treatment of the sacred subject. In addition, it was dramatically colorful, with the angel's wings and the Virgin's halo a striking red and the background foliage, bright blues and greens.

Appropriate to Arts and Crafts ideals, which deemed "art a primary means to cultivate taste and socialize children and immigrants," the Image poster was part of a series made for use in settlement house nurseries, hospitals, and schoolrooms to bring beauty and color into institutional settings. Its border, partially visible behind the two figures in the photo, is circumscribed with the words from which Käsebier derived her title: "And the angel came in unto her, and said, Hail thou that art highly favored, the Lord is with thee: Blessed art thou among women." As the art historian Kristin Schwain points out, Progressive Era reformers "believed the home—its architecture and material culture—had the power to shape the character of its inhabitants." Hanging as it did in the Lee

FIGURE 10. Selwyn Image, "Blessed Art Thou among Women" poster, from *The Studio*, April 1893, p. 29.

household, the print is evidence of the family's devotion to Christianity as well as to the aesthetics and principles of the Arts and Crafts movement. In selecting the biblical passage as the title of her portrait, Käsebier was working within a well-established tradition. The turn of the twentieth century was rife with images of the Virgin Mary, and representations could be found in "art galleries, exhibition spaces, museum and print collections, and popular periodicals." In fact, "those who relied on Marian associations at some point in their careers [made up] . . . a virtual who's who of American Art" at the time, even among photographers.[24] Käsebier's *Blessed Art Thou among Women,* then, was a product of artistic vision and serendipity: the mother and child, their own home, the image in the background, and the photographer who was able to recognize the banality yet transcendence of the moment. As a later acquaintance observed to Lee, the photo perfectly captures "the child with the guardian angel's arm about her looking through the doorway to a new life."[25]

The portrait was immediately deemed a masterpiece. Alfred Stieglitz reproduced the image as a photogravure in the July 1900, issue of *Camera Notes.* Likely already in production at the time of Peggy's death, the issue was distributed in early June, less than a month after the family's loss. Francis Watts Lee, who had previously written of the journal to Stieglitz, "I devour the whole thing with avidity the moment I get it," acknowledged receipt of the issue and portrait on June 6. "The reproduction of my wife and the dear little one whom we see in the flesh no longer is very beautifully done," he wrote, "and I am glad to think that its presence in Camera Notes may be the means of giving others pleasure beside us."[26] Lee's choice of words is telling and provides insight into his state of mind and worldview. Clearly heartbroken in his reference to "the dear little one whom we see in the flesh no longer," he seems to be asserting that he will see his daughter again, either in memory alone or in an afterlife. Lee's devotion to Christian principles and its firm assurance of an afterlife likely helped him withstand the tragic events that had so recently transpired. His beliefs allowed him to gain comfort rather than pain from the image, and his wish that it "may be the means of giving others pleasure" seems a generous and heartfelt one.

An original platinum print of *Blessed Art Thou among Women* was first hung in October 1900 in the third Philadelphia Photographic Salon, where it was called "unquestionably one of the most perfect and beautiful pictures of the Salon" by the critic Joseph T. Keiley. "In subject, composition, line, tone and feeling, it is singularly beautiful." The critic then discussed not only the photograph itself but also the relationship it represented. He began by describing "the beautiful solicitude of the delicate, charming mother, and the almost indifference of the child." As Keiley interpreted the scene, the child "accepts the maternal devotion as a matter of course, and looks straight ahead, as though forgetful of the mother in the contemplation of what is before it"—symbolically, a lifetime.

He then argues the appropriateness of the emotions depicted. "It is natural that the mother should look solicitously to the child—it is also in accordance with the laws of nature that the child should look beyond and be even indifferent towards the mother."[27]

Keiley had been one of the first critics to recognize that Käsebier's best work was achieved "not through the brain, but through a direct and irresistible appeal to the heart" and that her "real inspiration" seemed to be motherhood.[28] Michaels believes that "Käsebier had begun to consider motherhood as a basis for her art" while attending classes at the Pratt Institute. "The subject not only had a long tradition in the form of madonnas and children, but it was generally popular in the late nineteenth century."[29] In addition, Pratt had exposed Käsebier to the theories of Friedrich Froebel. Froebel, a German philosopher and educator, believed that children have distinct needs and abilities. He devoted himself to preschool child education, coined the word "kindergarten," and advocated for the kind of playthings and activities that later progressive educators embraced. His liberal, child-oriented methods became popular in U.S. teacher training centers like Pratt and helped solidify the belief in the nurturing mother whose kindness and support would educate and introduce young children into the adult world.[30]

In her own life Käsebier embraced this view of, as one historian described it, an "educated motherhood that stressed an insightful, rational approach to maternal duties" and progressive child-rearing techniques.[31] In her work she became known for her artistic studies of motherhood, childhood, and domesticity. She depicted the construction of motherhood, widely adopted by her class, which saw mothers as, in C. Jane Gover's words, "the cornerstone of the late nineteenth century value system that professed a commitment to traits of diligence, faith, individualism, and a trust in moral advancement."[32] Käsebier was an interpretive portraitist who favored compositions, including *Mother and Child* (1897), *The Picture-Book* (1903), and *The Hand That Rocks the Cradle* (1913), which utilized religious iconography or references. She had absorbed Symbolist ideals, wherein the artist, according to William Innes Homer, "preferred to suggest rather than to describe in a realistic manner" or to make explicit spiritual representations.[33] Thus, *Blessed Art Thou among Women* remains a contemporary double portrait with a biblical allusion rather than an explicitly religious statement.

Seeing in *The Manger*, another of Käsebier's maternal images, "the radiant, pure, holy love of the young mother as she feels the little being in her arms," Keiley emphasized that in *The Manger* as well as *Blessed Art Thou among Women*, "it is always the eloquence of the mother that floods out to you from these pictures." In *Blessed Art Thou among Women*, Keiley senses that it is only proper "that the mother should give all as a matter of nature, and the child accept everything as a matter of course . . ." He identified the image as "full of maternal love" and, more striking, "suggestive of the maternal sorrow that in the depth and silence of her own heart every mother feels at the seeming unresponsiveness of the child."[34] It is the mother's duty to delight, educate, and encourage her child; it is the child's duty to draw strength and confidence from the relationship and step boldly into adulthood, almost thoughtlessly leaving behind the nurturing maternal figure.

At the time he wrote this review, Keiley was undoubtedly aware of the depth of the sorrow that Agnes Lee was facing in reality. The American pictorialist community was a small one, and word of the child's death would certainly have reached Keiley through either Stieglitz or Käsebier herself. This knowledge may well have contributed to his detailed and compassionate assessment of the portrait. In this light, the critique reads like a letter of condolence to the Lees. The photo "is charming in rendering and truly beautiful in sentiment," Keiley concluded, and "is a picture that will long remain in the memory of those who have once seen it."[35] Keiley implies that the lost child will, in some way, be kept alive by those who have gazed upon and been affected by the image.

Soon enough the tragedy of Peggy's death was public knowledge. A 1904 profile of Gertrude Käsebier in *New Idea Woman's Magazine* by Sarah Slater called particular attention to *Blessed Art Thou among Women*. The journalist commented that "the clinging tenderness of the lines in the drooping figure of the mother are prophetic." Referring to Peggy as "the sturdy little form . . . already on the threshold of life," Slater continued, "even before the picture was printed she had slipped from the detaining grasp of love into the Beyond."[36] Although employing a rather maudlin tone and sonorous rhetoric, Slater understood that reality had transformed the image from portrait to a kind of mourning picture.

The scholar Karen Sánchez-Eppler explains that "from the first the miracle of photography has been understood as a miracle of memorialization, the capacity to preserve a bit of the present, to let us see again, . . . a moment that is in all other ways irretrievably past." Although taken for granted and considered unremarkable today, this ability of the photograph to, in a way, resurrect the dead, was "felt with gothic intensity" from the beginning of the daguerreotype era.[37] It was only natural that images which outlasted the living subject would come to be utilized and valued as anamnestic objects. Since ancient times, people have sought means to retain in memory the physical appearance of their departed loved ones, and items created by the bereaved to memorialize their dead have a long history.

In the early nineteenth century mourning embroideries and paintings were commonly displayed in American homes, particularly after the death of George Washington, whose demise inspired a commercial industry of commemoration. Uniquely embroidered and painted pictures on silk began to disappear in the 1830s and mass-produced prints took their place. These were characterized by willow trees, urns, mortuary obelisks, and generic allegorical mourning figures with a blank space for the appropriate name to be inserted. Between 1830 and 1860 a more elaborate and personal portraiture flourished, completed by artists called in at the time of death to sketch and then paint a picture of the deceased, usually as in life.[38]

With the advent of photography, postmortem portraits posed in the bedroom or in the casket, sometimes called "Last Memory Pictures," were commissioned. The tranquillity of these images would provide reassurance to the bereaved, the social historian Audrey Linkman explains, especially when "the final illness had been particularly painful, or if death was due to an accident or an act of violence."[39] Although unsettling today, these posthumous images were often the only means available to create and preserve a visual representation of a beloved child or spouse who may not have been photographed during their lifetime. For example, the British poet and critic Matthew Arnold requested a postmortem photo of his sixteen-month-old son, Basil, because "we should else have had no picture of him whatever."[40] Once photography became more common, pictures taken during the deceased's lifetime began to be used as memorial portraits simply by adding vital statistics (birth and death dates) or a verse to commemorate the passing. Often sized to be inserted into photographic albums, the pictures were given to family and friends as keepsakes.[41] Commercially printed nonphotographic cards began to appear as well. As

Sánchez-Eppler explains, the practice of sharing these mementos enabled an "extension and demarcation of mourning and memorialization well beyond the immediate circle of the bereaved."[42]

Although *Blessed Art Thou among Women* was not commissioned as a mourning picture or memorial, there is evidence that the Lee family decided to use it as a commemorative piece. Shortly after the image appeared in *Camera Notes*, Francis Watts Lee wrote to Alfred Stieglitz asking if he might purchase "extra impressions" of the photogravure. "I have coveted more . . . ," the grieving father admitted, "but could not bear to ask dear Mrs. K[äsebier]." Since Käsebier was a close friend, Lee was also aware "it was no use to try and talk money with her" under such circumstances. Acquiring duplicates through Stieglitz in a business transaction, Lee noted, would be "a simple and easy way out." Because Francis requested "50 impressions" and suggested that "a trifle more margin than it has in the magazine would improve it for framing," it is apparent that the Lees planned to give the portrait to relatives and acquaintances as a remembrance of their daughter.[43]

Given the relatively high rate of childhood mortality, any number of pictorialists' portraits could have been converted into memorial keepsakes. The Allen sisters made a number of evocative studies of neighbors and townspeople in their rural community. *Roana Sweeping*, a photo of their young neighbor Roana Andrews, then almost three years old, was one of their most charming. A few months later the child died of cholera, making all the more poignant the study image of the little girl in a long dress and bare feet sweeping the ground with a broom too large for her.[44] Gertrude Käsebier herself was touched by another distressful event involving her photography. Among her famous portraits of Native Americans are images of Sioux children, Mary Lone Bear and Willie Spotted Horse. Because the Sioux feared that any depiction of a child would cause harm or even death, it took Käsebier years and a "special friendship" with the Sioux before the family allowed her to photograph Mary Lone Bear. Shockingly, the girl died six weeks later.[45] Neither Käsebier's nor the Allens' image was intended to be a mourning picture, yet, in some sense that is what they became. There is no record of how Roana's parents viewed the photo after her death, and it is certain that the family of Mary Lone Bear drew no consolation from her image. For the Lees, however, the photograph of their daughter Peggy was a blessing. "If dear Mrs. K only knew what all those pictures she made when she was last here now mean to us," Francis wrote to Stieglitz, "she would be more glad than ever that she had done it."[46]

Käsebier continued to show *Blessed Art Thou among Women* at important photographic exhibitions, including *The New School of American Photography* mounted by F. Holland Day in London and Paris in 1900 and 1901. Always an admirer of the portrait, Alfred Stieglitz placed the work in the first Photo-Secession exhibition at the National Arts Club in New York in 1902, at his Little Galleries of the Photo-Secession in 1905, and in the final Photo-Secession Exhibition at the Albright Art Gallery in Buffalo, New York, in 1910. And, when Clarence White formed the Pictorial Photographers of America in 1916, Käsebier lent fifteen of her works including *Blessed Art Thou among Women* to the group's inaugural exhibition at the National Arts Club.[47]

With continuing public display, the work began to influence artists and others. The noted photographer Imogen Cunningham recalled that early in the twentieth century she had seen a reproduction of the photograph while a high school student. The image stayed with her and "inspired her to become a photographer" and even to seek Käsebier's counsel when she returned home from her studies in Europe in 1910.[48] In 1922, Agnes Lee received a request from a woman who was writing "a series of 'fairy-tales' of the origins of life for mothers and children." Having seen *Blessed Art Thou among Women*, the author wrote that "it seemed as though this picture symbolized all that I would have them say."[49] Unaware of the portrait's widening audience, Agnes wrote that she was "glad to have her use Lady K[äsebier]'s picture" but "was at a loss to understand how she could have seen the picture."[50] For Agnes, it was a cherished family photo, sent lovingly to close friends and relatives; perhaps she had forgotten it was also a work of art.

Käsebier produced several platinum prints of *Blessed Art Thou among Women*. Although she often manipulated her prints or experimented with multiple developing processes, she printed this image time and again with little tonal variation.[51] These additional platinum copies as well as the photogravure prints made it possible for museums, public institutions, and individual collectors to acquire the image, thereby increasing its audience and renown. The photograph was much sought after and was added to several significant public collections. As Käsebier's reputation continued to grow, the portrait became part of the emerging American photographic canon, and it has become one of the most recognizable images in pictorial history. In 1997, the United States Postal Service proposed to issue a pane of stamps featuring "notable pictures made by major American photographers over a span of some 120 years."[52] Among the twenty images selected was *Blessed Art Thou among Women*. On the verso of the semi-jumbo stamp was printed: "Eminent portrait photographer Gertrude Käsebier (1852–1934), whose best known images are those of mothers and children, pioneered an evocative soft-focus style that established her as a guiding force in the pictorialist movement. *Blessed Art Thou among Women*—a sensitive and artistic portrayal of author Agnes Rand Lee and her daughter Peggy—was made in 1899."[53] With the production and distribution of these stamps, the image gained further notoriety as it became part of philatelic history. The portrait can now be obtained in any size from a postage stamp to a poster and is likely to continue attracting new admirers.[54]

At its most elemental level, however, *Blessed Art Thou among Women* remains the portrait of a particular mother and child. More than a century after it was posed, Agnes Lee continues to lean protectively toward her daughter Peggy, who is eternally seven years old, looking expectantly into the future.

# *Chapter 5*

## THE DAUGHTERS OF FRANCIS WATTS LEE

Francis Watts Lee publicly displayed his photographic work for only four years beginning with the Linked Ring's London salon in September 1898 and ending with that organization's tenth exhibition in the fall of 1902. His artistic output was small, and he submitted several of his images to more than one venue. Most were portraits of men and women, with a few allegorical studies considered by one British writer "quite in the American vogue." All were praised for their "splendid colour and tone," and taken together were a pleasing collection of carefully constructed and executed character studies distinguished by Lee's ability to experiment with process and paper.[1] As one critic noted, the results were generally "fine examples of honest portraiture, dignified in style and evidencing a nice appreciation of the characteristics of the subjects—and admirable as such rather than as works of art."[2] Although beautiful, Lee's work seemed to some viewers more cerebral and technically proficient than emotionally engaging, with the exception of *The Vision* (plate 1), a haunting portrait of his wife Agnes, the elegant *Miss E. H.* (plate 2), and *Magdelena Meditans* (plate 7), a stunning picture in gray tones.

At the Third Philadelphia Photographic Salon, held in fall 1900, however, Lee made a significant change from his previous submissions. For the first time he exhibited images of his children; in fact, Peggy and Alice were the subjects of all four studies. Two of these, *Sisters* and *Stephana,* were straightforward portraits of the girls taken a few months before Peggy's death. They were, in Joseph T. Keiley's words, "very simply rendered, very directly."[3] The others were quite different in style and presentation. These photos featured an unclothed Peggy posed in marshy terrain looking like some elusive water sprite. Other pictorialists photographed and exhibited portraits of the girls as well, making Peggy and Alice significant models in the early years of artistic photography. Their images were also fitting examples of the depictions of children in art, especially pictorial photography, at the close of the nineteenth century.

Children have always been represented in art, yet for centuries European art academies deemed portraiture, particularly child portraiture, of lesser importance than works that addressed grand-scale narratives of religion, mythology, or history. Within the subgenre of portrait painting, a work's relative merit depended as much on the significance of the sitter as it did on the artist's skill or reputation. As the art historian Barbara Dayer Gallati has noted, unless the subject was a child "of royal or noble birth," portraits of children were the most marginalized of subjects and had "comparatively limited appeal."[4] By the end of the eighteenth century, influenced by the theories of John Locke and Jean-Jacques Rousseau, childhood was regarded more positively and artistic representations of children symbolized their uncorrupted state. This elevation of the subject was short-lived, however. As the nineteenth century progressed, cloying sentimentality began to replace innocence in child portraits. At the same time women artists, who had been virtually excluded from academic life classes, were encouraged to pursue subjects thought appropriate to their "more emotionally intuitive" natures and experiences. By the final quarter of the century, portraits of children were generally both inconsequential and "the province of women and of men of lesser talents and ambitions."[5]

In many ways the work of John Singer Sargent (1856–1925) transformed childhood and adolescence as subjects in the visual arts. Maturing within this academic construction of artist and subject, Sargent was nonetheless affected by emerging psychological and sociological theories about the stages of life, and he was a keen observer of the particular cultural settings that would provide a child distinct experiences according to societal values and economic conditions. Sargent and others began to recognize and depict cultural character types in their art. This was certainly true with regard to the idealized American child, who represented an independence, optimism, and confidence that differed from the more staid British prototype. As one contemporary observer wrote, "While the English children are sturdy and stolid, the German healthy and phlegmatic, the French nervous and attenuated, the American child combines a little of all those characteristics fused in the heat of the vivacious American temperament into brilliancy of mental power and faultlessness of physical proportions."[6]

Americans saw their children and their culture evolving toward modernity and perfection, and artists reflected these beliefs. Gallati contends that "Sargent's imagery reveals a synergy with the 'picture' of childhood promoted by progressive social reformers"—in essence, the "sheltered child," a product of urban middle- and upper-class beliefs, increased financial resources, and liberal child-rearing techniques. Sargent's portraits were imbued with these "culturally conditioned ideas of childhood."[7] Thus, the informality of the young people Sargent included in his genre paintings *Neapolitan Children Bathing* (1879), *Beach at Capri* (1878), and the later *Gypsy Encampment* (c 1912) have little in common with the personality, confident assurance, and obvious affluence of *Cara Burch* (1888) and *Dorothy* (1900). In 1888, Sargent's solo exhibition at Boston's St. Botolph Club contained child portraits that reflected the strong and secure character of the American child. Among these were the "clear-eyed directness" of *Ruth Sears Bacon* (1887) and the self-possessed yet mysterious *Daughters of Edward Darley Boit* (1882), a composition that reverberated among artistic Bostonians for some time.[8] It seemed that cherished and romanticized young people were taking center stage. "This is the age of the child," one critic noted in *Cosmopolitan*. "Never before has society taken so much interest in its bringing up." With this new focus, he continued, "portraiture [of children] . . . has almost become a necessity of modern life."[9] And, the creation of these portraits was rapidly becoming the domain of the photographer.

While much commercial photography remained stilted and artificial to the eye, practitioners who embraced the fine art aesthetic argued that photography too was a medium of creative expression and, in the proper hands, could result in both accuracy and artistic depth. By emulating painters, American pictorialism, according to the art historian George Dimock, "promoted the medium's capacity to convey the intimations and imaginings of the artist-photographer" through "a careful orchestration of signs and symbols all pointing to higher, more abstract and allegorical levels of meaning" within their images.[10] Pictorialism also helped democratize aesthetic child portraiture at the same time that it was expanding notions of fine art. An artistically conceived photograph was much more affordable and accessible than a painted portrait, which remained a viable option only for the elite. Additionally, as photography gained acceptance as a legitimate art form, it sparked, in one historian's words, "arguments regarding the relative truthfulness of painted and photographed images and forced painters to reevaluate their philosophical and technical strategies in that respect."[11] Images of one child gave a face to that discussion.

Helen Sears, the daughter of Sarah Choate Sears, a wealthy, well-connected Bostonian and multitalented artist who worked most notably in watercolor, pastels, and photography, was a frequent model for her mother.[12] Sarah photographed Helen from the time she was a baby, and the child was also the subject of portraits in oil by Abbott Henderson Thayer (in 1891–92) and John Singer Sargent (in 1895). The same year Sargent completed his portrait of Helen, a full-length study of the child in a white dress surrounded by flowering hydrangeas, Sarah photographed her daughter in the identical outfit holding a Japanese lantern. When Sarah shared the photograph with him, a generous Sargent alluded to the inadequacy of his own work: "But how can an unfortunate painter hope to rival a photograph by a mother? Absolute truth combined with absolute feeling."[13] Although the accuracy of Sargent's modest statement can be debated—the young girl certainly holds a graceless pose and expression in the photograph—his remark calls attention to what Dimock calls the "personal circumstances and emotional entanglements" that characterized much of the pictorialists' product.[14]

Achieving painterly effects through darkroom manipulations (with brushes and tools), processes (soft gum and oils), and varied papers, pictorialists created unique prints. But to capture the desired image itself, the photographer required the cooperation of the sitter. The faces full of affection, pleasure, and openness that could be created or re-created by an artist in oils or watercolors had to be unequivocally present when the camera was the medium. This was no easy task, and advice on how to achieve success could be found in most photographic journals. "It seems to be a case of selection," wrote one practitioner. "The children must love him. They have intuitive perceptions, and cannot be deceived

FIGURE 11. F. Holland Day, *Peggie*, 1898, platinum print. National Media Museum/Royal Photographic Society/Science & Society Picture Library.

by smooth words and pretty gifts."[15] Indeed photographers soon learned that children were more likely to be relaxed and their faces express affection before a person with whom they were familiar. Because of this it was common for pictorialists to use friends and family, as Sears did, rather than hire models for their art. Their goal was to capture "deeply treasured, carefully nurtured" children who were "perfectly at ease and natural." The best sitters for this endeavor were youngsters the photographer already knew and loved.[16]

From an early age, Peggy and Alice Lee were accustomed to being the subject of the artist's eye and thus, like Helen Sears, they were in Gallati's words, "more conscious of the act of self-presentation than most children."[17] Pictorialists, particularly in Boston, were a close-knit community. They collaborated in the studio and on outdoor expeditions, shared darkrooms, and traded glass plate negatives and prints. By the time the girls were four and five, they were the subject of portraits not only by their father but by his artistic colleagues and friends F. Holland Day, Frank W. Birchall, Herbert Arthur Hess, and Frederick Haven Pratt. Next to Käsebier's *Blessed Art Thou among Women,* the most well-known image of Peggy was a portrait by Day taken sometime in 1898 when she was about six (figure 11). Part of a series completed in the artist's studio, the image pleased Day enough that he sent a print to the English photographer Frederick Evans with a dedication written on the verso: "Mistress Peggie, to my dear friend Evans, August, 1898, FHD."[18]

Standing beside Day's hobnailed leather chair, his theatrical leopard skin draped across it, Peggy wears a spotless white dress with lace-trimmed collar and cuffs. As usual, Day has placed significant accessories in the composition. In this instance, a portrait of an elderly bearded man sits on the console behind Peggy's left shoulder. Possibly the depiction of a biblical character, the rather disconcerting image lends a certain solemnity to the portrait. The copy of Louis-Maurice Boutet de Manuel's *Joan of Arc,* which Peggy holds, is opened to an illustration of the peasant Joan encountering a vision of her future self. It was likely placed there by Day to suggest a similarly inspirational path for Peggy. This is not the portrait of a girl engaged in frivolous child's play. Instead, she stands straight-backed, gravely staring into the camera as her immaculate dress gleams with an aura similar to the visionary light on the open page just under her hand and the whiteness that surrounds the prophet staring over her shoulder. There is something reminiscent of eight-year-old Mary Louisa Boit from Sargent's famed portrait of the Boit sisters in Peggy's solitary stance and serious expression. Although two years younger than Mary Louisa at the time the image was created, Peggy too challenges the viewer with her upright posture and matter-of-fact gaze. As she does in Käsebier's *Blessed Art Thou among Women,* Peggy appears ready to meet whatever life brings.[19]

Peggy is more at ease in photographs taken of her with other family members. In images assumed to be the work of Frank Birchall, Peggy sits contentedly on her father's lap, a shy half-smile on her face (figure 12), and, in another, she stands comfortably beside her mother. Birchall, a friend of Francis Lee's, had a professional studio in Boston and advertised as both a commercial and

FIGURE 12. Frank W. Birchall, Francis Watts Lee and Peggy, c. 1896, reproduction print from glass plate negative. Massachusetts Historical Society, Frank W. Birchall Photographs, no. 1068/1277.

artistic photographer. As such, he was likely quite skilled in all aspects of child portraiture.[20] Gertrude Käsebier completed several images of the family, including photos of Peggy sitting with her grandfather William H. Rand playing checkers and examining his pocket watch. Each of these portraits reflected the prevalent pictorialist vision of childhood.

In his book *Priceless Children*, George Dimock notes that pictorialists' children were "well dressed and beautifully behaved, never angry, scared, or overtly unhappy, but often wistful or solemn." Meanwhile the adults were "invariably benevolent and attractive," solicitous and encouraging with an affectionate look, encircling arm, and patient demeanor. Peggy is engaged in the activities that pictorialists focused on as well: posing with relatives, "reading or just holding a book, and playing children's games."[21] Still, these photographers meant their

FIGURE 13. Frank W. Birchall, Agnes Rand Lee and Alice, c. 1896, reproduction print from glass plate negative. Massachusetts Historical Society, Frank W. Birchall Photographs, no. 1071/1281.

work to be considered "art" and often composed images in homage to a recognized artist of the brush. For example, in his *New School* exhibition of 1900 Day included a portrait titled *Mrs. F. W. L. and Daughter,* described by the French critic Robert Demachy as "well worth studying" as an example of expertise in portraiture. "The composition is most carefully thought out. Notice the spot of light on the face of the child and the arm of the mother—it is the same scheme as in 'A Ray of Sunlight,'" a portrait by American painter John White Alexander.[22]

The Lees' second child, Alice Stephana, also learned "the 'activity' of stillness" early.[23] Although she spent several months a year in residential schools for the deaf, she remained an integral part of the family. Portraits of her in what was apparently a favorite nautical-themed dress were completed by Frank Birchall and Gertrude Käsebier. In Birchall's composition, Alice stands next to her mother, who is dressed in a fitted gown with lace at the collar and cuffs; both figures are looking

FIGURE 14. Gertrude Käsebier, Francis Watts Lee and Alice Stephana Lee, c. 1899, platinum print. (LC-DIG-ppmsca-39436)

at a book they hold open together (figure 13). The mother's arm encircles the child tightly with her hand visibly supporting her daughter's elbow and arm. Similarly, in Käsebier's portrait, Francis holds his daughter securely. Seated at a craft table, Alice, clasping her hands before her, leans close against her father, who holds her affectionately, his right hand on her arm (figure 14). Both look directly into the camera. The print bears Käsebier's signature and may be the "fine portrait of 'Mr. Lee and Daughter'" that Demachy praised at the *New School* exhibition.[24]

Perhaps the earliest portrait of Alice is one in which her father holds her on his lap (figure 15). Likely completed at the same sitting as the photo of Francis with Peggy similarly posed, the young Alice is not really aware of the camera as she looks unsmilingly off to the side while her father gazes down at her. Outfitted in dark leggings and a plaid dress with large bib collar and lace-trimmed cuffs, Alice clutches tightly to her doll. The pose is suggestive of Julia Boit, who sits unceremoniously on the carpet at the center of Sargent's portrait of the Boit

FIGURE 15. Frank W. Birchall, Francis Watts Lee and Alice with doll, c. 1896, platinum print. (PR13 CN2015.052.567)

Figure 16. Herbert Arthur Hess, Alice Stephana Lee, c. 1900, platinum print. (LC-DIG-ppmsca-39460)

FIGURE 17. Frederick Haven Pratt, Alice Stephana Lee, c. 1905, platinum print. Library of Congress, Prints and Photographs Division, Gift of Stephen Davis Pratt and Elisabeth Pratt Cheeley, 2000 (LC-USZ62-139479).

sisters; she too does not meet the artist's eye.[25] Unlike Julia, however, Alice is stabilized not by empty space but by her father, who supports her with his own body. As the art historian Susan Sidlauskas notes in her analysis of the Boit portrait, "Julia is not yet able to articulate her inner life" and she seems to identify with the doll she holds.[26] Approximately the same age, Alice too grasps her toy as a reassuring anchor and, with her short cropped hair, she even resembles the object of her affection. Furthermore, Alice was profoundly deaf, exacerbating her inability to articulate her thoughts and feelings. Alice Stephana's world, and her place in it, was largely a tactile and visual place. It is the comforting touch of her father and the familiar feel of her doll that will pacify and console rather than the soothing tones of a parent's voice. Most of the extant portraits of Alice as a small child show her in proximity to her parents, demonstrating a physical intimacy that would have been especially significant to the child.[27]

As she matured, Alice Stephana continued to be the subject of pictorialist portraits. Herbert Arthur Hess, a Northampton, Massachusetts, native, took up photography around 1899 and exhibited in the Philadelphia Photographic

FIGURE 18. F. Holland Day, Alice Stephana Lee with braids, c. 1905, platinum print. Library of Congress, Prints and Photographs Division, Louise Imogen Guiney Collection (LC-USZC4-8159).

Salon and in Day's *New School* exhibition. At some point around 1900 Hess made a rather formal portrait of Alice in a dark dress and heavy shoes with floral branches in her arms (figure 16).

Later, around 1904 Frederick Haven Pratt also took a photographic interest in then ten-year-old Alice (figure 17). Pratt, a professor of physiology at Boston University, had taken up photography as a hobby while in medical school. His father, Frederick Sumner Pratt, was a trustee of the Worcester, Massachusetts, Art Museum and was acquainted with John Singer Sargent, who completed portraits of several Pratt family members.[28] Pratt was also a friend of William Rand, Agnes Rand Lee's brother, and, through these associations met F. Holland Day. During the summer of 1905, Pratt was invited to visit Day's home in Maine, and while he was there, he worked not only with Day but also with Clarence H. White and George Seeley, who were visiting as well.[29] For a few years Pratt mounted exhibitions in Boston and Worcester, at least one of which included a portrait titled *Stephana,* likely a picture of Alice.[30]

As she entered her adolescence, Alice Stephana continued to model for F. Holland Day. In one portrait (figure 18) she sits casually in a caned chair with hands folded, the light from the window to her right softly bathing her white frock and braided hair in sunshine. The bangle bracelet pushed up from her wrist emphasizes her strong arms and, along with the large bow fixed haphazardly on her gown, gives the portrait an informal air, the photographer catching her as her attention is drawn to someone or something off to her left. One of Alice's portraits particularly pleased her mother, who thanked Day in 1908 for the prints. "You already know how much I like Alice's portrait," she wrote, "It's her best for a long time." Preparing to send the photo to Francis as a birthday gift, she observed that "I think F[rancis] will like it, too."[31]

Peggy and Alice Lee were not the first in their family to be memorialized in art. Two of Francis Watts Lee's ancestors, Mrs. Samuel Watts and her daughter Mrs. Edward Watts, were the subjects of portraits by the eminent painter John Singleton Copley. Samuel Watts was born in England and arrived in Boston in 1710 at the age of twenty-two. A successful merchant, Watts was a ruling elder of his church, and, according to one source, "the most conspicuous citizen of Chelsea [Massachusetts] in his day," eventually becoming a Judge of the Court of Common Pleas.[32] At the time of his death in 1770, Judge Watts was an esteemed figure, surely the reason Copley was commissioned to capture the image of his third wife and widow.[33] In the portrait, the twice-widowed Sarah Osborne Oxnard Watts appears to be a refined woman of means dressed simply in black with a widow's cap. Sarah's daughter by her first marriage, Mary Oxnard, wed Dr. Edward Watts, son of Judge Samuel Watts and his second wife, Elizabeth Shute. Mary Oxnard Watts was painted by Copley sometime around 1765 shortly after her marriage.[34] The Copley portrait of Mrs. Samuel Watts, the great-great-great-grandmother of Francis Watts Lee, was passed down in the family for generations.[35] In 1895, while in the possession of Lee's mother, Mrs. Thomas (Alice Watts) Lee, it was part of an exceptional exhibition in Boston's Copley Hall. *Portraits of Women,* mounted for the benefit of the Boston Children's Aid Society, included hundreds of works by artists ranging from Gilbert Stuart and John Singleton Copley to James Abbott McNeill Whistler, Mary Cassatt, Sarah Choate Sears, and John Singer Sargent. The more than three dozen Copleys on display were described by a contemporary newspaper account as showcasing "fine and vigorous old colonial types." The newspaper also noted that many of the "good-looking descendants" of the subjects, presumably including Francis Watts Lee and his mother, attended the opening of the exhibition.[36]

In another encounter with early American portraiture, in 1805, Francis Osborne Watts, the grandson of Dr. Edward Watts, who had relocated his family to Portland, Maine, was the subject of a painting by the itinerant artist John Brewster Jr. Born a deaf-mute, Brewster was the son of a prominent Connecticut physician. Building on his native talent, he received instruction from Rev. John Steward, a clergyman and artist, and traveled throughout New England to earn a living; he was best known for his lively and sympathetic portraits of children. Standing in a serene landscape at evening with rather stylized pine trees in the background, the two-year-old Watts wears the short-sleeve gown and slippers customarily worn by small children of both sexes in the early nineteenth century. A bird is perched on the boy's raised right hand, a common accessory in Brewster's compositions.[37] The grandfather of Francis Watts Lee, F. O. Watts attended Harvard and was a devout Episcopalian and first president of the YMCA in Boston.

While having a Copley portrait of a family member had become a source of pride by the 1890s and Brewster's primitives were gaining notice as early American artifacts, art, and culture were benefiting from the popularity of the Colonial Revival movement, artistic photography was still in its infancy. As part of their advocacy for the acceptance of photography as an art, prominent pictorialists explored subjects that historically had dominated other artistic media. Among these were nude studies. Although not unheard of, the propriety of the nude in photography was still a matter of discussion. Gleeson White, an English critic, book decorator, and the founding editor of *The Studio*, defended the legitimacy of the "undraped figure" in photography in an 1897 article.[38] F. Holland Day, whose own use of the nude in his early work was well known, responded to White's rather cautious endorsement with an unqualified declaration in support of artistic freedom of expression. Day stated that "we must admit no question regarding the righteousness or legitimacy of the undraped figure in Art in this year of grace any more than it was admitted by Praxitiles and Titian in earlier days." Not advocating for gratuitous nudity, however, Day argued that only "a well-planned, well thought out, well executed *motif* . . . with the proper figures, can be considered worthy to be called Art." He was emphatic in his belief that an artist must have a "*raison d'etre* . . . in the subject or composition—in other words if it be not a *picture*—its cause for existence is *nil.*"[39]

The contemporary critic and author W. I. Lincoln Adams concurred, writing, "A photograph of the nude or partially draped figure must always tell a story; there must be a good reason for the semi or undraped appearance of the model."[40] All agreed that situating nude figures as classical subjects in nature would "remove the idea of nakedness" and ease the discomfort that a nude photograph might ordinarily elicit.[41] *The Marble Faun, Morning, Evening,* and *The Bather,* all early studies by Day, fit these criteria, as did later photos completed in Maine by Day, Clarence White, Herbert Hess, and others. In an unpublished essay, Day emphatically tied these open-air photographs to classical images, emphasizing the ability of the photographer to suspend time and place in order to re-create a mythical environment. "In taking . . . figures out of doors [the] photographer has gone back to antique life," he wrote. "For the landscape has preserved for us the places where moved the contemporaries of Anacreon." Props such as panpipes, lyres, and laurel wreaths lent a further "classical" air to these motifs.[42]

Although both Adams and Gleeson White found the subject of female nudes fraught with "difficulty and absolute danger," the use of children within these tableaux was deemed acceptable and without controversy. "Children . . . may be said to present to the photographer the very best models for the nude," Adams wrote.[43] White agreed, noting that children, as a category for nude models, "might surely be discussed freely without fear of hurting anybody's feelings, i.e. so far as propriety is concerned."[44] As the art historian Anne Higonnet notes, "An association of beautiful child bodies with primordial innocence was a central theme of the entire Pictorialist photography movement."[45] Day, Clarence White, and Herbert Hess all experimented with compositions that included nude boys, a staging and depiction that the art historian Peter Bunnell called "perfectly acceptable" during this time, "since the adolescent male was seen to echo the Classical past."[46]

In keeping with these artistic practices and ideals, in 1898, Francis Watts Lee posed Peggy for a series of unclothed outdoor figure studies, two examples of which he displayed at the Philadelphia Photographic Salon of 1900. In these images Peggy is set off against a landscape that includes wild grasses, reeds, and

FIGURE 19. Francis Watts Lee, *Infantem, Nymphis jam nunc qui posset amari, Narcissumque vocat,* c. 1899, platinum print. (PR13 CN2015.052.559)

FIGURE 20. Francis Watts Lee, *Silvestrem tenui Musam meditaris avena*, c. 1899, platinum print. (PR13 CN2015.052.530)

marshland, and the prints were mounted "in gilt frames and with classical titles."[47] As in the work of other pictorialists, such elaborate framing and the use of Latin titles diminished the impact of the child's nude body by associating the images with the trappings of antiquity and myth. Peggy crouches amid flora at the edge of a pool of water in *Infantem, Nymphis jam nunc qui posset amari, Narcissumque vocat* (figure 19), a clear reference to Greek mythology and Narcissus's fascination with his own reflected image.[48] In the second of these "little bits of outdoor figure work," as one writer termed them, Peggy peers out from among tall grasses looking like a character from Charles Kingsley's popular children's book *The Water Babies*. Lee titled the image *Silvestrem tenui Musam meditaris avena* (figure 20), alluding to an otherworldly muse who is able to

FIGURE 21. F. Holland Day, *Puck (Child Nude)*, c. 1899, platinum print.
National Media Museum/Royal Photographic Society/Science & Society Picture Library.

create music from the surrounding reeds. Both photos were well received at the salon, with the critic from *Photo Era* calling them "gems worthy of the highest commendation."[49]

F. Holland Day accompanied Lee on this photographic expedition, one which Louise Guiney fully endorsed. "I think Peggy in scant garments would be exquisitely apposite," she wrote. For Lee's *Silvestrem tenui Musam meditaris avena* Peggy sits on Day's ubiquitous leopard skin prop; in another image by Lee, Peggy wears the headband and costume seen in Day's portrait of the child titled *Puck* (figure 21). A character in Shakespeare's play *A Midsummer Night's Dream*, Puck was a playful untamed woodland elf or fairy in English folklore. In Day's photo, Peggy has a mischievous half-grin as she clasps her hands behind her head and thrusts her elbows forward. Day exhibited this print at the Philadelphia Photographic Salon in 1899, a year before Lee displayed his photos of Peggy. Mounted with nine other works that varied from an allegorical triptych to several interestingly paired figures, *Puck* garnered an uncomplimentary mention in Joseph Keiley's review. Dismissing it as "a rather crude specimen of glycerine-developed print," the influential critic thought the image "was rather disagreeable from the fact that the child had moved during the exposure of the plate, thus giving to its figure two distinct outlines."[50] Day, however, may well have thought the double-image effect brought a charming, rather impish quality to the study. With *Puck* Day captured Peggy at a moment of youthful abandon; she seems joyful and at ease. In many respects it is a companion print to his later photograph of Ruth Ruyl, *On the Threshold of Life* (1909), in which the young, unclothed child heads down a stone walkway toward the camera with her arms outstretched, delighting in the open air, nature, and childhood.

Francis Watts Lee was quite adept at child portraiture. *Hildegarde* (figure 22), a composition in middle tones of gray, featured Alice Stephana and a very obliging dog. They make an enchanting pair: the somber child with an arm wrapped around the animal, stares straight into the camera while her canine companion stands calmly beside her. Alice's wide white sash is striking against the rough texture of her baggy clothes and the dog's sleek body. Still, one critic thought the child "too much lost in the background."[51] *Billy*, described by Charles Caffin in *Camera Notes* as "another agreeable use of light tones" was also well composed. It is a portrait of a young boy in a white suit, dark socks and shoes standing

FIGURE 22. Francis Watts Lee, *Hildegarde*, c. 1899, mercury platinum print. (PR13 CN2015.052.494)

with his arms folded at his waist. Caffin felt that "the comparative stiffness" of the boy's light attire "contrasts very pleasingly with the smooth brown face and colors." Lee used a technique in the development of the print which enabled the child's suit to melt into the lighter background, leaving the "honest little face," hands, lower legs, and feet in sharp relief. Caffin thought *Billy* was "a sunny picture, abounding in freshness." Herbert Taylor of *Photo Era* called it "a strong bit of child life," and the portrait was reproduced in that journal.[52]

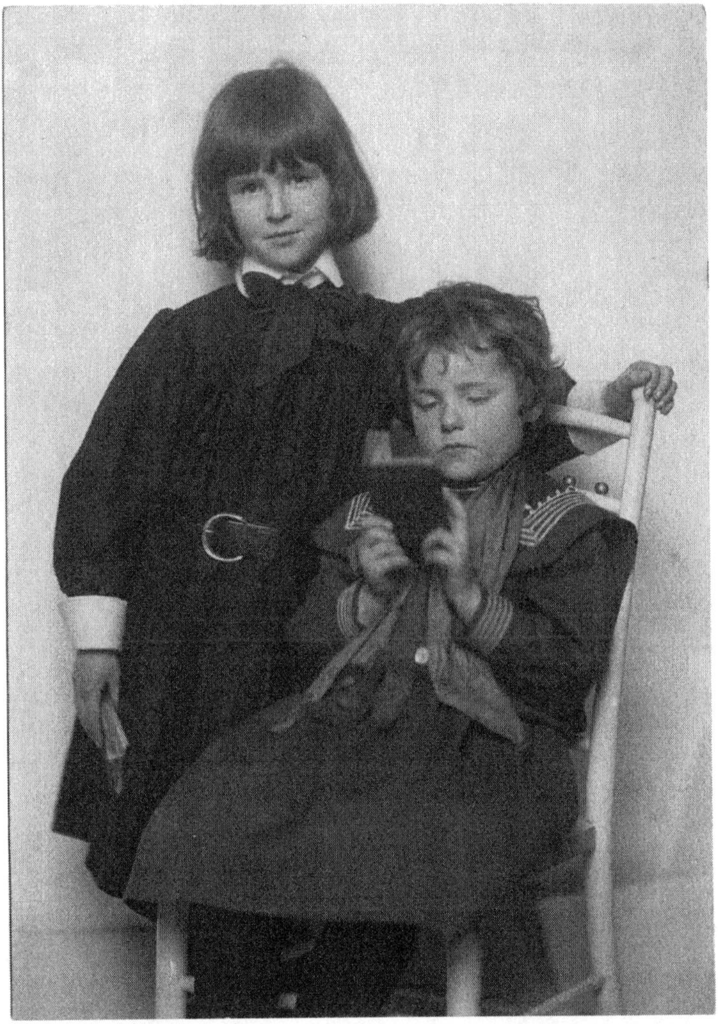

FIGURE 23. Francis Watts Lee, *Sisters*, c. 1899, platinum print. (PR13 CN2015.052.141)

Not surprisingly, Lee's portraits of his own daughters evoke the same "sweet, fresh simplicity" that critics recognized in his other child portraits.[53] In addition to the plein air photos of Peggy, the other two images that Lee exhibited at Philadelphia in 1900 received critical notice as well, with the *Photographic Times*'s reviewer writing that *Stephana*, a portrait of Alice, should be "awarded the sanction of praise."[54] The final photo of the group was simply titled *Sisters* (figure 23). In this portrait, elder sister Peggy stands beside the seated Alice.

She has one arm at her side holding a book; her other arm stretches behind her sister and her hand rests on the back of the chair. Peggy wears the same dress worn in Käsebier's *Blessed Art Thou among Women,* but here her posture and demeanor are more relaxed. She does not stand as straight, her hair is not quite so perfectly coiffed, and she looks with the beginning of a smile not into the distance but into the camera's (and her father's) eye. Alice, wearing her favorite nautical stars and stripes, has her eyes lowered, fixed on the small volume she holds in both hands.

No doubt painfully aware of the recent events that had forever separated the siblings—this exhibition was held five months after Peggy's death—Joseph Keiley focused on these two works in his *Camera Notes* review. "Of these four pictures, *Sisters* and *Stephana* are by far the most interesting," he wrote. "They are fine, unpretentious and sympathetic portraits of children." Acknowledging Lee's ability to see beyond the surface of his subjects, Keiley ruminated about the depths of a child's thoughts. "How much there is that is beautiful, that is pathetic, that is touching, in child life; that can be known only from the rapid play of expression that flits unrestrained over the sensitive little face." Although children may not be able to describe their own conceits or feelings, in the hands of a talented artist (and father) like Lee, Keiley believed, "in their earnest expressiveness they open up to us that undiscovered country—[childhood]—from whose bourne we all have come, yet which we do not know."[55]

Even more than *Blessed Art Thou among Women,* Lee's *Sisters* symbolizes all that was lost with Peggy's death. The two girls were the center of the Lee family and their parents' marriage. Devastated by Peggy's death, Agnes and Francis became isolated from each other in grief. They would spend the next half decade trying to reconcile their loss and repair their lives together.

1. Francis Watts Lee, *The Vision*, c. 1898, glycerine-developed platinum print. (PR13 CN2015.052.518)

2. Francis Watts Lee, *Portrait of Miss E. H.*, c. 1898, platinum print.
(PR13 CN2015.052.495).

3. Francis Watts Lee, *Portrait of Mr. B.*, c. 1898, platinum print.
(PR13 CN2015.052.488)

4. Francis Watts Lee, *The Low Lying Sun of October*, c. 1900, platinum print.

Courtesy of the Trustees of the Boston Public Library, Leslie Jones Collection.

5. Francis Watts Lee, *The Cloister Door*, c. 1900, platinum print. (PR13 CN2015.052.02)

6. Francis Watts Lee, *Rev. James Otis Sargent Huntington*, c. 1898, platinum print. (LC-DIG-ppmsca-39447)

7. Francis Watts Lee, *Magdalena Meditans*, c. 1898, platinum print.
(LC-DIG-ppmsca-39445)

8. Francis Watts Lee, *Beata mea Domina*, c. 1900, platinum print.
(LC-DIG-ppmsca-39443)

# Chapter 6
## THE HERITAGE OF MOTHERHOOD

In the summer of 1904, Gertrude Käsebier created an image that Joseph Keiley described as "one of the saddest and most touching that I have ever seen."[1] As in *Blessed Art Thou among Women,* Agnes Rand Lee was the subject, on this occasion seated alone in a stark, isolated landscape. The voluminous dark textured wrap draped around her shoulders contrasts sharply with her light gown, and the elegance and sophistication present in the earlier portrait is gone. Seemingly unaware of the photographer, Agnes clasps her hands on her knees, with her eyes nearly closed, and her head thrown back as if in contemplation. Käsebier called the portrait *The Heritage of Motherhood,* a startling title given the sense of melancholy the image evokes. As one early reviewer commented, "What wild wastes of desolation, what barren paths of mental agony must a woman have trod to reveal to the camera this ghost of radiant motherhood!"[2]

The critic Giles Edgerton immediately considered the image an example of photography "as an emotional art" and confirmation of Käsebier's expertise in illuminating "the illusive mystery of character."[3] The artist had remarked to Edgerton, "I want to see what life is doing to other people," and in *The Heritage of Motherhood* she appeared to demonstrate how life had worn down Agnes

Lee. A few decades later in an interview for *Abel's Photographic Weekly,* Käsebier linked the image to Peggy's death. She recalled that "three days" after she had "photographed the mother and her little daughter in the doorway," the child had died and Käsebier had gone "with the mother out to a hillside in Maine" [and produced] "the Heritage of Motherhood." It was a portrait she reportedly had in mind for many years but instead of composing the photograph she had waited for the image to present itself. "The poignancy of grief, the lonely figure of the woman with the great waves beating around her—this was the 'model.'" It was, as Käsebier told the interviewer, the moment she had long sought.[4]

In reality, however, the circumstances were more complicated and far less immediate than the photographer's recollection. Peggy's death in 1900 had come several months after Käsebier had visited the Lees in Boston and taken the double portrait she titled *Blessed Art Thou among Women,* and it was more than four years later that she produced *The Heritage of Motherhood.* Also, although the tragedy of her daughter's death weighed heavily on Agnes for the remainder of her life, there was another dimension to her reverie that day on the Maine coast. Her marriage was in crisis, and she was planning to make a decision in the summer of 1904.

Because of Käsebier's title and narrative, it has been assumed that the emotion captured by *The Heritage of Motherhood* was a woman's grief at the death of her child. In addition, the fact that the Lees eventually divorced fueled later speculation that the couple had been unable to overcome that event.[5] The belief that the breakup of their marriage was due to the child's death was consistent with early research, which indicated that there was a high incidence of divorce among couples who had lost a child. One author estimated that "as high as 90% of all bereaved couples were in serious marital difficulty within months after the death of their child" and divorce frequently followed. It was a statistic that was difficult to ignore, although no relevant studies were cited.[6] Subsequent researchers who considered both "normal divorce rates and longitudinal designs" in their studies, concluded that while "the intense grief that each parent experiences, coupled with difference in grieving and coping . . . can hamper . . . communication, engender misunderstanding, and produce tension," divorce was not assured or even common. In many instances, despite these difficulties, husbands and wives found their union strengthened. After all, as Paul Rosenblatt noted, "no one else knew the child as well or could understand what was lost" better. Most experts believe, however, that this same history could accentuate a vulnerability; if there was existing discord in the marriage, a tragedy such as the death of a child could easily exacerbate the distress.[7] That may well have been the case with the Lees, for the few extant references found in the correspondence of their acquaintances hint at long-term incompatibility.

In a letter to Fred Day, Louise Guiney implied that the couple may have always been temperamentally unsuited. "I don't know what to say about dear Agnes and dear Francis. So many people no matter what their worth and their charm, are not fitted for domestic life at all."[8] Guiney, who remained single her entire life, had cast a jaundiced eye on marriage before, most notably a decade earlier in another letter to Day inquiring, "Why will people go and get married? Then complications begin and you have to keep remembering twice three is six, when you are used to dealing with once three which is three."[9] Guiney was not surprised, then, by the examples of marital breakdown she witnessed. "The wonder," she wrote, "is not that we have so many sad upshots in the affair, as that we have so few."[10]

It appears that the Lees' marriage reached a crisis point in 1902, for by the end of the year, they were estranged. Nothing had seemed out of the ordinary in May, when Agnes, vacationing with relatives in New Jersey, wrote to Fred Day, "This place is perfectly beautiful and the cool sweet air of the hills is soothing and delicious." Agnes often spent time with members of the Rand family in New York, New Jersey, Connecticut, and Martha's Vineyard during the summer months when Francis could not get away for extended vacations from his position at the Boston Public Library. In 1902 she had apparently left a sick household behind. "Not a word from a soul in Boston since I came away!" she reported to Day, "But I hope my pack of invalids are much better." Agnes may have had a touch of the illness herself, for she admitted that her "head still aches but not so badly as at home." In any event, she concluded, "I return on Saturday," giving the impression at least that the marriage was intact.[11]

By January 1903, however, Guiney, living in Oxford, England, had received news about some kind of problem between the couple and wrote to Francis. In his reply, written on April 19 of that year, he acknowledged the distress. "I have never had the heart to answer your sweet little note of last January, for the subject is one which, while never for one instant out of my mind or heart, is too bitter to speak of," he began. Lee did not explain the origin of their troubles, but he did urge Louise, whom he called "Dearest Imogen," not to blame "my darling wife for what she has done." Agnes may have asked for a trial separation but, whatever action she had taken, a contrite Francis declared the fault was his, not his wife's. "She bore with me far longer than most women would," he asserted, "and she had more than ample cause for the step she took." While Francis was not specific about his transgressions, when Agnes finally filed divorce papers in 1910, she indicated that Lee had "committed adultery with a woman . . . on the ninth day of September, 1902." Whether this was, in fact, the case or merely the mutually agreed upon grounds for an uncontested divorce cannot be ascertained. There is evidence, however, of at least the perception of impropriety on his part.[12]

Francis Watts Lee's studies of his daughters displayed at the Third Philadelphia Photographic Salon in October 1900 were the first new work he had exhibited in several years. He continued to rely on his existing images for submissions to exhibitions in London, Chicago, and Glasgow, Scotland, a practice acknowledged by a critic of the 1901 Chicago Salon, who noted that "Francis Watts Lee's 'Portrait of Miss H.,' a charming and delicate study of a head in profile, was also shown in the Philadelphia Salon of '99."[13] The only other exception to this pattern had been his depictions of "the beauty of the lighted and shadowed architecture" at the Boston Public Library shown at the Fourth Philadelphia Photographic Salon in November of 1901.[14] That salon had turned out to be a contentious event, with Alfred Stieglitz leading a boycott of the exhibition because "Old-School" Philadelphians had criticized his New York–centric notions and elitism. Following Stieglitz's lead, few major pictorialists had submitted their work, and Lee later apologized for his participation. "Finding my name has been used against the attitude of my very good friends in New York," Lee wrote to Stieglitz, "I want once more to make what amends I can. . . . I cannot tell you how much I regret having sent to Philadelphia." It was the final photographic salon held in that city.[15]

For the January 1902 San Francisco Salon, Lee reverted once again to exhibiting his previously well received portraits titled *Theodora, Billy,* and *Father Huntington.* At the Linked Ring's Tenth Salon held in London in the fall of 1902, however, he introduced two new studies: *Anacreon: Ode XL* and *Beata mea Domina* (plate 8). Writing for *Photograms of the Year 1902,* A. C. R. Carter noted that the first was "a very decorative study of a love-lorn figure" and the second portrait was "a somewhat tame view of a head and neck." Neither was for sale. The critic referred to the latter image as "'My Missis,' or rather *Beata mea Domina* according to Mr. Lee's resonant title," quite obviously believing the image of a lovely dark-haired woman in a frothy white gown, her hair swept up on top of her head, looking straight into the camera was a portrait of Lee's wife. But it was not. *Beata mea Domina,* or as the critic assumed, "'My Missis,'" was a portrait of Marion Lewis Chamberlain, a Fine Arts librarian at the Boston Public Library and the future second Mrs. Francis Watts Lee.[16]

Marion Lewis was first employed at the Boston Public Library (BPL) in 1896, shortly after her graduation from the Massachusetts Institute of Technology. A trained architect, she left the library in 1898 to pursue further study in Italy, married, and returned to the BPL a widow in 1899. Sometime in 1902, Lee completed a series of portraits of her, experimenting with both development processes and papers. *Beata mea Domina* was among them. Whether there was an affair, an infatuation, or merely a friendship at this point is conjecture. Lee seemed oblivious to gossip, if there was any, in 1903 when he requested that Guiney "find a little time to be nice" to Marion, who planned to visit Oxford. He described her as "a very sweet woman who has had her full measure of sorrow and hardship in life" and reminded Louise that she may have known Marion when both worked at the library in the late 1890s.[17] If there was talk at the BPL about Marion and Francis, Guiney would have been aware of it. She maintained a lively correspondence, which Lee knew, with several acquaintances who still worked there. In addition, Guiney was a close friend to Agnes as well. "In this particular case," Guiney had written to Day about the couple's troubles, "fond as I am of both, I can only feel and not form opinions; and I feel sore enough."[18] Given their history and relationship, it seems unlikely that Lee would put Guiney in the position of appearing to condone an affair by asking her to befriend the woman who had broken up his marriage.

Of course, if Lee had indeed committed adultery, as the divorce papers indicated, he may have been involved with another woman, and Marion had merely been a nonjudgmental friend. Lending some credence to this possibility, Lee admitted to Guiney that Marion was "almost the only person who has not turned away from me in the past few months," an indication not of her complicity but her willingness to overlook whatever actions had estranged Lee from his friends. Still, the development of an emotional attachment might be inferred from the fact that Marion resigned her position at the BPL in the fall of 1903 and left Boston. For his part, perhaps as an attempt to make amends to his wife, Lee withdrew from photography; the 1902 London Salon was his final public exhibition. Although accepting the burden of fault and acknowledging that Agnes "had more than ample cause for the step she took," Lee still professed his devotion to her. "Only God can know how different the result might have been," he wrote plaintively to Guiney, "could she have believed at the end that, in spite of all, I did and do most passionately love her."[19]

As the months passed, Lee garnered some sympathy from Edward B. Hunt, chief of the BPL's catalog department, who queried Guiney about Francis: "I would there were some possible way to amend the condition of things for him and his wife! Is there?" Lee had evidently taken the marital breakdown hard, for Hunt continued, "I think he is in [a] better frame than he was, but every now and then he gets desperate and I am in terror." Perhaps fearing his colleague might harm himself, Hunt was supportive concerning Lee's predicament. "I may be unjust and prejudiced but I cannot help feeling that in the wretched case F. W. is not wholly, if mostly, to blame." Acknowledging he might hold this view "because I'm a man," Hunt asked, "Tell me if you think anything can be done or if time even will bring any cure."[20] Guiney had expressed optimism about a reconciliation herself a few months earlier to Fred Day, writing, "I cannot conceive a permanent breach there," but by the summer of 1904 she was more skeptical, even as it appeared Agnes was considering taking Francis back. "I dare not say I am for or against the reunion," she wrote, admitting reconciliation "would certainly seem a blessing for him." Despite Hunt's assessment of Francis's state of mind, however, Louise was not convinced Lee had earned his wife's trust, stating she would be "interested to learn (if only I might) in what particular he has so improved his character?" As Day prepared to welcome Agnes Lee and Gertrude Käsebier to his Maine retreat in July 1904, Guiney sent her final words on the matter. "I still love Francis too," she conceded, "but my poor Agnes knows best."[21]

Louise Guiney's beloved father, Patrick Robert Guiney, had been raised in Portland, Maine, and it was she who discovered the untamed beauty of Five Islands, in 1897. She described the landscape to Rev. William H. van Allen as reminiscent of "the coast of So. Devon, only far finer: all steep cliffs facing seaward, of whitest granite, caves, beaches, pasture-lands, and great tidal rivers running inland, abreast, for perhaps twenty miles. . . . I know Maine well; but there's nothing so wild in it, or so lovable, as that neighborhood." She derived great pleasure from the fresh air, cold nights, and outdoor activity of the "wild seacoast place," as she called it.[22] Guiney returned to the spot the following year and eventually purchased the property, house, shed, and extra land for $1,000. Although "bare and primitive," the humble two-story, shingled former fisherman's home was substantial enough to have survived decades of Maine's freezing winters and sundrenched summers. Guiney immediately filled it with friends and acquaintances in the summer of 1898, including van Allen, Alice Jordan of the BPL, and Fred Day, whom Louise enticed with the promise of sights to photograph. "It is certainly a Wild Paradise, if there be one on this earth," she observed, and the cool pine woods, blue water, precipitous cliffs, and rocky shoreline were a delight to her guests.[23] Day began calling the modest house "Castle Guiney" in her honor, although Louise objected. "Do you know my shanty's proper name is Water End?" she wrote later. "I protest against your magniloquent Castle Guiney." But Day persisted and the name stuck, as did the moniker "Little Good Harbor," a backhand tribute to the port's narrow inlet and shallow floor.[24]

After Guiney's move to England, the property was unused until 1903, when Fred Day returned, at her insistence, with friends, photographers, and protégées following in his wake. Among Day's visitors that first summer was the future poet Kahlil Gibran, who, upon returning home to Boston's North End, wrote: "It seems all but a dream.... You do not know how bad it seems to be under the elevated railroad while thinking of the calmness of Fife [*sic*] Islands.... [T]hink of me when the waves caresses [*sic*] the gray rocks, and when the pines stretches [*sic*] their arms to the waves below." The idyllic setting, later enhanced in 1912 by a large chalet Day commissioned (he purchased the property from Guiney in 1909), inspired many of Day's artistic colleagues, including Clarence White, who opened a summer school of photography nearby, Frederick Haven Pratt, George Seeley, and Gertrude Käsebier.[25]

Käsebier completed several noted works during her visits to Maine, and they were, as William Innes Homer wrote, "marked by an increasing fondness for solidity of form."[26] Two of these images were created inside Day's large chalet, erected on the site of Guiney's cottage, perched overlooking the rocky inlet of Little Good Harbor and the open water beyond. *The Hand That Rocks the Cradle* and *The Widow*, both taken in 1913, featuring her friend the artist Beatrice Baxter Ruyl, emphasized, in Barbara Michaels words, "the contrast of light and dark in an emotionally intense interior."[27] In the former, Ruyl is seated in the semi-darkened large open parlor of Day's chalet, directing her gaze on the child in the cradle at her feet. She has captured the infant's attention by holding up two fingers to simulate rabbit ears in a child's finger game. The sharp edges of the cradle, door frame, and windows contrast with the soft folds of the mother's dress and baby's blankets. The interesting geometric line of the door and window, illuminated by day's last light, and the deepening darkness that encircles the mother and cradle imbue the scene with calm and quiet. As Homer notes, Käsebier has caught the mother's hand symbolically "positioned almost in a gesture of benediction," and the waning but still strong sun which falls across the image "seems to beatify the entire subject."[28] Likely adding to the poignancy of the image for Käsebier, Day, and others in their circle was the gesture's subtle reference to Agnes Lee's book *The Round Rabbit* and the memory of an earlier mother-daughter portrait.

*The Widow* was a timely allegorical study that Käsebier produced at the height of public discussions about the plight of widows and fatherless families, a debate that only became more immediate as World War I took its toll. In "a pose uncharacteristic of Käsebier's mothers," as Michaels points out, Ruyl stares with distressed intensity at the camera while embracing her child protectively.[29] Seated sideways on a wooden bench and caught between a built-in table and a bowl- and crock-filled cupboard, she is literally backed into a corner, the encroaching shadows threatening to swallow both mother and child. The window situated behind a jumble of pots and cups in a tray on the table emits a cold, pale glow that chills the scene. Yet a strong bright beam emanating from an unknown source strikes the figure with the same blessed rays that illuminate the mother in *The Hand That Rocks the Cradle.* It is as if the grace and power of motherhood creates its own internal sacred light. Käsebier projected a "confident idealism" regarding motherhood with these later familial portraits, and together, in Michaels's view, they seem "less portraits than a consummation of the mother and child theme."[30] She had begun the series nearly two decades earlier, with *Mother and Child* (also titled *Adoration*) (1897), *The Manger* (1899), *Blessed Art Thou among Women* (1899), and *Real Motherhood* (1900), a serene portrait of the photographer's daughter and grandchild. As one scholar commented, each of these images, including the later two images, "convey an intimate relationship in which the woman, through her posture, facial expression, or both, expresses reverence for the child."[31]

*The Heritage of Motherhood*, however, represented an enigmatic anomaly at the center of this thematically connected series. It is the only photo in the group that was taken out of doors, thus removing the maternal figure from her domestic habitat, and there is no child present to affirm the maternal role. "Its gloomy tones, [and] simple barrenness" as Homer describes the image, acts as "a visual equivalent of the loneliness, perhaps tragedy, experienced by the woman who has become a mother."[32] Even *The Widow*, a fictional study of a worried, suffering mother, has more shared sentiment with the other photos in the mother series than *The Heritage of Motherhood*, which stands alone in its desolation.

Gertrude Käsebier had arrived at Five Islands in late July 1904. She had stopped in Boston on her way from New York to Maine, probably to join Agnes Lee and her daughter Alice for the latter part of the journey. Guiney at least believed the two women were traveling together when she wrote Day on July 27, "Tell me when Agnes is due with Mrs. Käsebier, and I shall write to her then."[33] They would have been greeted not only by Day but by a number of friends and fellow photographers, for Castle Guiney had simultaneously become a vacation paradise and an artistic retreat. Day had made sure there was a diversity of visitors: artists and amateurs, old and young, skilled and unskilled, all sharing their pleasure in the picturesque landscape. At some point during their stay Käsebier and Agnes Lee ventured out together on the rugged terrain near the Little Good Harbor property where Agnes, clothed in a light-colored, long-sleeved, free-flowing dress protected from the elements by a generously large dark shawl, sat on the flat rocks at the water's edge and looked out toward the horizon. Ever watchful for an effective subject to present itself, Käsebier made a handful of negatives. Years later Agnes confirmed that the photographer had caught her by surprise with the portrait "by the sea." Hoping the image was not "too poetical or fantastical" for a small literary exhibition, she wrote, "By-the-way I did not know it was being taken when Mrs. K. snapped the camera at me."[34] In addition to the plate that became *The Heritage of Motherhood*, Käsebier took a number of photos on the shore that day, including a few in profile and one as Agnes turned to face the camera (figure 24). The artist recognized that she had captured the picture she "had been waiting for fifteen years to secure" but transforming the image of Lee seated in the barren landscape into a symbol of a mother's heartache took a tour de force of skill and manipulation.[35]

The original glass plate negative (figure 25) is visually sharp and distinct with

FIGURE 24. Gertrude Käsebier, *Untitled* [Agnes Lee], 1904, platinum print. Portland Museum of Art, Maine. Museum purchase with support from the Friends of the Collection (2010.8.6).

"everything from the stitching and texture of the cloak to the freckles on Lee's face" apparent, and "the different textures of cloth, skin, rocks, sky," and hair clearly delineated.[36] Like many pictorial photographers, Käsebier employed multiple printing methods and techniques to lessen the mere documentary aspects of their work and enhance its artistic, even painterly effects.[37] Experimenting with platinum and gum bichromate processes would add tonal and textural dimension to an image. The gum print in particular could resemble a charcoal drawing, as the artist might "subdue and eliminate unimportant detail" to further the aim of artistic expression instead of reproduction.[38] For *Blessed Art Thou among Women*, Käsebier had used the relatively straightforward and stable platinum process, but to convey the internal turmoil of *The Heritage of Motherhood* she turned to the more variable gum. One photo historian notes that Käsebier, using the negative almost like a canvas, "subjected the image to any number of interventions, including enlargements, reversals, painting on the negative, and manipulation of the gum surface of the print."[39] First, she flipped the negative, then minimized physical details by softening the distinctions

FIGURE 25. Gertrude Käsebier, *The Heritage of Motherhood*, 1904, reproduction print from glass plate negative. Library of Congress, Prints and Photographs Division, Gift of Mina Turner, 1964 (LC-K2-27).

between sky, rocks, earth, and water. The jagged outcroppings of stone and the tonalities of skin, hair, and fabric are muted and blended, blurring textural differences and making the landscape less harsh and Lee less identifiable. Yet the emotional force of the image was not diminished but enhanced. William Innes Homer thought these manipulations gave the portrait "monumental dignity," while another later scholar remarked that by "brushing away the platinum emulsion of the negative, scraping and roughening the surface," Käsebier seemed to be "accentuating the trauma of bereavement."[40] Once again, the allusion to Christian imagery was unmistakable.

Agnes's head tilts upward as if in supplication, her eyes are unseeing as if in deep reflection, and her hands are joined as if in prayer. "Lee's posture and facial expression, as well as the tension of her hands, suggest sorrow," the art historian Susan L. Taylor points out, and with these gestures and developing techniques, Käsebier universalized the picture until the photograph is no longer simply "a portrait of Agnes Lee but rather the expression of the relationship of her pain and that of every mother, to the suffering of the Virgin."[41] The Stabat Mater (translated from a hymn) was the depiction of the mournful Mary, the mother of Christ, standing at or near the base of the cross during the crucifixion of her son. It was a common subject in medieval and Renaissance art, particularly in paintings, and became an emblem of grief, yet faith. Käsebier purposely linked her portrait to this well-established convention of Marian imagery by the insertion, in at least one print, of three crosses on the distant horizon to the left of Lee, a symbol of the all-encompassing grief the woman felt at the death of her child (figure 26). As if in preparation for the role, Agnes Lee had already demonstrated a deep comprehension of a mother's burden in her own work, especially in her poem "Motherhood," which dramatized the maternal love of both Mary and the mother of Judas. The introduction of the hand-drawn crucifixes placed the work within the tradition of Christian art; yet Käsebier eliminated this augmentation in several other prints, perhaps broadening the image's appeal. "By omitting the crosses in other copies," Barbara Michaels contends, "Käsebier achieved a subtler yet more intense result, a picture that recalls the Romantic and Symbolist tradition of showing a solitary contemplative person alone in an uninhabited landscape."[42]

The strength and emotional intensity of *The Heritage of Motherhood* was immediately recognized. It was shown at the Vienna Camera Club in February 1905, in Cincinnati and in Philadelphia in 1906, in several Photo-Secession exhibitions, and in Alfred Stieglitz's summary International Exhibition of Pictorial Photography in Buffalo, New York, in 1910. Käsebier proved that the image and subject held great significance for her by continuing to rework the print for decades. In 1916, she tightened the perspective, eliminated most of the terrain, and boxed in the figure to create, in Michaels's opinion, "a more expressionistic psychological portrait."[43] Five years later she printed a variant of Lee in profile looking out to sea. This time she produced a silver-based emulsion on tissue, a reworking that further emphasized the fragility of the scene and the vulnerability of the woman.[44] The details of the inlet shore are intact, but the sea and sky have become almost indistinguishable. Absorbed in her thoughts, Lee stares out across the water at something—or nothing.

Agnes Lee intended to make a decision about her future in the summer of 1904, and she was at least entertaining the idea of returning to the marriage. She had a difficult decision to make, for while the Lees were assured that they would

FIGURE 26. Gertrude Käsebier, *The Heritage of Motherhood*, 1904, platinum print with some additions by hand. Detroit Institute of Arts, USA/Founders Society Purchase, Henry E. & Consuelo Wenger/Foundation Fund & John S. Newberry Fund/Bridgeman Images.

not be outcasts among their own social circle since extant correspondence indicates the liberality of their friends, she needed to consider larger cultural and religious realities.

Divorce rates had increased dramatically in the last decades of the nineteenth century, "up 70% between 1880 and 1890 and another 67% the following decade," according to one study, and it was the subject of much debate.[45] Social scientists saw these increases as the result of changing social and economic mores rather than an indication of "moral laxness."[46] More women were obtaining higher levels of education and working outside the home. They were therefore able and willing to leave a troubled marriage since they were no longer economically dependent on their husbands. Under these evolving circumstances, civil divorce laws varied from state to state and were in continual flux. On the other hand, however, organized religions had a different view. The Roman Catholic Church had been and remained staunchly opposed to divorce, and many Protestant churches agreed, arguing for a limitation on the acceptable grounds for divorce action. While these debates escalated, more significant for a couple such as the Lees, who were devout Episcopalians, were church regulations regarding remarriage. Although infidelity was an acceptable reason to end a marriage, a mid-nineteenth-century ruling by the Episcopal Church allowed only the "innocent party" in such a divorce to remarry in the Church; the guilty partner, in the words of one historian, "had to live with the consequences of remarrying civilly or remaining unmarried." In 1907, the Episcopal Church made the regulation even more restrictive by establishing a year-long waiting period even for the innocent.[47]

However complicated or heart-wrenching the decision, Agnes ultimately did not return to the marriage. Although it took years for the separation to be finalized by divorce, the couple never lived together again. Agnes remained at the house on Peter Parley Road while Francis took up residence at Technology Chambers, a modern rooming house situated a few blocks from the Boston Public Library. Their divorce was finalized by the Commonwealth of Massachusetts on November 12, 1910. Agnes was awarded full custody of their surviving daughter, Alice; however, Francis was given generous visitation privileges, including several weeks in the summer. In addition, he agreed to pay $500 per year to Agnes for Alice's care, an award that was to continue to be paid to Alice herself once she reached maturity, certainly a concession to her disability.[48]

Six months later, in May 1911, Agnes Rand Lee married Dr. Otto T. Freer, a well-respected Chicago physician. In July 1911, Francis Watts Lee followed suit, marrying Marion Lewis Chamberlain, former colleague and the model for *Beata mea Domina,* in South Kingstown, Rhode Island. Neither couple was wed in an Episcopal Church. Agnes was married at her brother's home in Rye, New York, by a Methodist minister; Francis and Marion were wed in a Congregational service.[49] By that time, Alice Stephana Lee was nearing eighteen, and it is not unreasonable to assume Agnes and Francis had waited for their daughter to reach maturity before finalizing the dissolution of the family. Within a year, Alice Stephana Lee finished her formal education and, with the support and encouragement of her parents, extended family, and friends, she began to build a life of her own.

# Chapter 7
## ALICE STEPHANA LEE

In February 1898, Louise Imogen Guiney wrote to Rev. William H. van Allen, "Did I tell you I am going to the gymnasium this winter? . . . I could always run and vault better than I could sew, or scan!" In the midst of her always lively correspondence, however, Guiney slipped in a few more somber lines. "I get sight of our Lees, now and then," she noted. "Agnes looks very tired, since she left Chicago and her dear baby."[1]

Alice Stephana Lee, the couple's second child, was born on December 26, 1893, a little over a year after Peggy's birth. Like her sister, she was surrounded by love and parental attention. In her poem "Stephana," Agnes wrote of the girl's appealing temperament and beauty: "No laugh is so bright as Stephana's laugh, / No eyes are so clear and blue." The same verse captures her sense of abandon and joyful adventure as the "merry-wild" child scurries to the "high hill-top" where "We thought her running never would stop." Yet "Stephana" also alludes to a more affecting circumstance with the lines:

> She rises out of the hush of dark
> Into a hush of day.

She may not hear the song of lark,
Nor your resounding play.

While still an infant Alice had lost her hearing. In her poetry Agnes transforms this event into a magical occurrence. She imagines the little girl drawn to nature in order "To hear the secrets we may not know, / That fairies whisper to her" and concludes, "Ah, this is why no smile is so sweet / As the smile of Stephana!" In spite of their delight in the exuberance of their "merry-wild" daughter, soon enough Agnes and Francis had to make a decision about Alice Stephana's education. Perhaps influenced by the Rand family's familiarity with Chicago, the Lees chose the Chicago Kindergarten Home for the Deaf as their child's first formal educational experience.[2]

Deaf education had become contested territory in nineteenth-century America with two opposing perspectives vying for dominance in the field. The first school for the deaf, the American Asylum for the Deaf at Hartford, Connecticut, was founded by Thomas H. Gallaudet in 1817. Educated in France, Gallaudet envisioned a school in which deaf individuals could live together, learn a common language of signs, and create a distinct community among themselves. The pedagogy that developed, a combination of sign language, finger-spelling, and written English, was referred to as "manualism."[3] It remained the chief mode of instruction until after the Civil War, when political and cultural attitudes about national unity and homogeneity shifted.

Confronted by the need to reconstitute a divided nation and, at the same time, assimilate an ever-increasing number of immigrants, reformers condemned any perception of group isolation. Unlike manualists, whose teachings seemed to segregate the deaf by giving them a unique form of communication, "oralists," as they came to be known, promoted the integration of the deaf into the broader society through the use of lipreading and articulation. Although most manualist schools added lessons in speech and lipreading, oralists maintained that any curricula that depended primarily on sign language encouraged the deaf to remain separate. As one scholar explained the two viewpoints, "Manualists perceived deafness as a human difference, best accommodated through a special language; oralists saw it as a handicap to be overcome, with speech and lip reading allowing access to normal society." Adopting the language of nativist reformers who demanded the unequivocal assimilation of immigrants into the American way of life, oralists advocated for a total secession of the teaching of "the foreign language of signs."[4]

Beginning with the Clarke School in Northampton, Massachusetts, in 1867, and the Horace Mann School for Deaf-Mutes in Boston in 1869, oralism began its ascent aided by parents who saw articulation as the means for their offspring to "acquire the graces and be able to speak and understand the speech of others."[5] Sarah Fuller, who founded the Horace Mann School, for example, championed the belief that deaf children "were not deviant or dependent" but rather inherently capable and deserving "of an education identical to that provided hearing children." Following this precept, nearly a dozen institutions offering exclusively articulation and lipreading had opened by 1880. From that time on, the oralism movement gained momentum.[6]

Residing in Massachusetts, where both the Clarke and Horace Mann operated, and eager to ensure the most liberal and academically challenging education for their daughter, Agnes and Francis Lee enrolled Alice in oralist schools, beginning with the Chicago Kindergarten Home for the Deaf, a groundbreaking institution which served children (aged two to five) too young to attend any existing deaf-mute school. The Home accepted only eight boys and girls and paired them daily with hearing children from an affiliated kindergarten to create as natural an experience as possible. The *Chicago Tribune* praised the Home in October 1897, calling it "a kindergarten in pantomime." Each action, object, or person the pupils encountered was deliberately and consistently associated with the spoken and written word or name to reinforce learning. Because the children in this residential facility were so young and came from all parts of the country, maintaining a comfortable domestic atmosphere was paramount. The toddlers were never left alone; each shared a bedroom with one of the instructors and from the time they awoke the learning began. Meals were served in a homelike dining room where each activity and object was connected to language. Thus, the *Tribune* assured its readers, "The children are learning rapidly and unconsciously." Although "too young to be taught articulation scientifically," they nonetheless could "mimic" the physical motions of each utterance and eventually speak.[7]

Two deaf children were highlighted in the newspaper's glowing account of the Home; one was a two-and-a-half-year-old boy, the youngest pupil in the school, the other was "Alice Lee, a granddaughter of William H. Rand of

FIGURE 27. "Alice Lee, aged 5 years, One of the most promising pupils," from "Deaf Tots in School," *Chicago Daily Tribune*, 3 October 1897, p. 50.

Chicago" (figure 27). In an anecdote reminiscent of Helen Keller's famed revelatory moment, the *Tribune* recounted a poignant instance of comprehension by the child. "When in the play of taking care of the doll baby the teacher said she wanted a mamma to rock the baby to sleep, little Alice unexpectedly flew out of the room, and, returning with the picture of her own mamma, danced about in great glee, showing the picture to everyone and saying 'Mamma' many times over as plainly as anyone." Alice remained in Chicago for a few years at the Kindergarten Home and the McCowen Oral School for Young Deaf Children, where the customary arithmetic, grammar, spelling, reading, and writing were supplemented by classes in gardening, drawing, and painting. After a brief time at the Sarah Fuller Home for Little Deaf Children in Boston, Alice was enrolled at the residential Clarke School for the Deaf in Northampton, which she attended from 1899 to 1912.[8]

By 1906, the twelve-year-old Alice Stephana (as she signed her name) had grown into a beautiful, confident young girl. She retained the curiosity her mother's poem had described, and Clarke and its rural environs seemed to fit her well.

"Northampton is a very beautiful place," she wrote to the physician, amateur photographer, and family friend Frederick Haven Pratt. "I can see Mount Holyoke from my room and every morning I get up from my bed and look at the mountains." Pratt, just finishing his medical degree at Harvard, had been kind enough to send Alice a letter filled with anecdotes of interest to the child. Delighted with the correspondence, she opened her reply very formally, "I thank you very much for writing me a letter. I am very pleased with it." Her bright inquisitive temperament could not be contained, however, and Pratt likely smiled at her reaction to his news of a family wedding. "I am surprised that your sister Bessie is going to be married," Alice wrote. "Do you want to be married?" Then, concluding matter-of-factly as any child might, "If you will marry, you will be very happy in your new home, I think."[9]

Alice also introduced the subject of photography, a pastime she was well acquainted with having grown up surrounded by the work of her father and his colleagues. Perhaps modeling their behavior, Alice promised to send Pratt a photograph of the mountains of Northampton and "one picture of myself." And, she requested Pratt return the favor. "Will you please send me a picture of yourself some day because I like you very much." She also made a promise: "Next summer when I shall see you, I will probly [*sic*] take my camera to take you a picture."[10] Whether she fulfilled that promise is unknown, but she would see Pratt at Five Islands, Maine, where she and her mother visited Day.

Despite her deafness, Alice made friends easily and thrived in the uninhibited, informal environment of Little Good Harbor. As Jane White, wife of the photographer Clarence White, recalled, Day organized swimming, rowing, and eating contests; arranged fishing, berry picking, and hiking expeditions, and picnics. Evenings were given over to games of all sorts including "wit-stirring quizzes on various subjects."[11] During the summer of 1908, Day again took photos of Alice and her mother. "Thank you so much for the prints," Agnes wrote to Day in September of that year. "We are bursting with impatience to see proofs of the other things."[12] In one remarkably serene and graceful photo (figure 28), the beautiful adolescent wears a wide-brimmed straw hat, and her long wavy dark hair is curled across her shoulders. In near-profile, her perfect features and bright eyes are illuminated by the light reflected from her high-collared white dress.

Among the prints taken of the fourteen-year-old Alice Stephana that summer was the one that Agnes decided to send to Francis for his forty-first birthday, a gift Alice endorsed in her own letter to Day. "We are going to give my

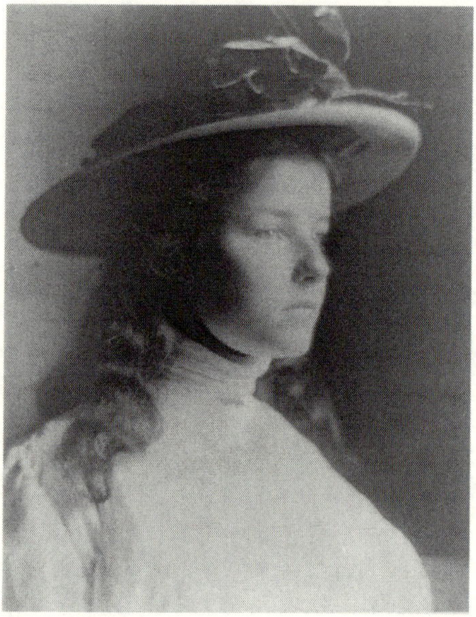

FIGURE 28. F. Holland Day, Alice Lee in white dress and hat, c. 1907, platinum print. Library of Congress, Prints and Photographs Division, Louise Imogen Guiney Collection (LC-USZ62-135751).

FIGURE 29. Mary Patten, Francis Watts Lee and Alice Stephana Lee, 1905, platinum print. (PR13 CN2015.052.555)

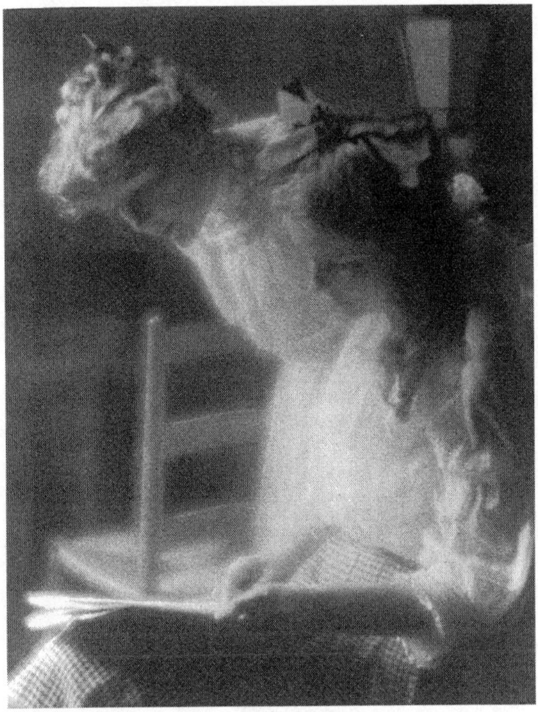

FIGURE 30. F. Holland Day, Agnes Rand Lee and Alice Stephana Lee reading, c. 1907, platinum print. Library of Congress, Prints and Photographs Division, Louise Imogen Guiney Collection (LC-USZ62-093640).

picture to Papa on his birthday," she wrote. "I think he will like it very much." But Agnes did have one reservation. "I do think he will feel that it is all too light. It gives the impression of a very fair blonde whereas Alice is quite dark—hair and skin," much like her father. A few years earlier Louise Guiney too had commented, "Stephana, I see, has grown more and more like her father." And, in a dual portrait of father and daughter, the resemblance is unquestionable (figure 29). Both formally attired—Alice in a belted, dark pleated wool dress with velvet accents, her father in a well-cut double-breasted suit—the two sit closely together. Alice holds a book while Francis places a reassuring hand on her wrist. The two stare forthrightly into the camera, and the likeness is undeniable, each with the same barely containable curling hair, straight brow, clear unflinching eyes, and slightly downturned mouth.[13]

Around the same time, Day composed a portrait of Alice with her mother (figure 30). The image is an effective study in reflected light. Wearing a white blouse and checkered pleated skirt with a large bow on the top of her head, Alice balances what appears to be an oversized magazine on her lap. Her mother, standing to her right dressed in a light gown, leans in to examine a page, her left arm encircling Alice in an embrace reminiscent of the maternal gesture captured in *Blessed Art Thou among Women*. At the portrait's center is the luminous white tone created by the light striking the fabric of the sitters' clothing. The bright warmth reflects up to their faces but dissipates before reaching the table to the distant left. The vase on the mantel to the rear and an empty rustic caned chair turned away from the figures at Agnes's right provide a solid angular contrast to the quietly ethereal shared moment between mother and daughter.

During the years of Alice Stephana's attendance, the Clarke School for the Deaf rose to prominence as the foremost institution of "pure oral" education in America.[14] Like similar schools, Clarke also began to hire female instructors in increasing numbers. It was believed that women were more capable of taking on the nurturing role expected of articulation instructors, who often worked with the youngest children. Manualists, chiefly men, objected to their schools becoming "nurseries" and argued that the academic subjects they taught, and the complex system of signs they depended on, required mature students.[15] Oralists, on the other hand, advocated for a "life-long habit of speech," a task best begun at an early age to ensure success. Pupils at the Chicago Kindergarten Home and similar schools, for example, were admitted as young as two years old. This required professional staff to maintain a "familial ambience" for the comfort and care of toddlers. As one scholar notes, preferred applicants for positions at oralist schools were "gentle, sympathetic, patient, firm, self-sacrificing, and devoted to their work," which consisted of intense and continual repetition and reinforcement. In addition, at residential institutions, duties often included sharing a bedroom with the youngest of the children, a proximity and relationship many thought improper for men. Summarizing these gendered expectations, the historian Douglas Baynton writes, "A female faculty made the boarding schools appropriate places for children, and at the same time young children made the schools appropriate places for women."[16]

There were also economic reasons for the increased use of female teachers. "The employment of women," Baynton points out, "would help to subsidize the higher cost associated with oral education." Articulation instruction was a dawn-to-dusk endeavor. Women, already considered culturally better suited for such an arrangement, were willing to work for far less than their male counterparts. Thus this confluence of cultural beliefs and economic realities resulted in the increased presence of women as instructors and advocates within the oralist movement.[17]

Clarke's curriculum was wide-ranging. In addition to speech, writing, and English, younger children were introduced to "Nature Work," a subject that continued into the intermediate classrooms. Upper-level students were engaged in the customary English, history, math, and literature courses as well as physical geography, physiology, zoology, physics, and chemistry offerings. Art was encouraged, and there were exhibitions of student work in basketry, printing, wood carving, needlework, and drawing. At the minimum, all boys and girls were required to take drawing and wood carving, subjects in which Alice excelled. At the school's 1912 Graduation Day ceremony, she was awarded a prize for her "Pen and Ink Work" but, as her mother wrote to a friend several years later, wood carving was "her *bent*."[18]

By the time Alice Stephana left Clarke, her parents were divorced and both had remarried. Alice returned to Chicago with her mother and stepfather, Dr. Otto T. Freer. She briefly attended the University School for Girls, a Lake Shore Drive finishing school for Chicago debutantes. Rather quickly, however, she followed her natural inclinations to Miss Church's School of Applied and Normal Art and then to the School of the Art Institute of Chicago, where she took the first of many classes in painting, still life, and lettering. Alice returned to the East Coast during the summer months, and, in 1916, she remained in Boston to study wood carving.[19]

Initially dominated by well-known immigrant craftsmen such as Hugh Cairns, John Evans, and John Kirchmayer, all of whom worked on large-scale figural, ecclesiastical, and architectural elements, wood carving in Boston was popularized by others who focused on the domestic arts and "recognized the value of carving to well-designed or artistic objects" including everyday items such as candlesticks, bookends, and frames.[20] "Frame reform" especially took hold in Boston, where the respected painters Charles Prendergast and Hermann Dudley Murphy advocated for the placement of their compositions "in custom frames" designed and created specifically "to harmonize with the picture." Murphy, who learned to carve and gild in order to present his own works effectively, opened a small studio called Carrig-Rohane in his Winchester home. As the demand for his frames increased, he eventually moved the shop to Boston, hired craftsmen to carve his sketched designs, and expanded his products to include not only picture and mirror frames but also "carved screens, panels, bookends, jewelry boxes, lamps, and even benches."[21]

Although she was introduced to the craft while at Clarke, there are no extant records of where Alice Stephana studied wood carving in 1916. According to the art historian Edward Cooke, however, since there were few institutional programs available for wood carving and gilding at that time in Boston, interested individuals "tended to learn through experiment, private tutorial, or books."[22] Writing later in *The Bulletin,* the newsletter of the Chicago League for the Hard of Hearing, Alice herself noted that "it would make a long story if I were to tell of all my experiences, how I looked about for teachers . . . and how I looked for an expert gilder to show me how to gild my articles."[23] Given that she was in Boston, she may have spent time at Carrig-Rohane, by then part of the Vose Gallery on Newbury Street. Although Murphy had withdrawn from the business sometime around 1911, he remained influential, and he was likely still in touch with Alice's father, who had been a Chauncy Hall classmate in the 1880s. At Murphy's studio she would also have encountered Sydney Sargent, who, like Alice, had been a photographic model for F. Holland Day.[24] Another family acquaintance who may had aided and encouraged Alice was Charlotte Hallowell. A friend of Francis Watts Lee's and sister to Emily Hallowell, the "Miss E. H." of Lee's photographs, Charlotte was a talented artist in wood. Her work was exhibited in Boston in 1912 and included chests, which were "artistic in design and splendidly carved," picture and mirror frames, candlesticks, and "dainty little boxes," all the type of pieces Alice Stephana later created.[25]

Wherever she studied, Alice Stephana had found her calling; she embraced it wholeheartedly, exclaiming, "I love my work," in her *Bulletin* article. "In the daytime I carve in my home," she wrote. "By a window where the sun pours in, stands one who is ever ready to welcome me from the outside world—my dear, broad, huge, faithful, responsive friend—my carving bench!" She went on to discuss much of her process with her readers. "It takes time to get acquainted with different kinds of wood," she explained. "Woods, like persons, have qualities of their own; some are even-tempered, some strong, some tricky or stubborn and some yielding, and those who know wood well from long experience choose the piece and kind with great care for a particular task." Her anthropomorphic attitude toward her materials was indicative of a skilled wood carver,

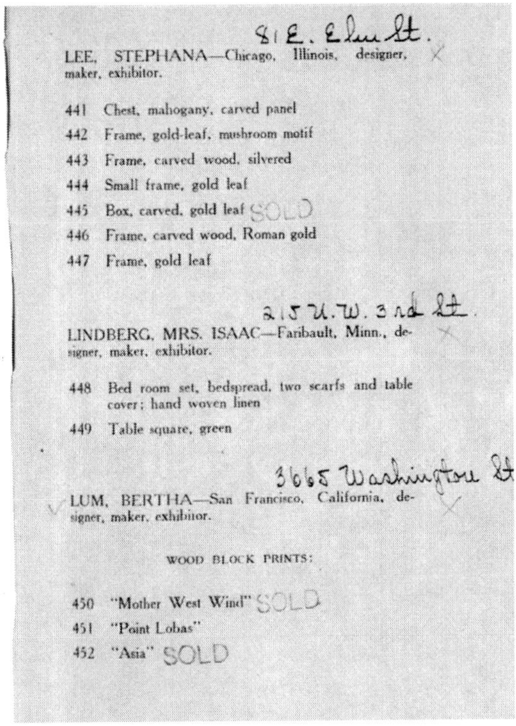

81 E. Elm St.

LEE, STEPHANA—Chicago, Illinois, designer, maker, exhibitor.

441 Chest, mahogany, carved panel

442 Frame, gold-leaf, mushroom motif

443 Frame, carved wood, silvered

444 Small frame, gold leaf

445 Box, carved, gold leaf SOLD

446 Frame, carved wood, Roman gold

447 Frame, gold leaf

215 N. W. 3rd St.

LINDBERG, MRS. ISAAC—Faribault, Minn., designer, maker, exhibitor.

448 Bed room set, bedspread, two scarfs and table cover; hand woven linen

449 Table square, green

3665 Washington St

LUM, BERTHA—San Francisco, California, designer, maker, exhibitor.

WOOD BLOCK PRINTS:

450 "Mother West Wind" SOLD

451 "Point Lobas"

452 "Asia" SOLD

FIGURE 31. "Stephana Lee—Chicago, Illinois, designer, maker, exhibitor. 81 E. Elm St." From Art Institute of Chicago, *Catalogue of the Nineteenth Annual Exhibition of Applied Arts and the Exhibition of British Art and Crafts* (1921). Ryerson and Burnham Libraries Book Collection, Ryerson and Burnham Archives, Art Institute of Chicago (dig. file #000000_1409022-001).

as was her insistence on perfection. "Often one meets with discouragement," she confessed. "I have failed and failed after working for hours over one article." But, she philosophically concluded, "in the long run the experience has counted; when success does come, I know how to appreciate its meaning."[26]

And Alice did succeed. In 1918, she became a member of the Society of Arts and Crafts, Boston (SACB) as a craftsman, a designation that included both designers and practitioners in some branch of applied decorative arts. To be admitted as a wood carver, as she was, she would have had to provide samples of her finished work as evidence of her skill. Although she never participated in SACB exhibitions, in 1921, Alice showed her work at the Art Institute of Chicago's Annual Exhibition of Applied Arts, a venue comparable to the SACB's expositions (figure 31).

Alice exhibited seven pieces, including a mahogany chest with carved panel, several carved frames with gold leaf, and a carved and gilded box. She sold the box during the exhibition itself and commented that "since then, I have been kept busy with orders." In the accompanying catalog, Alice was identified as "designer" as well as "maker and exhibitor," a significant distinction.[27]

One of the guiding principles of the Arts and Crafts movement was the appreciation and encouragement of hand work and artistry in an age when mass production had standardized and cheapened both materials and products. For wood carving in particular, as Charles Prendergast noted, the beauty of the "irregularities of hand labor" far surpassed the uniformity and "evenness" of the machine-made object. "Every wood-carver should be able to design his own work," he continued, lamenting that "we have unfortunately separated the designer and the craftsman." Alice Stephana agreed, remarking that "design is the foundation of all art. . . . What a pleasure it is to take a pencil and make a design smile out slowly from a block of wood!"[28]

Open discussion and honest assessments were encouraged among Alice and her colleagues. "And here I am not speaking for myself alone, but, I believe, for all of us who are trying to be true to our standards," she declared, "when I say that we welcome criticism, and are grateful for any suggestions which may broaden our minds or widen our outlook." Never pretentious about her skill or goals, Alice embraced her craft. "Many . . . seem to have heard of me as an artist who paints pictures. I am not," she stated. "I am simply a wood-carver, earning for each piece which I create the price it is worth."[29]

The 1920s was an especially active decade for Alice and her art. She continued to travel during the summer months, with the exception of 1918, when she chose to remain in Chicago and "swam in Lake Michigan every day."[30] In 1927, accompanied by her godmother Louise Graves, a Boston-bred artist whose calendar designs, illustrations, and bookplates were quite popular, she spent several months in Europe.[31] Keeping a diary while abroad, Alice wrote about her journey for *The Bulletin.* She began by explaining that she and her godmother generally "lived in pensions, something like what we call boarding-houses over here," and once "in a parish house of an Episcopal order" rather than in hotels. Venice captivated her artistic eye, and Alice recounted the stunning visual scenes that surrounded them. "The landscape is lovely in its colorings of faint purple and rose-color and gold at the watery horizon," she wrote. The travelers "glided through poetical jade-green canals" where they saw "sailing-boats with gray sails tinted here and there in burnt-orange, red and old gold . . . gliding prettily, attuned to the soft stir of the wind in a watery field of green-gold." Retaining the curiosity and spirit she had as a child, Alice viewed all she encountered with amusement and interest. On a night train to Rome, several Italian students "tried to flirt" with her "behind Godmother's back," one young man pointing to a line in his English language book, "You are fair with blue eyes and flaxen hair." Alice recalled, however, that she had been cautioned about such flirtations. "Before going abroad," she told her *Bulletin* readers, "I was warned not to look at Italian men lest I should fall in love with some villain." Thus, though she admitted that "most of the Italians' eyes are brown and soft and liquid," she did not succumb to their charms.[32]

Another of Alice's senses was tapped when she visited Naples. "It is beautiful and yet it is dirty and slothful with an unpleasant odor in the dark corners or alleys," she wrote, yet the city's picturesque qualities won her over. "Its beauty, at the Bay of Naples—a picture of Mt. Vesuvius purple-hued with a thin smoke of grayish-white curling upward, and the sea painted in rose-color—is so great that one forgets the ill-smelling odor." And, on Sicily, she was overwhelmed when she came upon an old Greek temple. "It was of a beautiful warm color—old gold mellowed with age—against the blue-green slopes of steep hills already heavy with golden fruit and purple iris in full bloom," she recalled. "It was all so beautiful that it hurt one's soul!"[33]

While in Florence, Alice took advanced lessons in carving and gilding. "I want to have the feeling that my designing, woodwork and gilding are mine entirely," she told her readers.[34] Back in the United States, Alice exhibited carved picture and mirror frames with unusual mushroom and tadpole motifs as well as boxes and book rests, all in gold and silver leaf, at the Chicago Woman's World's Fair (WWF) in 1928, and the Chicago League for the Hard of Hearing's own art exhibit in 1929. The Chicago Woman's World's Fairs, which ran each spring for four years (1925–1928), were part of a collective effort by the city's female reformers to highlight the entire spectrum of women's work. Initially held at the American Exposition Palace on Lake Shore Drive, by 1927 the mammoth enterprise was relocated to the Coliseum. In a conscious effort to surmount the race, class, and ethnic characterizations and divisions that had plagued the World's Columbian Exposition held in Chicago in 1893, the fair displayed all types of women's work, art, hobbies, and educational training opportunities. As one historian notes, "elitist metaphors" had no place in the fair. "Instead, industrial workers and peasants, governors, craftswomen, and prospectors all were equally celebrated as evidence of woman's ability to free herself through work." The WWF drew hundreds of thousands of visitors each year and even made a profit, which was donated to various causes.[35]

In the Chicago League for the Hard of Hearing booth at the 1928 Woman's World's Fair, along with her carved frames and accessories, Alice exhibited her Peacock sundial, a piece inspired by an Art Institute class assignment. Students were to read Hans Christian Anderson's "The Wicked Prince" and "make something out of clay to express the idea in the story." The tale of an evil nobleman who vowed to conquer even God inspired Alice to make the model for a sundial. A bronze bowed peacock sits on the dial's gnomon, itself decorated with stylized flowers, at the center of an octagonal base. Raised Roman numerals and the Latin phrase *Lucem Demonstrat Umbra* encircle the figure. There are tiny hearts on the bird's detailed tail feathers, and its body and crown are carefully carved. As Alice explained, the shadow falling on the dial was cast by the peacock representing "humanity forever bowing before the sun." She exhibited the original bronze at Tiffany's in New York and then presented it to Caroline Yale, then-retired principal of Clarke (figure 32). It was placed in front of Hubbard Hall at Clarke "as evidence both of her skill as an artist and of her affection for the school." Alice continued to show and sell bronze casts of the sundial with "great success."[36] Alice Stephana was not the only League member who was an artist, and in 1929 the organization held its own art exhibition. In addition to the work of "the elf-like Alice Lee, whose wood carving is the very essence of beauty expressed," the League promised an exhibition that showcased watercolor sketches, bronze statuettes, plaster models and casts, platinum and jewelry design, and photography.[37]

Alice Stephana Lee lived a well rounded, busy, and fulfilling life in Chicago. She continued to take classes at the Art Institute, was "one of the hardest workers" at Hearing League events, donated to the Field Museum, and visited and corresponded with family and friends. Nothing definitive is known about her relationship with her stepfather, but the household seemed to be a congenial and harmonious one. Born in Chicago, Otto Freer received his M.D. degree in

FIGURE 32. Alice Stephana Lee's Peacock sundial. Hubbard Hall, Clarke Schools for Hearing and Speech, Northampton, MA. Photo by author, 2010.

1879 from Rush Medical College, where his father, Joseph Warren Freer, had served as president for many years. Otto then continued his studies in Munich, Vienna, and Heidelberg, specializing in laryngology. Earning a worldwide reputation, Freer developed a groundbreaking surgical technique, a submucous resection of the septum, and invented a set of instruments for performing the procedure which are still in use today. A professor at Rush Medical College and a fellow of the Royal Society of Medicine of London, he published prolifically in both American and foreign journals, was a member of numerous medical societies in Europe, and served as secretary and chairman of the American Medical Association.[38]

Devoted to his career, Freer remained single until he wed Agnes Rand Lee in 1911. The event was not publicized, possibly because it was her second marriage. A year later, Agnes wrote to her colleague William Braithwaite, "I was married last May quietly in Rye, N.Y. at my brother's, to Dr. Freer of Chicago.

. . . There were no 'announcements,' otherwise of course you would have had one."[39] The couple, along with Alice Stephana, settled into one of the city's best neighborhoods. Their shared familiarity with both the city and Europe provided a bond, and it is also quite likely that the Rand and Freer families were previously known to each other in Chicago social circles. Agnes appeared quite content, at least to Louise Guiney, then living permanently in England. "Agnes Lee seems to be happy; I am so glad for her," Guiney wrote to Day. "There is some talk of herself and her Dr. coming over next winter."[40] Although there is no record of that particular trip, Agnes was a well-suited partner for this noted physician.

Freer's intellect and sophistication may have appealed to Agnes, and the Freer family was also well acquainted with the arts. Otto's brother, Frederick Warren Freer, was a multitalented artist who figured prominently in Chicago cultural circles, and his sister Cora was also a trained painter and teacher, suggesting that they would welcome a poet and artist into their extended family. In addition, Frederick Freer was left partially deaf after an illness contracted when he was a teenager, making Otto keenly aware of the challenges faced by the hearing-impaired. Compatible in many ways, then, the distinguished surgeon and professor and the admired poet and author created a quiet, successful marriage and surely made a cosmopolitan addition to Chicago's elite. Otto Freer died in 1932 of heart disease after a lengthy illness. As early as 1914 Agnes was concerned about her "tired husband" spending hours at night "at some bed of aches miles off" and, by 1928, she was "always anxious" about him. He was buried in the Freer family plot at Graceland Cemetery. Agnes and Alice Stephana remained in the East Elm Street home until Agnes's death in 1939.[41]

While Agnes was very close to and extremely protective of her daughter, referring to "my little deaf girl" even after Alice was an accomplished young woman who made her own way and traveled extensively, Francis Watts Lee played a lesser role in his daughter's life after his own remarriage. In fact, for a time the two were estranged, something Agnes attributed to Lee's second wife, Marion. According to Agnes, Alice Stephana did not visit her father's home "any more than she can help" because "Mrs. F. W., the wife, is insanely jealous of Alice and makes everything as disagreeable for the poor child as she possibly can," even forcing Lee to be "beastly to Alice, too."[42] Although this accusation was not repeated, there were indications that Marion Lee was indeed a complicated and troubled woman.

# Chapter 8
## MARION LEWIS CHAMBERLAIN LEE

Born in 1874 to Lucy Locke Lewis and her husband, Lothrop Lincoln Lewis, a grocery store clerk, Marion Lincoln Lewis was the eldest of six children. Said to be frail from birth, the girl was kept at home without schooling or instruction until nearly a teenager. This inauspicious beginning did not hold her back for long, however; two years later "she passed with the children of her age into High School" and went on to complete the work of four years in three. Even more impressive, as a friend and colleague recollected, "At the same time, at home by herself, she did the first year's work of the University and so entered the second year of [college] when she was seventeen." Her chosen field was architecture and her chosen university was the Massachusetts Institute of Technology.[1]

Incorporated in 1861, MIT quickly became known for a pedagogy that emphasized laboratory teaching, experimentation, and original student research. The institution opened a School of Architecture in 1867, where the curriculum was based on the "atelier" or studio system of the Ecole de Beaux-Arts in Paris. The school maintained a commitment to the humanities, however, promising that architectural students would gain not only thorough practical training but also an education in the liberal arts.[2] Working in tandem with the Boston Society of Architects, also founded in 1867, a professional organization that followed a decidedly English model, the school, according to one historian, "managed to blend the new French atelier system of instruction in the high arts with the English tradition of industrial arts."[3] MIT did not award its first BS in architecture to a woman until 1890, when Sophia Hayden earned her degree with honors. Hayden went on to design the Woman's Building at the 1893 World's Columbian Exposition held in Chicago.[4]

By the time Marion Lewis arrived at "Boston Tech," as the university was then commonly called, several more women had enrolled including, Marion Mahony, the second woman to receive an architectural degree from the school. Characterized by one scholar as "an architect of substantial creativity . . . deep convictions and profound spiritual experiences," the Chicago-born Mahony met Marion Lewis in a "dressing room" at the university, and they formed an immediate bond. "The conversation was so absorbing," Mahony later recalled, "that we both forgot and missed the classes at which we were due." During the years their MIT careers overlapped, "the two Marions," as Mahony referred to them, continued an intense exchange of ideas discussing a wide range of subjects including "the philosophies of the Western peoples, Kant's 'Critique of Pure Reason' and so on." A year following her graduation, in 1895, Mahony was hired by Frank Lloyd Wright as his first assistant and collaborator and continued in Wright's Oak Park studio for more than a decade. Remembering Marion Lewis as "one of the most interesting people of my acquaintance," Mahony described her "Boston pal" as "a most beautiful girl of the Burne Jones type." A formal portrait of Marion Lewis taken during her time at MIT captures a dark-haired young woman with handsome, even features, a long graceful neck, and deep pensive eyes (figure 33). She wears a light-colored dress with a Pierrot collar and layered sleeves, very simple and likely homemade. The intricate beadwork bib, perhaps an expression of her independent sense of style, does not appear to be stitched permanently to the bodice. Marion may have made this dress front herself to enhance her appearance for this photograph.[5]

While enrolled at MIT, the "beautiful, brilliant, and charming" Marion Lewis also became acquainted with Herbert Chamberlain, an extremely talented architect from Hudson, Ohio. After working as an under-draftsman and construction supervisor for the firm of Burnham & Root at the 1893 Columbian

FIGURE 33. G. Waldon Smith, Marion L. Lewis, 1896, glossy collodion, carte de visite. Private family collection.

Exposition, Chamberlain received a fellowship to MIT, where he earned an MS in 1896, the year Marion completed her bachelor's degree. Shortly thereafter Chamberlain won the Boston Society of Architects' annual prize and was employed by Cabot, Everett & Mead, where he produced the drawings for the restoration of the cupola on the Old State House. In September 1898, he and Marion married and traveled to Italy to pursue an advanced course of architectural study. Their intended creative partnership and marriage came to a tragic end only eight months later, however, when Herbert Chamberlain died in Siena, Italy, of acute peritonitis at the age of thirty-one. Now a widow,

FIGURE 34. Unknown photographer, *Boston Public Library, McKim Building,* c. 1900. Courtesy of Trustees of the Boston Public Library, Leslie Jones Collection (08_02_004232).

the twenty-five-year-old Marion Lewis Chamberlain returned to America and resumed employment in the Fine Arts Department of the Boston Public Library, where she had worked previously. It was the kind of position that was attractive to educated single women at a time of rapid social change.[6]

Before a new public library could be constructed in Copley Square as proposed, the city suffered through years of disputes and delays. Once commissioned, the New York firm of McKim, Mead & White sought to create a building that would stand on its own and yet architecturally complement its existing "motley and aggressive neighbors," including the Museum of Fine Arts and Trinity Church. The final design (figure 34) was deemed a great success by most critics, including Ralph Adams Cram, who described the building as evoking "a serene Classicism, reserved, scholarly, delicately conceived in all its parts, beautiful in that sense in which things have always been beautiful in periods of high human culture."[7] But when the library finally opened its doors in the winter of 1895, it was to, in one historian's words, a "raw, new urban-industrial society."[8] European immigrants and an uneducated rural population migrating into the city had increased the numbers and exacerbated the problems of an already disordered and unstable working class. Initially built to celebrate, serve, and promote the culture of the refined Brahmin elite, this "people's library" was immediately confronted with a more diverse populace. Librarians whose job qualifications had included "at least a knowledge of Greek and Latin" and preferably "a mastery of French and German" as well, and who were often openly "disdainful of public school curriculum, rote process, and unqualified instructors," found themselves providing supplementary readings to aid public school teachers and rudimentary literacy instruction at ancillary settlement house libraries. At the same time, as secondary education became more technical in order to provide young people with competitive occupational skills, librarians were to be "a civilizing influence," the arbiters of good taste, and the "custodians of cultural ideals" for the masses. Coincidentally, a growing number of women flooded into the field.[9]

The BPL hired its first woman clerk in 1852, but by 1878 two-thirds of its workers were female. As with teachers of the deaf, there were both economic and cultural reasons for this dramatic feminization of the profession. The last half of the nineteenth century brought about a proliferation of public libraries across the country to meet the needs of a changing demographic, and to face the challenges of industrial innovation and the rise of mass culture. Particularly in a city like Boston, the library was perceived as a great equalizer, an institution where knowledge, information, and learning were available and "Free to All." To keep pace with constituent demands, urban libraries, as one scholar wrote, were "in need of low-paid but educated recruits." Women were willing to accept these positions, a fact that once again perpetuated their lower economic status.[10] Still, the cultural and economic disruptions that had produced this new urban reality created opportunities for a generation of women who came of age desiring lives unlike those experienced by their primarily home-bound mothers.[11]

Although only twelve years apart in age, Agnes Rand Lee and Marion Lewis were on opposite sides of this occupational and social divide. In 1896, Agnes Lee, sheltered by her upper-middle-class upbringing, resided in a large suburban home, raising two daughters and writing poetry. In contrast, Marion Lewis exited MIT fully expecting to make her mark in the male-dominated profession of architecture. Instead, soon after her graduation she was hired by the BPL as "second assistant" in "Special Libraries," a newly formed department that encompassed arts, music, architecture, photography, and much else deemed "important to the study of Art." Under the direction of the librarian Otto Fleischner, the department not only fulfilled the customary clerical and reference duties but also mounted exhibitions, initiated collections in photography and prints, and offered instructional programs for school children. Thus, for the time being Marion likely found satisfaction in a position which, although not strictly in her field, was relevant to the arts, offered steady employment, and was "rewarding work."[12] Earning less than $8.00 per week and alone in the city, Marion either shared expenses and lodgings with other self-supporting young women or rented an inexpensive room in one of the many boardinghouses that sprang up around Copley Square. Single, peer-oriented, and adventurous, Marion fit the description of late-nineteenth-century society's emerging "New Woman," who was said to be "young, well-educated, probably a college graduate, independent of spirit, highly competent, and physically strong and fearless." Marion Lewis and others like her embraced educational parity, self-determination, and mobility. Capitalizing on their wide-ranging interests, these modern women sought employment and leisure activities aimed at "intellectual self-improvement."[13]

One type of association that enabled these women not only to enrich their minds but also to associate with one another was the "study club." As the historian Theodora Penny Martin observed, the Civil War "proved to be the hothouse which forced the organizational development of women," and by the end of the century hundreds of women's clubs emerged focusing on art, history, literature, education, and civic improvements. Club women consciously saw these organizations as "agents of personal growth and transformation."[14] Explaining that she had "a personal interest" in the women's study club movement, Marion Lewis used the phenomenon for her 1896 senior thesis in architecture at MIT. Titling her project "A Women's Club House," she proposed a structure "for the various women's clubs of Boston and vicinity to be built on the Back Bay district in the neighborhood of the Public Garden." The proposal contained scale drawings and detailed plans for a formidable multistory Italian Renaissance–style building combining retail, office, and large public spaces (figure 35). Cognizant of the need to make the "club house" self-sustaining, she suggested that the ground-floor area "be let as stores and another story for offices" to help in "defraying the expenses of the building." Marion argued for "a great hall seating not less than six hundred people" to be used by the clubs or rented out for "parties and theatricals" ensuring further income. She also proposed another public space "seating at least three hundred . . . for lectures, receptions and banquets" as well as "reception rooms and tea rooms." Clearly understanding

FIGURE 35. Marion L. Lewis, architectural design drawing, c. 1896. Massachusetts Institute of Technology, Architecture and Design Collection, Courtesy of MIT Museum.

the constituency she was designing for, she was emphatic that "there must be a library centrally located and always open for the use of members." There were also parlors, dressing rooms and toilet, club offices, and bedrooms.[15] Although Marion's "Women's Club House" was never built, perhaps in the BPL's Special Libraries Department her expertise in art, architecture, and philosophy at least enabled her to be of assistance to the clubwomen of Boston.

Upon her marriage to Herbert Chamberlain, Marion resigned her position, but according to the BPL's 1900 Annual Report, she was "re-engaged after an absence of one year." Her marriage and the death of her husband were not specifically mentioned, however; the report noted only that her time away had been "mostly devoted to study in Italy."[16] She remained in the Special Libraries Department for another four years, and at some point Francis Watts Lee began to take photographs of her. In one she wears a dark peasant-style dress with an equally dark open weave shawl draped around her shoulders (figure 36). She has gathered her hair loosely in Gibson-girl fashion with a bun on top of her

FIGURE 36. Francis Watts Lee, Marion Chamberlain, c. 1902, platinum print. (LC-DIG-ppmsca-39444).

head and one small curl escaping. Her hands lightly hold the shawl in place and a thin shy smile indicates her discomfort or amusement at taking on the role of model. Her dark hair and clothing are absorbed into the even darker background, accentuating the flawless skin of her face, neck, and hands. In contrast, a second portrait of Marion is all gentle lightness as the frothy, layered fabric of her gown and her modified pompadour hair style with its soft fullness on the sides blends smoothly into the textured background creating a delicate, dreamy image. This is the photograph that Lee exhibited in the 1902 London Salon as *Beata mea Domina* (plate 8).

How close Marion and Francis became during this time is uncertain. It is possible the two found consolation with each other in their grief. Lee was aware of Marion's loss and had written to Louise Guiney that her "early widowhood was one of the saddest things I have ever known." During these same months, Lee himself was still trying to cope with Peggy's death. In 1903, Marion spent her vacation in the north of France and in England, where, at Lee's suggestion, she met Louise. Lee had requested that Guiney assist "Mrs. Chamberlain . . . as much as you are able" during her stay in Oxford, where, since she was "an architect by profession," he felt "the beauties of the place will doubly appeal."[17] Marion did enjoy her time in Oxford and wrote a note of appreciation to Guiney. Expressing gratitude to Louise for advice and "eatables," she reported, "I have tramped the streets all day," and concluded, "I am so happy, it does not seem real."[18] Despite this respite and a promotion that brought her salary to just under $700 per year, Marion resigned from the BPL in October 1903. Perhaps her time in Oxford had renewed her architectural ambitions or perhaps she chose to absent herself from Boston, and Lee, as he attempted to reconcile with his wife. Whatever her reasons for leaving, Marion headed to Illinois and the studio of Frank Lloyd Wright.[19]

At the turn of the twentieth century, architecture remained a male-dominated and chiefly patriarchal profession in which "women architects," as one scholar wrote, "were frequently viewed with contempt and suspicion, not only by fellow practitioners but also by members of the building trades and potential clients." These attitudes made apprenticeships and entry-level positions difficult for women to find, and it was decades before true parity was reached.[20] Although rarely given the credit she deserved, Marion Mahony had become the de facto "superintendent of the office force" at Oak Park. In that role she oversaw the creation of many of Wright's presentation drawings and organized much of the business workflow.[21] Undoubtedly owing to Mahony's friendship and encouragement, Marion Chamberlain, seven years out of MIT and close to five years since her brief stint in Italy, began work at Wright's studio in the fall of 1903.

"The head of the Fine Arts Department is on from the Boston Public Library, studying," observed Charles White Jr., a young Vermont native who likewise arrived at Oak Park that fall, "also a well-known Chicago painter, so the environment ought to be fine." White's initial impressions of the studio were mixed. "I have seen Mr. Wright, and had many good talks with him," the young man wrote to his former employer back home. Although pleased with the time Wright was spending with him, and the amount of business the studio handled, White had some reservations about Wright's work habits. "He is certainly the most impractical man—is way behind in his work, but calmly takes seven weeks to alter his office, and lets the work wait." And he was even more concerned with the architect's attitude toward those seeking his services. "It makes me nervous," White stated, "to think of the way he treats his clients, and yet he seems to get the work all the same."

While White seemed to thrive in such an environment and remained for three years, Marion Chamberlain did not. In May 1904, less than a year after her arrival, White reported to his friend "what news I have," chiefly that "Mrs. Chamberlain—she of the Tech, and Boston Pub. has left us and gone back east." White believed her departure was due to her lack of skill and Wright's lack of patience. "She seemed to have so little ability along Architectural lines," he explained, "that Mr. Wright frankly advised her to give up." Wright went even further by bluntly suggesting that she "try and get back into Librarianism," a phrase which delighted Charles White.[22]

Faced with this setback, Marion did return to library work. She was first employed at the Avery Architectural and Fine Arts Library at Columbia University, a position well suited to her education and experience.[23] Three years later she moved to the New York Society Library, a subscription library founded in 1754.[24] By 1906, Marion Chamberlain and Francis Watts Lee had renewed their acquaintance. His marriage was irretrievably broken, and he likely called on Marion as he traveled frequently to New York for business and political reform meetings. On these journeys, he often visited friends like Gertrude Käsebier and would have had considerable time to spend with Marion.[25] In September of 1909 Marion Chamberlain became librarian and dean of the first women's dorm at Rhode Island State College in Kingston, Rhode Island. The administration was pleased to employ Mrs. Chamberlain for this dual position, believing that her MIT degree, her library experience, and her familiarity with foreign travel

FIGURE 37. Francis Watts Lee, Marion Lee and Lucy Lee in Walpole, 1913, platinum print. (LC-DIG-ppmsca-39446).

would provide a sophisticated outlook to the school's young women. She held this post for two years until July 1, 1911, when Marion Lincoln Chamberlain of Kingston, Rhode Island, married Francis Watts Lee of Boston, Massachusetts. On the same date, she resigned from the college.[26]

Since this was the second marriage for each, the couple took "no real honeymoon and wedding journey."[27] Instead they settled immediately in Walpole, Massachusetts, a town of 5,000 located about thirteen miles south of Boston. Founded in 1724 and known for its combination of successful industrial enterprises near the town's center and flourishing farms on its less populated outskirts, Walpole was home both to a politically well-connected elite and a growing working-class population. The Lees took up residence on "Halfway Farm," an eight-acre parcel of land with a rambling old farmhouse, barn, silo, and outbuildings. Francis retained his position at the Boston Public Library, commuting six days a week while Marion remained at home. A year after their marriage, a daughter, Lucy, was born, and three years later, a son, Francis Lincoln Lee.[28]

Initially the marriage was a happy one. The rather rural setting seemed to agree with Marion, who relished being a mother, judging by a photograph of her and one-year-old Lucy (figure 37). Unlike the ceremonious mother-daughter tableaux that Agnes shared with her children, the image is indicative of this new family's more casual lifestyle. The two are out-of-doors, on a grassy area surrounded by untamed shrubbery, dappled sunlight showing through the trees. There is a rustic gate in the background, connected to a fence, nearly lost in the vegetation that has grown unchecked around it. Wearing a loose, comfortable dress with her sleeves rolled up, Marion crouches over a metal wash basin, her hands and lower arms wet from her efforts to bathe her daughter, who clings to the edge of the bucket. Marion is aware of the camera and laughs heartily as she squints into the sun while supporting the baby's back, keeping her upright in the tub. It is a homely scene, intimate, easygoing, and joyful. The homespun atmosphere, pastoral setting, and less formal mother-child relationship captured in this photo attest to twentieth-century cultural change, particularly with regard to children.

Between the years when Peggy and Alice were born and the arrival of the two younger Lees, universal and mandatory public education, the expectations of more nurturing parents, an awareness of child labor issues, and the rise of popular culture had prolonged the economic dependency of the young. Yet these shifts resulted in a new kind of independence. An emerging consumer culture, mass media, and extended time with peers caused shifts in customary family dynamics. Sons and daughters sensed they had far more options than their parents had, and they were increasingly influenced by the opinions and values of their contemporaries. The hours beyond the usual school day were seen as open-ended recreational time, allowing children to entertain themselves with little adult supervision. Childhood as a distinct period was becoming culturally codified.[29] These new ideas were beneficial to the quality of children's lives, particularly in semi-rural areas like Walpole. Lucy and Francis enjoyed exploring the woods, waterways, and fields around their home, as demonstrated by a photograph of the two playing in a leaf-strewn glen. In contrast to the formal, genteel portraits of Peggy and Alice Lee, orchestrated by famed pictorialists, this snapshot catches two modern siblings unaware (figure 38). Hair disheveled, hands soiled from play, and dressed in comfortable clothing—the boy in a corduroy one-piece coverall, the girl in bloomers and a generous

FIGURE 38. Francis Watts Lee, Lucy Lee and Francis Lincoln Lee at play, c. 1919, platinum print (PR13 CN2015.052.486)

overblouse—they huddle together absorbed in their examination of a camera, undoubtedly belonging to their father. What had once been an instrument of artistic expression was now a toy.

As time passed, however, Francis and Marion remained aloof from the local community. They joined the Episcopal Church but were not active members, and there is no record of their involvement in the civic or social life of the town. In many ways, the family became isolated and disconnected. Agnes Freer thought it was "a queer atmosphere," and offered her opinion to Fred Day that "the whole story is like a Balzac novel," perhaps alluding to the family's struggles amid trying circumstances.[30] Raising two very young children in middle age was difficult, and Francis admitted to his wife that "neither of us can deal with the children . . . as we could if God had given them to us while we were younger." In addition, Francis was the guardian of his institutionalized sister, Constance. The couple also had the care of Lee's aged mother, who joined the household soon after their marriage. And, of course, his daughter Alice visited, sometimes for several weeks at a time. The emotional and physical toll of these multiple responsibilities fell primarily on Marion, since Francis was away from home close to twelve hours a day.[31]

Sometime in 1921 Agnes heard "quite unofficially . . . that a separation had been threatening between [Francis] and his wife" but dismissed it as "mere rumor." Although the marriage remained intact, the family dynamic did seem to deteriorate. Eventually under a doctor's care for "emotional tension," Marion at times turned her anxiety and frustration on others, and Francis acknowledged that the children were subjected to "a verbal lash" and sometimes "physical violence" when their mother lost control.[32] Lucy, the eldest, was defiant and confident; as soon as she was able, she left home and finished high school in Springfield, Massachusetts, where she lived with Marion's sister Christine, an unmarried school teacher and suffragette.[33] Young Francis was a more taciturn child whom his father feared would be forced "more and more in upon himself" by his mother's erratic behavior. The boy found solace in his studies, however, and, inheriting his parents' technical abilities, excelled at engineering, eventually earning degrees at Stanford and MIT.[34]

The reasons for Marion's transformation from the "brilliant and charming" university student, the "very sweet woman" who worked at the BPL, and the delighted new mother into an unhappy and somewhat unstable wife and parent cannot be definitively determined.[35] Her symptoms included extreme irritability, unfounded suspicions, and high anxiety, however, and it seems possible that unprocessed grief over the death of her first husband and her thwarted career ambitions could have been exacerbated by postpartum depression or psychosis, a diagnosis unheard of in the early twentieth century. Whatever the cause, Marion struggled to overcome her apparently untethered emotional swings. She amassed a personal collection of "psychiatric books" and sought assistance from various physicians, including Dr. C. Macfie Campbell, the medical director of the Boston Psychopathic Hospital and professor of psychiatry at Harvard.[36] Born in Scotland, Campbell received his medical degree in Edinburgh, completed postgraduate studies in France and Germany, and held numerous posts both in Scotland and in the United States. Characterized as a "charming, incisive, and erudite man," Campbell was a recognized expert in the still-nascent field of psychiatry.[37] He was instrumental in introducing Freudian analysis into American hospitals and medical schools, and according to one source, he was "responsible for a large group of his students becoming psychoanalysts and dynamic psychiatrists." Like Sigmund Freud and Adolf Meyer, with whom he worked, Campbell believed that the root cause of mental illness or disturbance could be traced to previous life experiences and trauma. He thus "exhaustively probed the patient's entire life" to understand the origins of an illness within "a broad and experiential context."[38] In spite of Campbell's ministrations, Marion's distress continued and seemed to peak in August 1928, when she insisted on taking an ocean voyage alone. The journey carried her from New York to Havana, through the Panama Canal and up to California, where she planned to stay for six months of total rest. Her decision "disturbed" her brother Gardner and made her sister Christine "gravely anxious," but Marion was convinced that the trip would bring her "physical and psychical relief."[39]

It was perhaps on this journey that Marion wrote a self-reflective creative composition she called "The Lure of the Question Mark." In it she likened her past to "a shabby textile" which she had "rolled up and put away and never want[ed] to set eyes on again." Yet, encouraged by Dr. Campbell, who would have supported such self-scrutiny, and, as she put it, "for the children's sake," she felt she must do the work of self-examination. She took out this "shabby, dark coarse old life . . . and unrolled it." As Agnes Lee had exorcised her grief through her poetry, Marion sought to understand herself through this thinly veiled autobiographical musing, part memoir and part allegory. "At first it seemed a dingy web," she began, "the warp a succession of hardship—iron poverty, followed by a small scarcely living wage—days of labor, evenings of drudgery; a little more salary, and the tiny surplus all put into education for younger brothers and sister. . . . And the woof, boundless ambition, little accomplishment." This extended metaphor illuminated her young adult years, when she saw her hopes frustrated by familial responsibilities and her high ambitions stymied by unfulfilling occupational choices and failure. As she continued to study this symbolic unfurled fabric, she saw that "both warp and woof were cut in places by terrible tears." Perhaps for the first time, Marion identified the "frightful rents" in her past as "The Hole in the Italian Hillside, the Hole in the Wall, the Nettle, and the Break in the Stairway." While "The Hole in the Italian Hillside" was a clear reference to the untimely death of Herbert Chamberlain, the other images are more elusive and difficult to interpret but certainly refer to significant disappointments or stressors.[40]

Recognizing that this torn cloth was "a sorry piece of goods on which to work," she recalled that "in the old days" when she could not afford a new dress, she would "take someone's old, worn out, cast off garment and fashion it over." Now, she saw that she had "only one piece of material to work with," her "old life." Determined to make herself whole, she wrote, "I was used to fashioning from poor material, so I went at it." Comforted by the logic and stability of architecture, a language and art she understood instinctively, Marion began to envision a drawing "somewhat like the 'cross-section' of a building." She began to plot floor and stairways until she perceived a certain pattern to her life; "that each choice in some measure determined the succeeding choice; that there was plan, echo, and proportion in it all." "I saw," she wrote, "that it had depth and perspective. Then, at last I sensed the organic quality of Life" and the future that "must rise from the hearthstone of the Tatterdermalion Cottage." It was an image that could only stand for the rustic homestead she inhabited with Francis and their children. Perhaps filled with renewed hope and purpose, Marion returned to her family and together they persevered.[41]

In the succeeding years, Lucy went off to Vassar and Francis prepared for college; Alice Stephana, now in her late thirties, continued to visit occasionally. "Alice saw F. W. L. when she was in Boston last autumn, and also saw his two children," Agnes Freer wrote to a friend in 1931. "I must say they seem to be very fine children." Returning to the family touchstone, she remarked, "I liked their photographs, which Alice had," and she observed that young Francis "looks very like Alice, to judge by his picture."[42] Meanwhile, Marion sought recreation in "design, travel, and needlework." In a photograph taken of her in middle age, the strength of her personality and unique style are undeniable (figure 39). Dressed in a low-cut loose-fitting blouse and silk robe with stunning designs across the shoulders and down the lapels, she wears an extraordinary necklace, brooch,

FIGURE 39. Unknown photographer, Marion Chamberlain Lee, c. 1925, silver gelatin, copy print. Private family collection.

and accompanying drop earrings. The deep oriental-inspired design and strong trimming on the robe indicate the influence of the Aesthetic movement, as does the elaborate medieval revival jewelry. The fashionable yet somewhat bohemian ensemble, along with her unruly graying hair and the tilt of her chin, give the impression of a proud and competent woman. Likewise, her direct gaze into the camera, challenging yet with a tinge of sadness, reveals an iron will perhaps tempered by experience. Sadly, despite her best efforts Marion continued to grapple with the anxieties and outbursts that threatened to ruin her relationship with those closest to her.[43]

In the midst of the Depression and nearing the BPL's mandatory retirement age of seventy, Francis sought a scholarship to ensure his son's education when he could not provide the necessary funds. "Had I been a younger man the problem would not [be] so serious;" he confessed, poignantly adding that the reason for the financial deficiency was that "I have spent my life in a minor mechanical position in the civil service."[44] If he actually felt this to be true, it was a heart-wrenching coda to the aspirations of his youth.

# Chapter 9
# FRANCIS WATTS LEE

By the last quarter of the nineteenth century American book publishing in general had become a tasteless, commercial industry. Books were inexpensive and plentiful, but the lack of concern for beauty and balance in typography, layout, and decoration had resulted in unattractive, rather shoddy products. The reasons for this decline were many. A rapidly expanding urban middle class, an increase in primary and secondary schools and the accompanying rise in literacy rates, the proliferation of public libraries, and a population with at least some leisure time all fostered a demand for books. At the same time, the Industrial Revolution had brought about the mechanization of all aspects of bookmaking, from the production of ink to paper manufacturing, typesetting, and bookbinding, as well as the use of inferior materials to keep costs down while meeting the increased demand.[1]

Francis Watts Lee was part of the generation that came of age in 1890s Boston who saw themselves surrounded by this rapid industrialization and uninspiring design and were determined to make a change. Just as he was attracted to a religious doctrine that embraced social reform, he sought a similar intensity of experience in his occupational life. As T. J. Jackson Lears describes it,

"Instead of the small workshop, the dominant mode of economic organization was becoming the monopolistic corporation," which left the ordinary worker without a meaningful connection to a fulfilling occupation, one from which the worker might derive satisfaction and pride.[2] Through F. Holland Day, his former Chauncy Hall classmate, and Ralph Adams Cram, who shared his Anglo-Catholic and social reform leanings, Lee was drawn into the convivial Pewter Mugs dining club and invited to join the more exclusive and somewhat outlandish Visionists. These youthful romantics, recognizing a spiritual void in modern life, challenged one another to believe passionately in a cause or an ideal and to dedicate their lives to it. In some ways theirs was, as Stephen Maxfield Parrish concludes, "a revolt against modernism—against the intrusion of rational science and industrial progress upon the calm and the leisured harmony of an earlier age." But, this cohort, including Lee, was more confident and optimistic than Parrish implies. Instead of withdrawal, they dared one another to bring about a "new renascence" through their writing, architectural design, publishing, printmaking, photography, and music. "To us it was a golden age, with the promise of high fulfillment," Cram recalled. "Everything seemed to open out around us like the bursting of fireworks. We thought that we were chosen people in a chosen time."[3]

An intense, driven man who, according to Louise Imogen Guiney, kept "his enthusiasms at white heat," Francis Lee was undoubtedly an active participant in the earnest discussions and high-minded intentions of the Visionists.[4] They began by jointly producing two periodicals, *The Mahogany Tree* and *The Knight Errant*, through which they expressed their philosophy of life. *The Mahogany Tree* ran weekly from January through July 1892, and, although its typography was not striking and its format was conventional, liberal margins, a good grade of paper, and its intimate tone gave the magazine some distinction. As their collective interest in *The Mahogany Tree* waned, however, a smaller cohort of the Visionists issued a more ambitious, and as it turned out, more significant journal, *The Knight Errant*.

Chiefly under the direction of Ralph Adams Cram, Bertram Grosvenor Goodhue, whose elaborate design graced the magazine's cover, Fred Holland Day, and Herbert Copeland, *The Knight Errant* provided a vehicle for many of Boston's most influential cultural critics including Bernard Berenson, Charles Eliot Norton, Ernest Fenollosa, Arthur Wesley Dow, and Cram himself. Louise

Guiney, in a letter to Herbert Clarke, called the journal "as medieval as possible, by way of representing the rebound from progress and science and agnosticism and general modernity." In an essay titled "The Quest," the editors acknowledged that the Knight's purpose was no longer to slay dragons and rescue maidens but "to war against the Paynims of realism in art, to assail the dragon of materialism, to ride for the succor of forlorn hopes and the restoration of forgotten ideals," to restore beauty, "not only beauty in Art, but beauty in thought and motive, beauty in life and death."[5] To that end according to Cram, *The Knight Errant* "was to be not only an expression of the most advanced thought of the time . . . but, as well, a model of perfect typography and the printer's art." The responsibility for the journal's presentation fell to Francis Watts Lee, who, as Cram put it, "looked to the printing" at his Elzevir Press in Boston.[6]

Bearing a resemblance to the English periodical *The Hobby Horse*, *The Knight Errant* (figure 40) was a physically striking oversized journal printed on handmade paper. Although fellow Visionist Laurens Maynard may have engaged in a bit of hyperbole when he subsequently wrote that "the *Knight Errant* was of a significance corresponding to that of the founding of the Kelmscott Press in England," the quarterly was generally well received. The *Boston Transcript* commented on the attractiveness of the journal, and the British artist and book illustrator Walter Crane, who was well regarded in Arts and Crafts circles, praised the periodical and its creators. But, the most noteworthy endorsement came from the highly esteemed journal of letters *The Critic*: "It is to be hoped that this periodical will receive the support it so fully deserves. To lovers of the beautiful in paper, type, and margin, in illustration and design—to lovers, in short, of the bookmaker's art in its perfection, *The Knight Errant* appeals with irresistible force."[7]

One reviewer who strenuously disagreed with these positive assessments, however, wrote in the *American Bookmaker* that *The Knight Errant* "is really an offense against every accepted or acceptable rule for type display, page conformation, line spacing, punctuation, word breaking, paging and those minor and simple details which enter into the manufacture of a volume . . . justly claimed to be elegant." Referring to it as "this sudden freak of Francis Watts Lee," the critic had kind words for Goodhue's initial letter designs, the photogravure frontispiece, and the linen book paper, but, the final judgment was that the magazine "is a lamentable waste of time, labor and good material."[8]

FIGURE 40. *The Knight Errant*, cover design by Bertram Grosvenor Goodhue, 1892.
F. Holland Day Collection, Norwood Historical Society.

There is no record of Lee's reaction to this scathing review, but his own business left him little time for reflection. Since his return to Boston after his marriage to Agnes Rand, Lee had been employed in the printing industry, an occupation he shared with his father-in-law. Lee was first employed at the Rapid Printing Company, located at 106 Pearl Street in Boston, a full-service printing operation owned by the Willcox Manufacturing Company. Within a few years, however, Lee reported that he "had severed . . . all connections with the Willcoxes." The parting was apparently unpleasant. When Fred Day questioned the status of an order, Lee replied that "one of my last acts [at Rapid Printing] was to send . . . the paper and instructions to print. . . . The Willcox brothers will undertake to carry out all work in progress I think; but the feeling between us is not such as to render it *expedient* for *me* to make the request." Lee opened his own business at the same address, calling it the Elzevir Press after a much-celebrated seventeenth-century Dutch publishing house.[9]

*The Knight Errant* seemed to offer an exceptional beginning to Elzevir. Lee took charge not only of the hand printing of the journal in a run of five hundred, but kept the subscription and distribution lists and held the copyright; he even wrote a few pieces.[10] The first was "an enthusiastic notice" of Daniel Berkeley Updike's initial design effort, the privately printed *On the Dedications of American Churches*. The book's typeface, handmade paper, and ecclesiastical subject were all of great interest to Lee. As the print historian Susan Otis Thompson indicates, it was "a book, sober in content and design, destined, one would think, to obscurity" until Lee encouraged *Knight Errant* readers "to secure copies of it, notwithstanding the fact that it . . . is not for sale."[11] Lee also commented briefly on *Poems by the Way* by William Morris and *The Love Lyrics and Songs of Proteus* by Wilfred S. Blunt, both issued by Morris's private press. Acknowledging that most of the verses in each were reprints, Lee described the English reformer as a "great master of decorative art" and noted that "these beautiful 'Kelmscott' editions . . . mark a new era in the making of English books."[12]

Following up this praise, in the second number of *The Knight Errant*, dated July 1892, Lee wrote an article titled "Some Thoughts Upon Beauty in Typography Suggested by the Work of Mr. William Morris at the Kelmscott Press." After a brief history of the earliest printers and Roman characters, he examined Morris's contribution to the design of typeface, ornamental initials, and borders using several reproductions of Kelmscott pages. He concluded that the Kelmscott Press had produced books exquisitely "down to the smallest of those little but important details which go to make up the perfect book." So much so that "they may well be described, as they have been by one enthusiastic and competent judge, as, within the realm of the printer's art 'the crowning glory of the nineteenth century.'"[13]

Lee had great aspirations for his own printing as well. In September 1892, he wrote to Day of his "scheme to give up city life, retire into the country and operate a small hand press for art's sake only."[14] An adaptation of the phrase generally attributed to the French poet Theophile Gautier, "art for art's sake" was the statement of belief that art has an intrinsic value that needs no utilitarian or moral purpose. It was a term associated with the Aesthetic movement and certainly in keeping with the stated philosophy of the Visionists. Lee, however, clearly linked this particular "for art's sake only" phrase to his own Christian ideals as he continued, "I'm thinking of a six volume, . . . edition of the Book of Common Prayer as a chef-d'oeuvre round which other work may cluster. I'd like to talk it over with you." By November, however, a deeply disappointed Lee admitted "the book-publishing scheme was given up—knocking the wind all out of the sails of a long letter I had written to you in regard to the idea."[15]

Meanwhile, despite a "group of guarantors" Cram described as a "bluebook of the New England intelligentsia of the time" and a subscription list that included Stanford White, Augustus Saint-Gaudens, Bernard Berenson, and Thomas Bird Mosher, *The Knight Errant* survived for only four issues with its final number (January 1893) distributed "more than a year late."[16] Still, the journal did make a contribution to the revival of the book arts in Boston and was a factor in the establishment of four fine publishing houses: Stone and Kimball; the Merrymount Press; Small, Maynard and Company; and Copeland & Day. The respective principals, Herbert Stone, Ingalls Kimball, Daniel Berkeley Updike, Herbert Small, Laurens Maynard, Herbert Copeland, and Fred Holland Day all had been involved in, or greatly influenced by, the Visionists and their short-lived periodical. Stephen Maxfield Parrish contends that *The Knight Errant* was the coterie's "crowning artistic achievement" since "within a year or so after the knight had succumbed . . . the once tightly-knit esthetic vitality began to flag."[17] While these idealists did indeed drift away from one another in pursuit of their individual careers, Parrish fails to mention the external forces that proved insurmountable to these hopeful young entrepreneurs. More than anything else, it was the depression of 1893 that sounded the death knell for the Visionists.

Although parts of the southern and western United States had experienced disruption in the late 1880s, 1893 was the year that Wall Street and much of urban America were drawn into a "massive worldwide economic crisis." The stock market dropped precipitously, banks closed, and railroads went bankrupt in the panic that followed. Throughout the nation thousands of businesses were shuttered, and unemployment reached more than 20 percent in some cities.[18] As the depression deepened, labor unrest led to contentious standoffs and strikes across the country. Jacob Coxey led his "Industrial Army" to Washington to protest a lack of meaningful response by the federal government in 1894, and that same year brought the famed Pullman railroad strike. Taking place in the summer of 1894, the work stoppage was preceded by George Pullman laying off workers and lowering wages without a comparable rent reduction in his company housing on Chicago's South Side. Eugene Debs, who had founded the American Railway Union in 1893 as a result of the economic panic, brought his members into the city to organize Pullman workers who were not unionized. The ensuing boycott of trains carrying Pullman cars affected much of the country's railroad traffic, particularly in the West. After President Cleveland ordered the army to stop the action, violence broke out in many cities and the strike and boycott collapsed.[19]

As a declared Christian Socialist and member of the Church Association for the Advancement of the Interest of Labor, Francis Watts Lee had long decried the Episcopalian Church's upper-class sympathies and embraced the action of workers. He commemorated the Pullman strike by compiling a list of sources into something he called "Bibliographia Pullmanensis: An attempt to indicate some sources of information concerning the man, the town, and the system," which he published in *The Dawn*, a publication by the Society of Christian Socialists. He then assembled clippings of the bibliography into a pamphlet which he donated to the Boston Public Library.[20]

On a more personal note, the depression of 1893 likely caused the closure of the Elzevir Press. Lee had already expressed concern about the press as early as May 1892, when, returning from New York, he admitted to Day, "I fear my trip has been an ignominious failure from a business point of view."[21] Within a matter of months the economic crash and accompanying panic hit, and Elzevir ceased operation along with countless similar small enterprises. By this time Lee had a wife and two children to support. Fortunately he had a marketable skill as a talented, technologically capable printer with expertise in both the hand-operated fine art press and the modern mechanical printing press. He was also well known in Boston. In 1894 he accepted what was very likely a temporary position in the cataloging department of the Boston Public Library, knowing that with the opening of the new McKim Building on Copley Square, he would be made chief of the printing department. It was a remarkable opportunity as the BPL began a new era. Walter Muir Whitehill in his *Centennial History of the Boston Public Library* certainly gives the impression that Lee's appointment was part of the grand plan of the BPL's director, Herbert Putnam: "In reading Putnam's reports one inevitably feels that, almost by his very arrival, he brought the Public Library back to the heights . . . when important things had been happening in every direction at once. A Special Libraries Department was established under the care of Otto Fleischner. Francis W. Lee was transferred from the Catalogue Department to the charge of the Printing Department."[22]

Lee was responsible for a department handling a wide array of print projects for a busy, well-respected institution at the same time utilizing the most modern, cutting-edge technology available to the print industry. He spent the summer installing the library's first linotype machine purchased from the Mergenthaler Company.[23] A revolutionary step forward in printing, the linotype was introduced in the mid-1880s. The operator sat at a keyboard, adjusted the equipment for point size and line length, and typed the copy to be set. Pressing the keys activated the mechanism that released the matrices stamped with letters, numbers, or characters to a small conveyor belt to be dropped into the appropriate place in the line. Once each line was completed and justified, molten metal was pumped in and the line cast. This slug then moved on to be trimmed and delivered onto the galley. Meanwhile, the matrices were carried through a system of elevators and conveyors and returned to their original position, ready for repeated use.[24] The machine was complicated, loud, and abrasive to the ears. Within a few years Lee remarked of his department that "the continuous noise of linotypes constitutes a great nervous strain upon all of us."[25] The linotype was also a dangerous contraption with countless movable parts and metal heated to about 550 degrees Fahrenheit; a careless or inattentive worker could easily be injured. During the fall, Lee trained a compositor, pressman, and linotype operator, and, with the addition of a second linotype machine and compositor, the department gradually "took over the greater part of the library's printing."[26]

Francis Watts Lee was a very capable chief of the printing department, which by 1897 consisted of himself, "two compositors (women), one pressman, and one general assistant." These five employees worked on two Mergenthaler linotypes, three presses, and "the usual accessory equipment" to complete "all requisite letter-press and relief-plate printing" for the library.[27] In his first annual report,

FIGURE 41. Unknown photographer, Francis Watts Lee (center rear) in the Printing Department, Boston Public Library, 42 Stanhope Street, c. 1904. Courtesy of Trustees of the Boston Public Library, Leslie Jones Collection (08_02_004321).

Lee noted that since the linotype was invented "chiefly for newspaper work," adapting it for library use required matrices for multiple languages and unusual characters. Because of this unique need, Lee wrote, "during the past year the type with which we began work has been replaced by another and more suitable one made by the Mergenthaler Company from a design submitted by me." Lee also had a "specially cut and cast series of diacritical marks made" for use as accents, and even ingeniously devised a way of making certain unobtainable characters himself.[28] Lee's expertise in adapting the linotype to library use was quickly recognized. In 1897 he submitted the pamphlet *Memoranda concerning the Printing Department* as part of the BPL's exhibit at an international conference in London, and the following year Edwin H. Anderson, the librarian at the Carnegie Library of Pittsburgh, "acknowledge[d] our indebtedness" to him. "Mr. Lee is an expert printer," Anderson wrote, "and we profited by his advice and suggestions, generously given, in the installation of our plant."[29]

As foreman of the department, Lee shouldered more than simply administrative duties. In addition to ensuring the timely completion of hundreds of printing tasks, he was the hands-on expert, diagnostician, and problem solver, spending much of his time, as Guiney observed, "battling against his monster machine."[30] And the hours were long. He worked six days a week, "9 AM to 6 PM with one hour out for dinner," which meant a forty-eight-hour week.[31] In addition he was often required to be at the BPL late into the night, something which put outside plans in jeopardy. "I work both tonight and tomorrow and cannot promise to come," he wrote to Day, unless he was able to "get a swap" from another worker. And, if the machinery broke down, which was a common occurrence, Lee needed to be on duty. "My luck's against me," he explained in apology to Day in 1899. "I found that a careless boy had smashed the main driving pinion of one of the presses. This means repairs for me."[32] Mentally challenging, physically arduous, and seemingly without pause, the position made Lee almost indispensable at the library. "Francis floats in and out of the Catalogue Room, as usual," Guiney, who was working there in 1899, wrote to Rev. van Allen, "with his antiseptic sort of smile, and his blessed old finger-nails worn away" from his physical labors.[33]

As the department continued to expand and add machinery, in 1902, printing and binding were moved to rented space in a commercial building on Stanhope Street (figure 41). Lee noted in his annual report that although the additional square footage and better ventilation were "a real gain," the department was also a considerable distance from other departments, making communication more difficult. Still committed to workers' rights, in this same report Lee voiced his outrage over what he considered a "breach of faith" on the part of the library's administration. The previous year he had criticized the BPL for not allowing one employee to take all her earned vacation and for not giving another his promised salary increase. Now, he stated, "So far as I know no steps have been taken during the year to undo the injustice done to Miss Greeley last year and to which I referred in my last report." Apparently as some kind of gesture of solidarity, for the next decade Lee refused to submit any annual report except for an accounting of the department's yearly output.[34]

The linotype's constant clatter was not the only cause of "nervous strain" in Lee's life. Alice's deafness and her separation from the family to attend boarding school, the shock and grief of Peggy's death, the eventual institutionalization of his sister, and the breakup of his marriage to Agnes, each added a further emotional burden. Still, he continued to work "like a treadmill," as Guiney put it, seemingly burying himself in long hours of strenuous and exhausting work. Yet, he had not entirely given up on his dream to "retire into the country," and, in fact, this hope was renewed by his friend and fellow photographer Frank Birchall, who made the transition from city to country in 1905.[35]

Born in England, Birchall arrived in Boston sometime in the 1880s and became the proprietor of a photographic studio and the associate editor of *Photo-Era*, a well-respected journal in the field. Birchall and his studio were embraced by Boston pictorialists. He joined them on photographic excursions, developed negatives for them, and allowed others including F. Holland Day and Francis Watts Lee to use his equipment for their own work. In 1905, however, Birchall closed his business, packed up his equipment and negatives, and moved to Vaughn Hill Farm in rural Bolton, Massachusetts.[36] Three years later, Lee wrote asking, "How is your bucolic experiment turning out—well, I hope; for I think that you have chosen the only way to really *live*." Obviously still drawn to this lifestyle, Lee stated, "I am strongly inclined to follow your example—tell me, would you do it again?" Birchall emphatically replied that yes, he would certainly do it again. Although admitting his financial standing was rather precarious, he found working outside where the "wooded hill stretched away to the mountains of New Hampshire" to be both invigorating and liberating.[37]

In 1909, in a lengthy rather philosophical letter, Birchall elaborated on his decision to Lindsay Swift, a friend of Lee's and an accomplished writer and Editor of Library Publications at the BPL. Perhaps thinking of Francis Watts Lee and his stated desire to move to the country and "operate a small hand press," Birchall reflected on the prevailing "frightful method of setting a man to watch a machine do what his own hand should be doing."[38] Birchall tried to describe to Swift "the sense of freedom" he felt when working his land and the pity he felt for those trapped in the city. "And as I straightened up for a moment," he wrote, "[I saw] your weary-worn figure bending at its desk in the Editors room at the Library, dungeon like in its stone walls and floor and looking out upon an enclosed court so gloomy and shut in that it would be condemned even for a prison exercising yard." Swift, too, had inquired if he might be able to replicate Birchall's experience. The two agreed to meet so that Birchall might help Swift plan his escape from his "killing situation" to fashion his life into "something more nearly resembling what it ought to be."[39]

Although Lindsay Swift never made the move, Francis Watts Lee, who visited Birchall in Bolton and reported that he was "spending [his money] for books on farming," certainly may have been thinking of Birchall's escape when he purchased Halfway Farm in Walpole after his marriage to Marion Chamberlain. Perhaps he thought that, like Birchall, who was "laying lines to do printing of photographs during winter seasons," he might transition from his library position to a life of farming complemented by hand-press printing or even photography in the winter months. But it was not to be. While he may have had farming in mind when he and Marion decided to reside in Walpole, the arrival of two children, no matter how welcome, made such a drastic change less likely.[40]

As the size and scope of the BPL continued to increase, so did the work of the printing department, which supplied not only forms, circulars, catalog cards, signs, and miscellaneous other print jobs but also pamphlets and exhibition catalogs. One of these catalogs put Lee in touch with an old friend, Fred Holland Day. Although his commute from Walpole to Boston took him almost directly past Day's home in Norwood, Lee had lost touch with Day years earlier. Lee broke the long silence in 1921 when the BPL held an exhibition to commemorate the one hundredth anniversary of the death of the poet John Keats. Day was an avid collector of Keatsiana and loaned considerable material to the exhibit, which ran from February 21 to March 14. The library's printing department produced the catalog. On March 10, Lee sent a letter to Day with a copy of the finished product "as soon as it was off the press," assuring Day, "It was a good show and did you and us both credit." Still a perfectionist when it came to his printing, Lee's next sentence provided a sense of why he was sometimes labeled a "difficult man" in the workplace. "I could have wished the Catalogue were a little more in accord with my own ideas of how to do that sort of thing; but it is not always easy to arrange such things when the data given you at the start proves quite unlike the material furnished later after the type has been partly cast up. However it is what it is." In a passing reference to their former lives and activities, Lee added, "I'm glad you [*sic*] able to keep up your interest in these things & sorry I don't have a chance to see something of you these days even though I too have seldom a chance to expose a plate."[41]

Lee's printing department also produced more "popular publications" for the BPL. Beginning in 1919, the long-standing *Quarterly Bulletin* introduced "news of the library and information not purely bibliographical" to its pages. This

FIGURE 42. Workrooms of Frederick W. Horsman, Francis Watts Lee, 1928, silver gelatin print. Private family collection.

quarterly was replaced by a *Monthly Bulletin of Recent Books* in 1924, which was in turn superseded in March 1926 by a monthly titled *More Books*. In each issue of this journal, which was intended "for the general public," the list of new book purchases was supplemented by "several articles relating to the book treasures and manuscripts of the library."[42]

In 1928, while Marion cruised through the Panama Canal, Francis began to take stock of his life. "When one sees the end of the journey approaching," he wrote to his wife, "it is time to unsaddle!" A formal portrait taken that year shows a still carefully attired and distinguished Lee, now gray-haired and spectacled (figure 42). In an attempt to put his affairs in order, he sold the John Singleton Copley portrait of Mrs. Samuel Watts that had been in the family since 1770. Next, he turned to his pictorial equipment. "I am going to try to get together as much of my photographic apparatus as possible and dispose of it for what it will bring," he explained. He intended to do the same with his books. "I mean to get rid of what I can by gift to the O.H.C. [Order of the Holy Cross] and to others." Lastly, he proposed to Marion "either a sale or lease of the house" in Walpole and a two-year relocation to England for the entire family, where he hoped to renew "the rich fullness of our early love . . . not alone but with the children of our union." The move abroad did not take place, and soon enough both Lucy and Francis were enrolled in college.[43]

The couple eventually did rent their Walpole home, however, and took rooms in Boston close to the BPL, easing the lengthy commute for the sixty-seven-year-old Francis. Lee was growing ever more critical of the library, however. He complained in his 1934 annual report that considerable work "has been 'railroaded' through the Department unrecorded." Thus, Lee contended, the "production figures," which surpassed four million pieces, were "understated."[44] The following year he reiterated that "the output of catalogue cards, signs, blank forms, circulars, sundries, catalogues, pamphlets, and bibliographic programmes" was much higher than recorded. "It should not be forgotten," he continued cantankerously, "that the Chief of this Department has never been allowed any clerical help (though I recall no other department of which this is now true) and that in spite of the constant growth in volume of the Library's many activities the staff of this department is no larger (numbers one less in fact) than it was a generation ago. It is time that the implications of the fact were faced."[45] That report was dated January 30, 1936. Two days later, on February first, Lee began a three-month leave of absence with pay "for reasons of general health;" a leave that was imposed upon him. "This winter I was thought by others (I rather resented the thought myself) to be in poor shape physically," he wrote to an acquaintance, "and our Board very considerately voted me a leave which enabled us to escape" the Boston winter.[46]

Lee returned from his leave in May of 1936. A year later, just five months shy of his seventieth birthday, the library's board of trustees announced "the retirement of Francis Watts Lee, Chief of the Printing Department on May 31, 1937." Although the City of Boston presented Lee with a Certificate of Merit for his forty-three years of "faithful and meritorious public service" and the library's trustees recommended he be given the title of "Chief of the Printing

Department, Emeritus," neither mentioned his enormous talent or illustrious early work.[47] A dozen years later, however, Carl Purington Rollins, the famed designer, printer, and critic, recalled Lee and his talent in a letter to Zoltan Haraszti, then Keeper of Rare Books and Editor of Publications at the BPL: "Has the Library ever printed anything about its printer, Mr. Lee? If so, I should be grateful for reference to such an account. One of my treasures is a set of the Knight Errant."[48] But, there was no account. Francis Watts Lee had died four years earlier in total obscurity, the last of the bright, young, intellectual coterie of the 1890s to go. There was no obituary, only a two-line death notice in a Boston newspaper. He was buried at Mount Auburn Cemetery next to his daughter Peggy.[49]

# EPILOGUE AND ACKNOWLEDGMENTS

After his retirement, Francis Watts Lee and his wife Marion continued to rent out their home in Walpole. For a time they resided at the Riverside Apartment Hotel in Cambridge; in 1940, they sold Halfway Farm and relocated out of state to Parkchester, a "garden apartment community" in East Bronx, New York.[1] A year earlier, in 1939, Agnes Rand Lee Freer died in Chicago, her husband, surgeon Otto T. Freer, having predeceased her. After her mother's death, Alice Stephana Lee moved to a small apartment, where she lived alone and continued to travel, visit relatives, and participate in the activities of the Chicago Hearing Society. In 1943, Francis and Marion returned to Springfield, Massachusetts, to be near her sister, Christine.[2] That same year Francis had an extended stay in Pasadena, California, with his daughter Lucy and her family. According to letters from Lucy to her mother, who remained East, Francis, approaching seventy-six, was devoted to his grandson, Butch; Lucy's second child, Martha, was born while Francis was there. In her correspondence with Marion, Lucy sharply criticized her mother for questioning Francis's competence. "Old he is: ill, slow, forgetful," she wrote. "But there is nothing the matter with his ability to think when he does concentrate and is not tired, and he still is prepared to back his statements with facts, figures and logic."[3] On his return train trip across the country, Francis stopped in Chicago to see Alice Stephana, then nearing fifty, perhaps for the final time, and he remained with her when she was hospitalized for a minor operation.[4] After Francis's death in 1945, Marion lived with their son, Francis Lincoln Lee, and his family; she died in 1947, and her cremated remains were interred in the Lee family plot at Mount Auburn Cemetery. Alice Stephana Lee died in 1957 and was buried next to her mother and stepfather at Graceland Cemetery in Chicago.[5]

After graduating from Vassar in 1934, Lucy Lee attended graduate school at Columbia, where she met and married Charles Bridges. The couple had five children, Charles, Martha, Lee Thomas, Joseph, and Cristine. The family eventually settled in Vermont; Lucy and Charles later divorced. Very religious, Lucy converted to Catholicism and at some point considered entering a Benedictine convent; she ran a motel, was a substitute school teacher, and taught catechism in several parishes near her home. "A shrewd and opinionated observer of human nature," she, like her father, was known for her frequent contributions to the Letters section of local newspapers.[6] Francis Lincoln Lee attended boarding schools from a young age, including South Kent School, associated with Father Huntington's Order of the Holy Cross, and Phillips Exeter. He graduated from Stanford University, earned a graduate degree from MIT, and entered military service in 1942 as an ensign in the United States Naval Reserve. He utilized his expertise in petroleum engineering for a career in the oil business, moving his family frequently throughout Oklahoma, Kansas, and California before settling in Whittier, California, in 1950. Lee and his wife, Betty, whom he had known since childhood, had three sons, Francis Robert, John Bullard, and William Watts.[7]

Most of Francis Watts Lee's grandchildren were born after his death; none had a meaningful relationship with either Francis or Marion and, thus, knew little about their lives. There are, however, echoes of Francis Watts Lee in the life choices of this generation. One grandchild is a clinical social worker and a talented botanical artist. Two are "very oriented to art, architecture, and design" and are especially drawn to the Arts and Crafts aesthetic. Another built a career as a professor of law specializing in "civil legal aid and access to justice" for minorities and the disadvantaged. Yet another grandchild was a printer for more than thirty years. Particularly fond of fine art and screen printing, he received a patent for technological advancements in the field. Although unaware of his grandfather's connection to the craft, he was told by an early instructor that he seemed to have "ink in his blood."[8]

For my own part, during the years I spent researching and writing a biography of F. Holland Day, a man who surrounded himself with brilliant, artistic, and intriguing people, I was drawn to the Francis Watts Lee family. The little information that had been gleaned about Lee by scholars of Day's circle usually left him on the periphery, focusing instead on his wife and daughters and the stunning photographs taken of them. I wanted to look more closely at them all, to put some flesh on the bare bones story of a family so central to American photographic history and yet so elusive. And so, I began to pull gently on the thin threads of information embedded in the existing documents.

It was Agnes Lee who provided the key in her letters to Fred Day. In 1917, she mentioned that Lee lived in Walpole, Massachusetts; and in 1931 she wrote that his daughter, Lucy, was attending Vassar. Town of Walpole records confirmed his residence, and the names of his wife and children. Vassar retained some of Lucy's biographical data and an obituary, which provided the names of her children. The Internet helped me track down one of them who led me to the rest. They collectively provided me with a few photographs and family stories. Meanwhile, the letters from Alice Stephana Lee to Frederick Haven Pratt brought me to the Clarke School for the Deaf in Northampton. The school's archives provided more information on her life and her work, including the peacock sundial, which, in turn, confirmed Agnes's reference in her letter to Day in 1917 about Alice's artistic talent.

The chief issue remained the lack of any trace of the photographic work of Francis Watts Lee. I had combed through the exhibition catalogs at the Library of Congress to find when, where, and what photographs he exhibited but had little else. *The Photograms of 1898* and *Photo-Era* reproduced a few images of his works; these were still not enough. Finally, at my request, my brother, Charles, located the estate documents of Alice Stephana Lee in Chicago. These contained the addresses of her half-siblings, Lucy and Francis Lincoln Lee. Amazingly, the latter's son, William Watts Lee, still lived in the same house some fifty years later and very graciously offered me access to a chest that had stood unopened in the foyer of the home for decades. Inside, there was a bounty of photographs by Gertrude Käsebier, F. Holland Day, Herbert Hess, and, most important, Francis Watts Lee. It was this collection, which also included letters, a scrapbook of ephemera, and other items, that brought the threads of my research together. I am enormously pleased, as well, to write that this Francis Watts Lee Collection has been donated to the Library of Congress, where it joins the collections of other American pictorialists including F. Holland Day and Gertrude Käsebier, collections that already contain photographs and documents relating to Lee and his family. Here Francis Watts Lee's work and his place in American photographic history can be accessed and studied by future generations.

I must first thank the grandchildren of Francis Watts Lee. Martha Lucy Bridges, Cristine Bridges Piane, Lee Thomas Bridges, Francis Robert (Bob) Lee, and, especially William Watts (Bill) Lee and his wife, Geri, have all been extraordinarily generous with their time, encouragement, and support of this project. I am, as well, indebted to various people and institutions: the Fine Arts, Microtext, Rare Books, and Print Departments of the Boston Public Library, particularly, John Dorsey, Kimberly Reynolds, Aaron Schmidt, Henry Scannell, Kim Tenney, Jane Winton, Roberta Zonghi, and the late Janice Chadbourne, who offered encouragement at the start of my research; the staffs of the Library of Congress, Manuscripts Division, Prints & Photographs Division, and Rare Books Division; the Massachusetts Historical Society, especially Anna Clutterbuck-Cook, Elise Dunham, Elaine Grublin, Dan Hinchen, and Tracy Potter; the Clarke Schools for Hearing and Speech, especially Amanda Aliotta, Miriam Aylward, Rodney Kunath, and JennyKate Marble; the staffs at the Chicago History Museum and the Newberry Library; Sarah Campbell of the Archives and Special Collections at the College of the Holy Cross; Brother Adam McCoy, archivist, at the Order of the Holy Cross; the Art Institute of Chicago, especially Judith Barter and Nathaniel Parks; the staff at the Houghton Library, Harvard College; John and Sue Anderson of the Walpole Historical Society; Erin Damon at the Portland Museum of Art; Ruth Janson and Liz Reynolds at the Brooklyn Museum; Sophia Brothers of the Science & Society Picture Library; Jan Gardner Broske, University Museums, University of Delaware; Amber Sinicrope, MIT Museum; Kajette Solomon, Bridgeman Images, Detroit Institute of Art; and Hannah Harris, Spencer Museum of Art, University of Kansas.

I received invaluable assistance from the following friends and colleagues: Verna Posever Curtis, Gale Eaton, Trevor Fairbrother, Adrienne Lundgren, Barbara Michaels, Cashman Kerr Prince, Barbara Rand, Douglass Shand-Tucci, and Mary Ann Violette. Kate Allendorf, Karla Daddieco, Nancy Kreusel, Cheryl Meserve, and Mary Phinney, I thank for their friendship and encouragement.

I am grateful to the Center for the Advancement of Research and Scholarship at Bridgewater State University for their support, and am deeply appreciative of the encouragement of my colleagues Howard London, Rita Miller, Walter Carroll, Jodi Cohen, Bill Levin, Kim Mac Innis, and Michele Wakin.

I want to thank the University of Massachusetts Press, especially Bruce Wilcox and Brian Halley for their continued confidence in my work.

I am most grateful for the very able research assistance of Shelby Warner, Sarah Whittey, and especially Heather Cole. There would be no book without their enthusiastic contributions.

The unwavering encouragement and love of my late parents, Francis Patricia Balduf Fanning and Charles Frederick Fanning, and my brothers Charles and Geoffrey has always kept me going; and I cannot thank Charles enough for his expert research at crucial points in this project and his careful reading of various drafts of this work.

# NOTES

## INTRODUCTION

1. Joseph T. Keiley, "The Salon, Its Purposes, Character, and Lesson," *Camera Notes* 3, no. 3 (January 1900): 142; William Howe Downes, "Massachusetts Photographers' Work," *Photo Era* 4, no. 3 (March 1900): 72.

2. John Scott, *A Matter of Record: Documentary Sources in Social Research* (London: Polity, 1990), 110.

3. Penny Tinkler discusses this process in *Using Photographs in Social and Historical Research* (Los Angeles: Sage Publications, 2013), 24–25.

4. Douglas Harper, "An Argument for Visual Sociology," in *Image-based Research*, ed. Jon Prosser (London: Routledge Falmer, 2004), 29.

5. See Alan Sekula, "Reading an Archive: Photography between Labour and Capital," in *Photography/Politics: Two* (London: Comedia Publishing, 1986), Richard Bolton, ed., *The Contest of Meaning: Critical Histories of Photography* (Cambridge: MIT Press, 1989), and Pierre Bourdieu, *Photography: A Middle-brow Art* (Stanford, CA: Stanford University Press, 1990).

6. Alan Trachtenberg, *Reading American Photographs* (New York: Hill and Wang, 1989), xvi.

7. George Dimock, "Priceless Children: Child Labor and the Pictorialist Ideal," in *Priceless Children: American Photographs 1890–1925: Child Labor and the Pictorialist Ideal* (Seattle: University of Washington Press, 2002), 7.

8. Susan Sontag, *On Photography* (New York: Farrar, Straus and Giroux, 1977), 15.

9. C. Wright Mills, *The Sociological Imagination* (New York: Oxford University Press, 1959), 3.

10. Pictorial photographs that are referred to but not reproduced in the text are also available for viewing in these digital photographic archives.

11. Tinkler, *Using Photographs*, 108.

12. Trachtenberg, *Reading American Photographs*, xiv.

13. Tinkler, *Using Photographs*, 108–9.

14. Shawn Michelle Smith, *At the Edge of Sight: Photography and the Unseen* (Durham, NC: Duke University Press, 2013), 8.

## 1. FRANCIS WATTS LEE

1. Boston's Back Bay was created by draining wetlands and filling the area with gravel and earth from surrounding hillsides. The project took decades but was basically completed by 1888.

2. Copley Square was originally named Art Square. The name was changed in 1883.

3. Thomas J. Lee and Alice Haskell Watts Lee originally lived in Roxbury, Massachusetts, where Francis and his sister Constance were born. In the 1870s the family resided at Mountford Street in a section of Brookline called Cottage Farm. By the late 1870s, they had moved to Marlborough Street in the Back Bay.

4. For Chauncy Hall curriculum, see *Fifty-Fourth Annual Catalogue of the Teachers and Pupils of Chauncy-Hall School, 1881–1882* (Boston: David Clapp & Son, 1882).

5. Lewis Mumford, "The Significance of Back Bay Boston," *Back Bay Boston: The City as a Work of Art* (Boston: Museum of Fine Arts, 1969), 20.

6. Paul Dimaggio, "Cultural Entrepreneurship in Nineteenth-Century Boston: The Creation of an Organizational Base for High Culture in America," *Media, Culture & Society* 4 (1982): 34, 35. For more information of this time period, see Ronald Story, *The Forging of an Aristocracy: Harvard and Boston Upper Class, 1800–1870* (Middletown, CT: Wesleyan University Press, 1980) and Robert F. Dalzell Jr., *Enterprising Elite: The Boston Associates and the World They Made* (Cambridge: Harvard University Press, 1987).

7. Hina Hirayama, *"With Éclat": The Boston Athenaeum and the Origin of the Museum of Fine Arts, Boston* (Boston: Boston Athenaeum, 2013), 52.

8. Handwritten manuscript, Obituary of Francis Osborne Watts, no pagination, Library of Congress, Manuscripts Division, Francis Watts Lee Collection, Gift of the Francis Lincoln Lee Family (hereafter FWL-LC).

9. T. J. Jackson Lears, *No Place of Grace: Antimodernism and the Transformation of American Culture, 1880–1920* (Chicago: University of Chicago Press, 1981), 23–24.

10. Ibid., 24, 32, 23.

11. Ibid., 210. There was a family story that Lee spent the money that was set aside for his college education on his European journey.

12. Ralph Adams Cram, *My Life in Architecture* (Boston: Little, Brown, 1936), 19.

13. Ibid., 90, 13–14, 91–92. For more on these groups, see Patricia J. Fanning, *Through an Uncommon Lens: The Life and Photography of F. Holland Day* (Amherst: University of Massachusetts Press, 2008), and Douglass Shand-Tucci, *Boston Bohemia (1881–1900): Ralph Adams Cram: Life and Architecture* (Amherst: University of Massachusetts, 1995).

14. Francis Watts Lee (hereafter FWL) to F. Holland Day (hereafter FHD), 7

November 1892, F. Holland Day Papers, Library of Congress, Manuscripts Division (hereafter FHD-LC).

15. *Knight Errant,* 1, nos. 1–4. FWL's article appeared in no. 2 (July 1892), and Agnes Lee's poem "Parsifal" was published in no. 1 (April 1892).

16. Lears, *No Place of Grace,* 57.

17. Ibid., 198, 290.

18. Shand-Tucci, *Boston Bohemia,* 75–78; Douglass Shand-Tucci, *The Art of Scandal, The Life and Times of Isabella Stewart Gardner* (New York: Harper/Collins, 1997), 126–27.

19. Bliss relinquished his pastorate at the Grace Episcopal Church in South Boston and founded the Church of the Carpenter, under the aegis of Phillips Brooks and the Trinity Church in Copley Square. Richard B. Dressner, "William Dwight Porter Bliss's Christian Socialism," *Church History* 47, no. 1 (March 1978): 66.

20. Arthur Mann, *Yankee Reformers in the Urban Age, Social Reform in Boston, 1880–1900* (Chicago: University of Chicago Press, 1974), 90–95.

21. Dressner, "William Dwight Porter Bliss," 71.

22. Mann, *Yankee Reformers,* 91; "Heaving With Unrest," *Boston Daily Globe,* 14 April 1890, 2. The Church of the Carpenter held services at Brunswick Hall at 241 Tremont Street, a vacant building at 812 Washington Street, and in rooms off Boylston Street at 3 Boylston Place. A profile of the church in the *Boston Daily Globe* in October of 1892 paid particular attention to the "cooperative household" that occupied 23 rooms at 812 Washington Street in Boston, rooms that included a lounge, library, chapel, dining room, kitchen, office, and several bedrooms. In 1896 Bliss left Boston for a national position within the Church Social Union and with his departure the Church of the Carpenter and *The Dawn* both dissolved. See also Shand-Tucci, *Boston Bohemia,* 76–77.

23. FWL, "Some Thoughts Upon Beauty in Typography Suggested by the Work of Mr. William Morris at the Kelmscott Press," *Knight Errant* 1, no. 2 (July 1892): 53–54.

24. *The Dawn* 2 (1890) lists Mr. F. W. Lee as Associate Editor and notes that articles by him would be appearing. F. W. Lee, "Notes of the Social Teaching of the Christian Year," *The Dawn* 7, no. 1 (January, 1895): 13–15. The column also appeared in *The Dawn* monthly from February 1894 through January 1895. See by FWL: "Believing and Understanding," *Boston Transcript,* 3 August 1891, 5; "Ruskinian Political Economy," 20 June 1892, 6; "Philanthropy and Morality," 7 November 1892, 5; "Franklin Baths," 16 June 1893, 15. Letter in *St. Andrews Cross,* January 1894; book reviews in *St. Andrews Cross,* January 1894, January 1895. All in scrapbook, "Ephemeral Scribblings from the Pen of Francis Watts Lee," FWL-LC. The scrapbook contains clippings of writings by both Francis Watts Lee and Agnes Rand Lee. "Church Social Union Organized," *New York Times,* 20 May 1894; "Church Social Union Tenets," *New York Times,* 21 May 1894.

25. FWL to FHD, 14 April 1894, FHD-LC.

26. W. J. Ashley, M.A. *The Railroad Strike of 1894* (Cambridge, MA: Church Social Union, 1895); Francis Watts Lee, *A Proposed Constitution for the Church Social Union* (Boston: Church Social Union, 1894); Francis Watts Lee, *Suggestions for Reading on Social Reform* (New York: Church Social Union, 1895); Francis Watts Lee, ed., *William Morris, Poet, Artist, Socialist: A Selection from His Writings together with a Sketch* (New York: Humboldt Publishing, 1891), vii–xix. Most of Lee's brief introduction to these selections focused on John Ball,

the fourteenth-century English priest and revolutionary. Ball was of particular interest to Lee, who wrote an entry on the Englishman for *The Encyclopedia of Social Reform* produced by Bliss. See Francis Watts Lee, "John Ball," *The Encyclopedia of Social Reform* (New York: Funk & Wagnalls, 1908): 87–88.

27. Vida Dutton Scudder, *Father Huntington: Founder of the Order of the Holy Cross* (New York: E. P. Dutton, 1940), 129, 164–65. For a biography of James Otis Sargent Huntington, see Holy Cross Monastery, West Park, NY, website; Scudder, *Father Huntington*. Huntington was associated with the Society of St. John the Evangelist in Boston as well as the Church of the Advent and through these channels was connected with Ralph Adams Cram, Vida Dutton Scudder, Rev. Arthur Hall, Rev. William van Allen, and FWL. Robert Stockton Dod and James Cameron Gibbon were the other founders of the O.H.C. The community began its work in the 1890s in Westminster, Maryland. Within a few years Huntington, who had spearheaded the order's move to West Park, New York, withdrew into monastic life.

28. FWL began work at the Boston Public Library in 1894 in the Catalogue Department. The following year he became the first head of the BPL's in-house printing department. He remained there until his retirement in 1937. See detail on FWL as a printer in chapter 9. Of the four portraits, one is Father Huntington, one is Father Henry Rufus Sargent, and two others remain unidentified. Sargent graduated from Harvard in 1877, became a Cowley Father while in England, and became part of the O.H.C. soon after its inception. He remained with the O.H.C. until 1912. My thanks to Brother Adam McCoy of the O.H.C. for explaining the dating tied to the black cassock and white cassock. Lee also took portraits of Huntington and Sargent in white cassocks.

29. LIG to Rev. W. H. van Allen, 17 December 1897, *Letters of Louise Imogen Guiney*, ed. Grace Guiney, 2 vols. (New York: Harper & Brothers, 1926), 1:213 (hereafter *Letters of LIG*).

30. Cram, *My Life*, 14–15. For Guiney's connection to the Visionists, see Fanning, *Through an Uncommon Lens;* for Guiney biography, see E. M. Tenison, *Louise Imogen Guiney: Her Life and Works, 1861–1920* (London: Macmillan, 1923), and Henry G. Fairbanks, *Louise Imogen Guiney, Laureate of the Lost* (Albany, NY: Magi Books, 1972).

31. Lears, *No Place of Grace*, xix.

32. LIG to Rev. W. H. van Allen, 17 December 1897, *Letters of LIG*, 1:213. Guiney did finally meet Huntington, writing to van Allen: "Sometime I must tell you how Agnes arranged a 'meet' between Fr. Huntingdon [*sic*] and me; how we had to chase him about, from the Lee dinner-table, owing to a concatenation of funny circumstances. But we found him. He's perfect" (13 June 1898, *Letters of LIG*, 1:227).

33. Peter Henry Emerson, "Photography as a Pictorial Art," *Amateur Photographer* 3 (19 March 1886): 138–39.

34. Joseph Price Loud, "The Second Philadelphia Salon," *Photo Era* 3, no. 7 (December 1899): 512.

35. LIG to FHD, 22 September 1898, Louise Imogen Guiney Collection, Manuscripts Division, Library of Congress (hereafter LIG-LC). Perhaps Day agreed with their mutual friend's assessment; Day was his own model for Christ.

36. Francis James Mortimer, "The Work of the Year. A Fragmentary Retrospective," *Photograms of the Year 1898* (London: Dawbarn & Ward, 1898): 74. Founded in the spring of 1892 to protest the artistic inadequacy of the exhibitions mounted by the Royal Photographic

Society, the Linked Ring stood at the forefront of the redefinition of photography as a fine art. Membership could be obtained only by invitation. For a discussion of Lee's photography, also see Patricia J. Fanning, "Francis Watts Lee: A Reintroduction," *History of Photography* 36, no. 1 (February 2012): 15–32.

37. Mortimer, "The Work of the Year," 74.

38. Joseph T. Keiley, "The Salon, Its Purposes, Character, and Lesson," *Camera Notes* 3, no. 3 (January 1900): 141–42.

39. Ibid., 141–42.

40. William Howe Downes, "Massachusetts Photographers' Work," *Photo Era* 4, no. 3 (March 1900): 71–72.

41. Joseph T. Keiley, "The Salon," *Camera Notes* 4, no. 3 (January 1901): 212. On Lee's work hours and activities, see LIG to Rev. W. H. van Allen, 7 February 1898, *Letters of LIG*, 1:218; LIG to Rev. W. H. van Allen, 8 May 1899, *Letters of LIG*, 1:257. Constance Lee, FWL's sister, was eventually committed to Medfield State Hospital where she died in 1955. During most of that time, FWL was her guardian. The census of 1900 shows the Rands living with Lee and his family in their Jamaica Plain home. Guiney at least implied that William Rand had fallen on hard times. In a letter to FHD, Guiney writes, "Mr. Rand has been unsuccessful in all his late ventures, alas" (15 February 1901, LIG-LC).

42. Robert Demachy, "Exhibition of the New School of Artistic Photography at the Paris Photo-Club," *The Amateur Photographer* 33, no. 861 (5 April 1901): 275–77.

43. Downes, "Massachusetts Photographers' Work," 71–72; F. Holland Day, "Art and the Camera," *Lippincott's Monthly Magazine* (January 1900): 85.

44. Joseph T. Keiley, "The Philadelphia Salon: Its Origin and Influence," *Camera Notes* 2, no. 3 (January 1899): 125. Marmaduke Humphrey [Rupert Hughes], "Triumphs in Amateur Photography II—F. H. Day," *Godey's Magazine* 136, no. 811 (January 1898): 19. Alvin Langdon Coburn, "American Photographers in London," *Photo Era* 6, no. 1 (January 1901): 212. No extant original print of *A New England Saint* has been located. The image was reprinted in *The Photogram* 8 (January 1901): 11. For more on local colorists, see Josephine Donovan, *New England Local Color Literature, A Women's Tradition* (New York: Frederick Ungar Publishing, 1983). Not all of Lee's portraits drew universal praise, however. Critics were divided on the success of *The Convalescent*, an intriguing study of a woman (Emily Hallowell was the model) with long hair, dressed in a flowing white gown, and seated, apparently leaning against a wall. While Coburn termed the image "an excellent study," others disagreed. "Hopefulness should certainly be suggested by such a title as *Convalescent*," A. C. R. Carter wrote, "but the photographer apparently wishes to convey the fear that the patient is going to have a serious relapse." And, another reviewer in *Camera Notes* concurred: "We congratulate Mr. Lee's 'Convalescent' upon her hopeful condition, but we think she would have been seen to better advantage if she had been photographed when perfectly recovered." See Coburn, "American Photographers in London," 212; A. C. R. Carter, "The Two Great Exhibitions. The Photographic Salon," *Photograms of the Year 1900* (London: Dawbarn & Ward, 1900): 136; "The English Exhibitions of the 'American Invasion,'" *Camera Notes* 4, no. 3 (January 1901): 174.

45. "Pictures at the Exhibitions. The Photographic Harvest," *Photography* 28 September 1899, 654; "Some Random Notes on the Philadelphia Salon," *Photographic Times* 32, no. 1 (January 1900): 9.

46. Karen Evans Ulehla, ed., *The Society of Arts and Crafts, Boston: Exhibition Record 1897–1927* (Boston: Boston Public Library, 1981), 16. Regarding Lee's developing prints, he wrote to Day about his techniques: "I want to call your attention to the fact that Persulphate of Ammonia to which I have before spoken to you as an agent for *softening* negatives will if added to Oxylate developer give a *hard* Platinum print for an over soft negative" (FWL to FHD, Saturday, c. 1899, FHD-LC). In October 2014, participants in a symposium and workshop on platinum and palladium photographs organized by the Foundation of the American Institute for Conservation of Historic and Artistic Works, the National Museum of the American Indian, the National Gallery of Art, the Library of Congress, and the National Museum of American History were impressed by the variety of processes Lee was experimenting with. As Adrienne Lundgren, senior photograph conservator at the Library of Congress writes, "Lee produced a wealth of prints from the same negative utilizing various papers, additives, and processing techniques. The result is an ideal study collection for understanding the effects achieved through altering these variables" (e-mail to the author, 6 July 2015).

47. FWL to FHD, Saturday, c. 1899, FHD-LC.

48. Alvin Langdon Coburn, "The question of diffusion; A tribute to the P. & S. semi-achromatic lenses," in *'Smith' Soft Focus Lenses Semi Achromatic Visual Quality Synthetics, Sixth Series* (Boston: Pinkham & Smith, 1920), unpaginated. The story is repeated with elaboration in *The Cooke Portrait PS945 Soft-Focus Lens* (Leicester, UK: Cooke Optics Limited, 2002), 17. The history of the soft-focus lens is the subject of William Russell Young III, "The Soft Focus Lens and Anglo-American Pictorialism" (PhD thesis, University of St. Andrews, 2008).

49. FHD to unknown correspondent, 8 July 1921, FHD-LC.

50. Ibid.

51. Ibid.; FHD to Frederick H. Evans (hereafter FHE), 6 May 1908, 8 pages, handwritten, in the possession of William Russell Young III. Photocopy donated to Norwood Historical Society (hereafter cited as Young Photocopy). A full transcript of this letter is included in Young's thesis, "The Soft Focus Lens and Anglo-American Pictorialism," 107–9; FHD to unknown correspondent, 8 July 1921, FHD-LC. Day recounts in both letters that Lee later sold his lens to the Boston photographer Alice Austin and Day's was lost in a fire that destroyed his studio in 1904. Pinkham & Smith employees were under the impression that Day had received the first lens (Walter Wolfe, Pinkham & Smith to FHD, 13 January 1920, FHD-LC). In this letter Wolfe writes, "I wish I had the first Smith lens and your first picture. I would be ashamed of the appearance of the instrument, but certainly not of its product."

52. Charles E. Fairman, "The Fourth Philadelphia Photographic Salon," *The American Amateur Photographer* 13, no. 12 (December 1901): 536.

53. C. Yarnall Abbott, "The Fourth Philadelphia Salon," *Camera Craft* 4, no. 2 (December 1901): 79; Charles H. Caffin, "The Philadelphia Photographic Salon, 1901," *Camera Notes* 5, no. 3 (January 1902): 209. Lee came to regret his decision to participate in this salon. Stieglitz led a boycott of this exhibition; Day sent his work, as did Lee, who was perhaps influenced by Day's decision. However, FWL later wrote to Stieglitz, "I cannot tell you how much I regret having sent to Philadelphia" (FWL to Alfred Stieglitz, 15 December 1901, Alfred Stieglitz / Georgia O'Keeffe Archive, Series I, Correspondence, box 30, folder 706, Yale Collection of American Literature, Beinecke Rare Book and Manuscript Library, Yale University). Fairman, "The Fourth Philadelphia Photographic

Salon," 536; Herbert W. Taylor, "Fourth Philadelphia Photographic Salon," *Photo Era* 7, no. 6 (December 1901): 210.

54. *Second San Francisco Photographic Salon*, 9 January–23 January 1902; *Tenth Photographic Salon, London*, 19 September–1 November 1902, both catalogs in Library of Congress, Prints and Photographs Division.

55. Keiley, "The Salon, Its Purposes," 141–42.

## 2. AGNES RAND LEE

1. Yvor Winters, "Agnes Lee," *Poetry*, September 1939, 336.

2. "W. H. Rand, Publisher, Dies," *New York Times*, 22 June 1915. Most of the biographical information on William H. Rand comes from this obituary.

3. The reference to Charles Edwin Rand as "an unlucky son" is from a 29 March 1928 letter to the Harvard Alumni Directory from Mitchell Follensbee. Follensbee included Rand's brief obituary in the correspondence. Harvard University Archives. Information on the Rand siblings, especially William H. Rand Jr., is gleaned from Agnes Rand Lee's letters. Agnes also wrote a poem about her brother William: "Colonel William Rand," *Under One Roof* (Chicago: Ralph Fletcher Seymour, 1940), 141. This is a posthumously published collection which contains most of Lee's best-known poems.

4. Geraldine Udell to Barbara Michaels, 26 June 1978. My thanks to Barbara Michaels, biographer of Gertrude Käsebier, for sharing this letter.

5. Susan L. Taylor, "The Heritage of Motherhood and the Agony of Agnes Lee," *Bulletin of the Detroit Institute of Arts* 75, no. 2 (2001): 18.

6. Details of the Rand-Lee wedding in *Chicago Daily Tribune*, 24 December 1890.

7. Wendy Clauson Schlereth, *The Chap-Book, A Journal of American Intellectual Life in the 1890s* (Ann Arbor: UMI Research Press, 1982), 1; "Ephemeral Scribblings from the Pen of Francis Watts Lee," no pagination, FWL-LC.

8. Wendy Simonds and Barbara Katz Rothman, *Centuries of Solace: Expressions of Maternal Grief in Popular Literature* (Philadelphia: Temple University Press, 1992), 37.

9. Harriet Monroe, "Comment: Agnes Lee," *Poetry*, March 1932, 325.

10. LIG to W. H. van Allen, 18 October 1898, *Letters of LIG*, 1:240; LIG to W. H. van Allen, 9 July 1898, *Letters of LIG*, 1:231.

11. Emily Stipes Watts, *The Poetry of American Women from 1632 to 1945* (Austin: University of Texas Press, 1977), 142, 140.

12. Eunice Tietjens, "An Old, Old Garden," review of *Under One Roof* by Agnes Lee, *Poetry*, August 1941, 269.

13. Agnes Lee, "A Lonely Man," *Under One Roof*, 47; "Black Flowers and White," *Under One Roof*, 126.

14. Agnes Lee, "The Asphodel," *Under One Roof*, 181; Tietjens, "An Old, Old Garden," 270.

15. Winters, "Agnes Lee," 336–37.

16. Ezra Pound, "A Retrospect" (1918) and "A Few Don'ts" (first published in *Poetry*, March 1913, as "A Few Don'ts by an Imagiste"), available online at www.poetryfoundation.org.

17. Winters, "Agnes Lee," 337.

18. Agnes Lee, "A Statue in the Garden," *Under One Roof*, 3.

19. Winters, "Agnes Lee," 336.

20. Pound, "A Retrospect"; Agnes Lee to Josephine Preston Peabody, 10 January 1914, Josephine Preston Peabody Collection, Houghton Library, Harvard University.

21. Agnes Lee, "A Nesting Linnet," *Under One Roof*, 10.

22. Tietjens, "An Old, Old Garden," 269–70. Agnes's speech impediment is mentioned in a letter from Geraldine Udell to Barbara Michaels, 26 June 1978. I thank Barbara Michaels for sharing this letter with me.

23. Winters, "Agnes Lee," 336; Tietjens, "An Old, Old Garden," 269.

24. LIG to FHD, 16 May 1899, LIG-LC; LIG to W. H. van Allen, 2 January 1897, *Letters of LIG*, 1:165.

25. "Ephemeral Scribblings." FWL-LC.

26. Agnes Lee, "The Round Rabbit," *The Round Rabbit and Other Child Verse* (Boston: Copeland & Day, 1898), 1.

27. Nancy Finlay, "The Round Rabbit and Other Child Verse," *Artists of the Book in Boston* (Cambridge: Department of Printing and Graphic Arts, Houghton Library, Harvard College, 1985), 65. For these associations also see Patricia J. Fanning, *Through an Uncommon Lens: The Life and Photography of F. Holland Day* (Amherst: University of Massachusetts Press, 2008).

28. "I get sight of": LIG to W. H. van Allen, 7 February 1898, *Letters of LIG*, 1:218; "I am awfully concerned": LIG to FHD, 19 April 1899, LIG-LC.

29. "lot to bear": LIG to FHD, 12 May 1899, LIG-LC; "too busy socially": LIG-FHD, 16 May 1899, LIG-LC; "gymnasium": LIG to W. H. van Allen, 17 December 1897, *Letters of LIG*, 1:213; "three dear dears": LIG to FHD, 28 June 1898, LIG-LC.

30. Gertrude Käsebier (hereafter GK) to FHD, 12 June 1899, FHD-LC.

31. GK to FHD, 21 June 1899, FHD-LC.

32. Joseph Keiley to Alfred Stieglitz, 2 September 1899, Alfred Stieglitz / Georgia O'Keeffe Archive, Series I, Correspondence, box 27, folder 635, Yale Collection of American Literature, Beinecke Rare Book and Manuscript Library, Yale University.

33. GK to FHD, 3 July 1899, FHD-LC.

34. *An Exhibition of Prints by The New School of American Photography Supplemented by an Additional Collection of One Hundred Examples of the Work of F. Holland Day of Boston* (London: Royal Photographic Society, 1900).

35. Agnes Lee to FHD, 26 December 1892, FHD-LC.

36. Charles Caffin, "The Philadelphia Photographic Salon," *Harper's Weekly*, 3 November 1900, 1061. There is a reproduction of this image accompanying this article.

37. See Fanning, *Through an Uncommon Lens*, 216, n67.

38. Ibid., 38–39.

39. FWL to FHD, 26 February 1892, FHD-LC.

40. Agnes Lee, "Rossetti's Wife," *Under One Roof*, 70. Lee prefaces the poem with a synopsis of the events.

41. Fanning, *Through an Uncommon Lens*, 3–4, 96–97; Roger B. Stein, "Artifacts as Ideology: The Aesthetic Movement in Its American Cultural Context," in *In Pursuit of Beauty: Americans and the Aesthetic Movement*, ed. Doreen Bulger Burke et al. (New York: Metropolitan Museum of Art and Rizzoli, 1987), 20.

42. See Marilee Boyd Meyers, foreword to *Inspiring Reform: Boston's Arts and Crafts*

*Movement* (Wellesley, Mass: Davis Museum and Cultural Center, 1997), 14–15.

43. Lears, *No Place of Grace*, 70.

44. Edward S. Cooke Jr., "Talking or Working: The Conundrum of Moral Aesthetics in Boston's Arts and Crafts Movement," in *Inspiring Reform*, 17–31.

45. As noted in chapter 1, FWL was the secretary for the Church Association for the Advancement of the Interests of Labor. He maintained his pro-labor stance throughout his life.

46. FWL, "Franklin Baths," *Boston Evening Transcript*, 16 June 1893, 15. Lee is advocating for Franklin Fund monies to be spent on public baths and wash houses for public laundries.

47. Marianne Carlano, "Anti-Fashion in Boston: Rational, Hygienic, and Artistic Dress during the Second Half of the Nineteenth Century," *Textile and Text* 13, no. 3 (1991): 37. See also Sally Buchanan Kinsey, "A More Reasonable Way to Dress," in *"The Art that is Life": The Arts and Crafts Movement in America, 1875–1920* (Boston: Little, Brown, 1987), and Gayle V. Fischer, *Pantaloons and Power: A Nineteenth-Century Dress Reform in the United States* (Kent, OH: Kent State University Press, 2001).

48. See Christian A. Peterson, "American Arts and Crafts, The Photograph Beautiful 1895–1915," *History of Photography* 16 no. 3 (Autumn 1992): 193.

49. Kinsey, "A More Reasonable Way to Dress," 361.

50. Tietjens, "An Old, Old Garden," 270.

## 3. HARRIET TEMPLETON "PEGGY" LEE

1. LIG to Rev. William van Allen, 17 December 1897, *Letters of LIG*, 1:213.

2. Sam B. Warner Jr., *Streetcar Suburbs: The Process of Growth in Boston 1870–1900* (New York: Atheneum, 1976), 15.

3. Ibid., 17.

4. Map of Jamaica Plain, Massachusetts, 1896, Jamaica Plain Historical Society. Peter Parley was the pseudonym of Samuel Griswold Goodrich (1793–1860), the author of history and schoolbooks for children. In 1833 he bought land in Roxbury and built a home in the area now known as Jamaica Plain. Goodrich later moved to New York and his property was sold and subdivided. "Samuel Goodrich, Alias Peter Parley," Jamaica Plain Historical Society website, originally published in the *Boston Daily Globe*, 23 September 1906. My thanks to Henry Scannell of the Boston Public Library for a photograph of 63 Peter Parley.

5. David I. Macleod, *The Age of the Child: Children in America 1890–1920* (New York: Twane Publishers, 1998), 2–4.

6. Ibid., 23; Bernard Mergen, "Made, Bought, and Stolen: Toys and the Culture of Childhood," *Small Worlds: Children and Adolescents in America, 1850–1950*, ed. Elliott West and Paula Petrik (Lawrence: University Press of Kansas, 1992), 183.

7. Mary Ellen Chase, *A Goodly Heritage* (New York: Henry Holt, 1932), 61, 66.

8. Ibid., 72; Edna Ferber, *A Peculiar Treasure* (New York: Doubleday, Doran, 1939), 52.

9. Anne Scott MacLeod, *American Childhood: Essays on Children's Literature of the Nineteenth and Twentieth Centuries* (Athens: University of Georgia Press, 1994), 119. According to MacLeod, it was not until the 1910s that adult and children's literature diverged. Adult fiction veered into realism while children's literature remained genteel and romantic.

10. Chase, *A Goodly Heritage*, 72.

11. On the mother's role, see Macleod, *Age of the Child;* Philippe Aries, *Centuries of Childhood: A Social History of Family Life* (New York: Vintage Books, 1962); Viviana Z. Zelizer, *Pricing the Priceless Child: The Changing Social Value of Children* (Princeton, New Jersey: Princeton University Press, 1985).

12. Macleod, *Age of the Child,* 9–10.

13. Zelizer, *Pricing the Priceless Child,* 3.

14. Agnes Lee, "Motherhood," *Under One Roof* (Chicago: Ralph Fletcher Seymour, [1940]), 93.

15. Agnes Lee to FHD, 26 December 1892, FHD-LC.

16. LIG to Rev. William van Allen, 13 June 1898, *Letters of LIG,* 1:226. References are made to Peggy's garden in poetry by Agnes Lee ("Under Peggy's Window" and "In the Spring").

17. Most of these sitters stayed in touch with Day well into adulthood. See Patricia J. Fanning, *Through an Uncommon Lens: The Life and Photography of F. Holland Day* (Amherst: University of Massachusetts Press, 2008).

18. Verna Posever Curtis, "F. Holland Day: The Poetry of Photography," *History of Photography* 18, no. 4 (Winter 1994): 319 n. 54.

19. Barbara L. Michaels, "Portraits of Friendship: Fred Holland Day, Gertrude Käsebier, and Their Circle," *New Perspectives on F. Holland Day,* ed. Patricia J. Fanning (North Easton, MA: Stonehill College, 1997), 75 n. 11, 27.

20. Sara Bustin to FHD, 30 December 1930, FHD-LC; Michaels, "Portraits," 27.

21. Agnes Lee to FHD, 17 April 1918, FHD-LC.

22. Michaels, "Portraits," 31.

23. Joe W. Kraus, *Messrs. Copeland & Day* (Philadelphia: George S. McManus, 1979), 87, 168; Barbara L. Michaels, *Gertrude Käsebier: The Photographer and Her Photographs* (New York: Harry N. Abrams, 1992), 49.

24. Agnes Lee, "Under Peggy's Window," *The Round Rabbit* (Boston: Copeland & Day, 1898), 17.

25. My thanks to Charles Childress of the Boston Public Schools for trying to track down these records.

26. James Frederick Hopkins, *Outline of Lessons in Drawing, 1898–1899* (Boston: Boston Public Schools, 1898), 3–9.

27. Macleod, *Age of the Child,* 38; Samuel H. Preston and Michael R. Haines, *Fatal Years: Child Mortality in Late Nineteenth-Century America* (Princeton, NJ: Princeton University Press, 1991), 3. There were three major causes of death among the very young. Deaths within the first month or so, referred to as neonatal mortality, and considered inevitable, included children born prematurely, or with some physical deformity, or injury at birth. Gastrointestinal problems resulting in severe diarrhea, dehydration, and death were commonplace among babies, while respiratory and childhood infectious diseases such as measles, scarlet fever, and diphtheria more often struck down children who had survived past the age of one (Preston and Haines, *Fatal Years,* 3–9).

28. Entry for Alice Stephana Lee, "The Alumni," *Clarke School and Its Graduates: A Memorial Volume Issued to Commemorate the Fiftieth Anniversary of the Founding of the School, 1867–1917* (Northampton, MA: Alumni, 1918), 119. Scarlet fever, for example, often left survivors with permanent disability.

29. Certified Copy of Record of Death, Registry Division, City of Boston, No. 4747, 12 May 1900.

30. Thea Cooper and Arthur Ainsberg, *Breakthrough: Elizabeth Hughes, the Discovery of Insulin, and the Making of a Medical Miracle* (New York: St. Martin's Press, 2010), 1.

31. Donald M. Barnett, MD, *Elliott P. Joslin, MD: A Centennial Portrait* (Boston: Joslin Diabetes Center, 1998), 16.

32. Eric J. Ruby, MD, telephone conversation, 27 February 2009; Cooper and Ainsberg, *Breakthrough*, 1.

33. Barnett, *Elliott P. Joslin*, 18.

34. Cooper and Ainsberg, *Breakthrough*, 3.

35. Barnett, *Elliott P. Joslin*, 18.

36. Birth, Death, and Marriage Records, Commonwealth of Massachusetts Archives; Certified Copy of Record of Death, Registry Division, City of Boston, No. 4747, 12 May 1900.

37. Barnett, *Elliott P. Joslin*, 7. I thank Dr. Donald M. Barnett for checking Joslin's patient ledger.

38. Lot 3277 burial documents, decedent cards, and ancillary materials, Mount Auburn Cemetery, Cambridge, Massachusetts, enclosed with a letter to the author from Caroline Loughlin, 19 June 2008.

39. For the history of Mount Auburn, see Blanche M. G. Linden, *Silent City on a Hill: Picturesque Landscapes of Memory and Boston's Mount Auburn Cemetery* (Amherst: University of Massachusetts Press / Library of American Landscape History, 2007).

40. Martha V. Pike and Janice Gray Armstrong, *A Time to Mourn: Expressions of Grief in Nineteenth Century America* (Stony Brook, NY: Museums at Stony Brook, 1980), 26.

41. Thomas Lynch, *The Undertaking: Life Studies from the Dismal Trade* (New York: W. W. Norton, 1997), 51.

42. Pike and Armstrong, *A Time to Mourn*, 26–27; Alan C. Swedlund, *Shadows in the Valley: A Cultural History of Illness, Death, and Loss in New England, 1840–1916* (Amherst: University of Massachusetts Press, 2010), 232 n. 47.

43. Swedlund, *Shadows in the Valley*, 187.

44. LIG to FHD, 15 February 1901, LIG-LC; LIG to FHD, 5 May 1901, LIG-LC.

45. Emily Stipes Watts, *The Poetry of American Women from 1632–1945* (Austin: University of Texas Press, 1977), 85; Wendy Simonds and Barbara Katz Rothman, *Centuries of Solace: Expressions of Maternal Grief in Popular Literature* (Philadelphia: Temple University Press, 1992), 49.

46. Simonds and Rothman, *Centuries of Solace*, 22.

47. Harold K. Bush Jr., "'Broken Idols': Mark Twain's Elegies for Susy and a Critique of Freudian Grief Theory," *Nineteenth-Century Literature* 57, no. 2 (September 2002), 246.

48. Agnes Lee, "Before Sleep," *Under One Roof*, 23.

49. Agnes Lee, "In the Spring," ibid., 11.

50. Agnes Lee, "The Diary," ibid., 23.

51. Simonds and Rothman, *Centuries of Solace*, 50.

52. LIG to FHD, 5 May 1901, LIG-LC. For biography of Watson, see Linda K. Hughes, *Graham R.: Rosamund Marriott Watson, Woman of Letters* (Athens: Ohio University Press, 2005).

53. Bush, "'Broken Idols,'" 252–54.

54. LIG to FHD, 5 May 1901, LIG-LC.

55. William Canton, *The Invisible Playmate, W. V. Her Book, and In Memory of W. V.* (New York: E. P. Dutton, n.d.), 123.

56. Macleod, *The Age of the Child*, 15, 160 n. 34.

57. Agnes Lee to FHD, 10 March 1919, FHD-LC.

58. Agnes Lee to FHD, 17 March 1919, FHD-LC.

59. Agnes Lee to FHD, 14 November 1920, FHD-LC.

60. Agnes Lee to FHD, 15 December 1920, FHD-LC; Agnes Lee, "The Death of Louise Imogen Guiney (A Vision)," *Under One Roof*, 142. Guiney lived in Auburndale, MA, when she met the Lee family.

61. FWL to Marion Lincoln Lee (MLL), 6 January 1934, FWL-LC.

## 4. *BLESSED ART THOU AMONG WOMEN*

1. Laura Wexler, *Tender Violence: Domestic Visions in an Age of U.S. Imperialism* (Chapel Hill: University of North Carolina Press, 2000), 191.

2. Ibid., 191.

3. For biography of Käsebier's early years, see Barbara L. Michaels, *Gertrude Käsebier: The Photographer and Her Photography* (New York: Harry N. Abrams, 1992), 13–20.

4. Käsebier quoted ibid., 14; ibid., 28.

5. C. Jane Gover, *The Positive Image: Women Photographers in Turn of the Century America* (Albany: State University of New York Press, 1988), 17, 20.

6. For biography of Frances Benjamin Johnston, see Verna Posever Curtis, "Frances Benjamin Johnston in 1900: Staking the Sisterhood's Claim in American Photography," in *Ambassadors of Progress: American Women Photographers in Paris, 1900–1901*, ed. Bronwyn A. E. Griffith (Giverny, France:: Musée d'Art Américain Giverny in association with Library of Congress, Washington, DC, 2001; dist. by University Press of New England, Hanover, NH), 24–37.

7. For biography of the Allen sisters, see Suzanne L. Flynt, *The Allen Sisters: Pictorial Photographers, 1885–1920* (Deerfield, MA: Pocumtuck Valley Memorial Association, 2002; dist. by University Press of New England, Hanover, NH).

8. Quoted in Michel Poivert, "A Taste of the Avant-Garde: The Reception of American Women Photographers in Paris (1900–1901)," in Griffith, *Ambassadors of Progress*, 47.

9. Michaels, *Gertrude Käsebier*, 18; Sadakichi Hartmann, "Gertrude Käsebier," *Photographic Times* 35, no. 5 (May 1900): 196.

10. Poivert, "A Taste of the Avant-Garde," 47; R. A. Cram, "Mrs. Käsebier's Work," *Photo Era* 4, no. 5 (May 1900): 134.

11. Cyrille Menard, quoted in Poivert, "A Taste of the Avant-Garde," 47–48.

12. Michaels, *Gertrude Käsebier*, 28.

13. Ibid., 18.

14. Arthur Wesley Dow, "A Note on Japanese Art and What the American Artist May Learn Therefrom," *Knight Errant* 1, no. 4 (January 1893): 114–17; Ernest F. Fenollosa, "The Significance of Oriental Art," *Knight Errant*, 1, no. 3 (October 1892): 65–70.

15. Michaels, *Gertrude Käsebier*, 26–27; William Innes Homer, *A Pictorial Heritage: The Photographs of Gertrude Käsebier* (Wilmington: Delaware Art Museum, 1979), 19.

16. Homer, *A Pictorial Heritage*, 19.

17. Arthur W. Dow, "Mrs. Gertrude Käsebier's Portrait Photographs," *Camera Notes* 3 (July 1899): 22.

18. Cram, "Mrs. Käsebier's Work," 136.

19. H. Snowden Ward, "Gertrude Käsebier and Her Work," *Amateur Photographer & Photographic News*, 13 December 1910, 591.

20. Käsebier quoted in Michaels, "Portraits of Friendship," 30.

21. Giles Edgerton [Mary Fanton Roberts], "Photography as an Emotional Art: A Study of the Work of Gertrude Käsebier," *Craftsman* 12 (1907): 92.

22. Ibid., 88.

23. Ibid., 88.

24. "The First Publication of the Fitzroy Picture Society," *Studio* 1 (1893): 28–29. Kristin Schwain, *Signs of Grace: Religion and American Art in the Gilded Age* (Ithaca, NY: Cornell University Press, 2008), 128; 110–11. For more on the image of the Annunciation, see Estelle M. Hurll, *The Madonna in Art* (Boston: L. C. Page, 1897), and Maria Vassilaki, *Images of the Mother of God* (London: Ashgate, 2005).

25. Ellen May to Agnes Lee, 22 September 1922, FHD-LC.

26. FWL to Alfred Stieglitz (AS), 3 April 1900; FWL to AS, 6 June 1900, both Alfred Stieglitz / Georgia O'Keeffe Archive, Series I, Correspondence, box 30, folder 706, Yale Collection of American Literature, Beinecke Rare Book and Manuscript Library, Yale University (Yale).

27. Joseph T. Keiley, "The Salon," *Camera Notes* 4, no. 3 (January 1901): 222.

28. Ibid., 222.

29. Michaels, *Gertrude Käsebier*, 17.

30. Ibid., 17–18.

31. Judith Fryer Davidov, *Women's Work: Self/Body/Other in American Visual Culture* (Durham, NC: Duke University Press, 1998), 64–65.

32. Gover, *The Positive Image*, 111, 104.

33. Homer, *A Pictorial Heritage*, 22. For a discussion of symbolism in pictorial photography, see also Edwin Becker, "F. Holland Day and Symbolism," in *F. Holland Day*, ed. Pam Roberts (Amsterdam: Van Gogh Museum, 2000), 53–64.

34. Keiley, "The Salon," 222.

35. Ibid., 222.

36. Sarah E. Slater, "Profitable Industries for Women, V.—Photography," *New Idea Woman's Magazine* 10 (February 1904): 30.

37. Karen Sánchez-Eppler, *Dependent States: The Child's Part in Nineteenth Century American Culture* (Chicago: University of Chicago Press, 2005), 119, 112. Similarly, Roland Barthes remarked on "that rather terrible thing which is there in every photograph: the return of the dead" (Roland Barthes, *Camera Lucida: Reflections on Photography*, trans. Richard Howard [New York: Hill and Wang, 1981], 9).

38. Jay Ruby, *Secure the Shadow: Death and Photography in America* (Cambridge: MIT Press, 1995), 115; Martha V. Pike and Janice Gray Armstrong, *A Time to Mourn: Expressions of Grief in Nineteenth Century America* (Stony Brook, NY: Museums at Stony Brook, 1980), 67.

39. Audrey Linkman, *Photography and Death* (London: Reaktion Books, 2011), 62; 17.

40. Ibid., 18, 194 n. 14.

41. Ibid., 131; Ruby, *Secure the Shadow*, 120–28.

42. Sánchez-Eppler, *Dependent States*, 144.

43. FWL to AS, 6 June 1900, Yale. In the letter Lee also writes, "I shall be very glad to pay for them whatever is right. This is of course supposing that Lady K has no objection but I hardly think she could object."

44. Alan C. Swedlund, *Shadows in the Valley: A Cultural History of Illness, Death, and Loss in New England, 1840–1916* (Amherst: University of Massachusetts Press, 2010), 53.

45. "Some Indian Portraits: Photographic Portraits by Gertrude Käsebier," *Everybody's Magazine* 4 (January 1901): 12. For a further discussion of these images, see Wexler, *Tender Violence*, 177–208.

46. FWL to AS, 6 June 1900, Yale.

47. Michaels, *Gertrude Käsebier*, 88; 111; 134; 156.

48. Ibid., 158.

49. Ellen May to Agnes Lee, 22 September 1922, FHD-LC.

50. Agnes Lee to FHD, 8 September 1922, FHD-LC.

51. Michaels, *Gertrude Käsebier*, 107.

52. George Amick, "37¢ Masters of American Photography (20 Designs) Classic Collection Series," *Linn's Stamp News, U.S. Stamp Yearbook, 2002* (Sidney, OH: Amos Press, 2003), 60.

53. Ibid., 57.

54. When I was studying for my PhD at Boston College in the early 1990s, I was surprised to see a print of the image hanging in the office of one of my professors. She had purchased it in a shop at Faneuil Market in Boston.

## 5. THE DAUGHTERS OF FRANCIS WATTS LEE

1. A. C. R. Carter, "The Two Great Exhibitions. The Photographic Salon," *Photograms of the Year 1899* (London: Dawbarn & Ward, 1899), 103; "Pictures at the Exhibitions. The Photographic Harvest," *Photography*, 28 September 1899, 660.

2. Joseph T. Keiley, "The Salon, Its Purposes, Character and Lesson," *Camera Notes* 3, no. 3 (January 1900): 141.

3. Joseph T. Keiley, "The Salon," *Camera Notes* 4, no. 3 (January 1901): 212.

4. Barbara Dayer Gallati, "Great Expectations: An Introduction to John Singer Sargent's Paintings of Children," in *Great Expectations, John Singer Sargent Painting Children* (New York: Bulfinch Press and Brooklyn Museum, 2004), 19.

5. Ibid., 20.

6. W. I. Lincoln Adams, *In Nature's Image: Chapters on Pictorial Photography* (New York: Baker and Taylor, 1898), 85; Claire Perry, *Young America: Childhood in Nineteenth-Century Art and Culture* (New Haven: Yale University Press, 2006), 4–6.

7. Gallati, "Great Expectations," 30; David I. Macleod, *The Age of the Child: Children in America 1890–1920* (New York: Twayne Publishers, 1998); Gallati, "From Souvenir to High Art: Childhood on Display," in *Great Expectations*, 82.

8. Gallati, "Posing Problems: Sargent's Model Children," in *Great Expectations*, 195.

9. Sadakichi Hartmann [Sidney Allan], "Children as They Are Pictured," *Cosmopolitan Magazine* 43, no. 3 (July 1907): 235.

10. George Dimock, "Priceless Children: Child Labor and the Pictorialist Ideal," in *Priceless Children: American Photographs 1890–1925* (Greensboro, NC: Weatherspoon Art Museum, 2001), 10–11.

11. Gallati, "Posing Problems," 203.

12. On Sarah Choate Sears, see Erica E. Hirshler, *A Studio of Her Own: Women Artists in Boston, 1870–1940* (Boston: MFA Publications, 2001). Sargent also painted Sarah Choate Sears (Mrs. J. S. Montgomery Sears).

13. John Singer Sargent to Sarah Choate Sears, quoted in Gallati, "Posing Problems," 237 n. 53. Despite Sargent's generosity and modesty, as Gallati observes, "ironically, . . . it is the painting that seems less posed than the photograph" (203–4).

14. Dimock, "Priceless Children," 10.

15. Eva Watson-Schutze, "Portraits of Children," *The Photographer* 1 (4 June 1904): 93.

16. "Deeply treasured": Dimock, "Priceless Children," 12; "perfectly at ease": Hartmann, "Children as They Are Pictured," 242. On pictorialists' use of children of friends as models, see also Judith Fryer Davidov, "The Geometry of Bodies: Gender and Genre in Pictorialist Photography," in *Women's Work: Self/Body/Other in American Visual Culture* (Durham, NC: Duke University Press, 1998), 45; Dimock, "Priceless Children," 7–10; Hirshler, *A Studio of Her Own*, 59.

17. Gallati, "Posing Problems," 203.

18. Verna Posever Curtis, "From New Athens to Arcadia," in *F. Holland Day, Selected Texts and Bibliography*, ed. Verna Posever Curtis and Jane Van Nimmen (Oxford, UK: Clio Press, 1995), 18 n. 24.

19. Curtis notes the still-unidentified "prophet"; the identification of the book in Peggy's hand was made by Sue Welsh Reed (ibid., 20 n. 25). Whether the book was in French or English is unknown. Agnes Rand Lee spent several years in France and may have been fluent in French.

20. The image was found in the Frank W. Birchall Glass Plate Collection at the Massachusetts Historical Society. Other plates within the collection have been identified as taken by Francis Watts Lee, Gertrude Käsebier, Sarah Choate Sears, and F. Holland Day. It appears that Birchall both printed for others and allowed them to use his studio for their own work.

21. Dimock, "Priceless Children," 12.

22. Robert Demachy, "The American New School of Photography in Paris," *Camera Notes* 5, no. 1 (July 1901): 42.

23. Gallati, "Posing Problems," 203.

24. Demachy, "The American New School," 36.

25. My thanks to Trevor Fairbrother for bringing the comparison to my attention.

26. Susan Sidlauskas, *Body, Place, and Self in Nineteenth Century Painting* (New York: Cambridge University Press, 2000), 80.

27. Davidov, in "The Geometry of Bodies," 67–68, notes the importance of this kind of physical connection.

28. Frederick Haven Pratt (FHP), biography, Pratt file, FHD-LC.

29. FHP to FHD, 12 August 1906, FHD-LC. Gertrude Käsebier, White, and Seeley all visited Day in Maine in the summer of 1905.

30. *Photographic Studies by Frederick Haven Pratt,* at the studio of J. Edw. B. Greene, 657 Boylston St., Boston, 23 January to 4 February 1905. Pratt file, FHD-LC.

31. Agnes Lee to FHD, 1 September 1908, FHD-LC.

32. For biographical information on Mrs. Samual Watts, see Frank W. Bayley, *The Life and Works of John Singleton Copley* (Boston: Taylor Press, 1915), 257; Sotheby's, Lot 62, *Mrs. Samuel Watts (Sarah Osborne):* www.sothebys.com/en/auctions/ecatalogue/lot.pdf.N08449.html/f/62/N08449-62.pdf.

33. On Copley as a society painter, see Paul Staiti, "Character and Class: The Portraits of John Singleton Copley," in *Reading American Art,* ed. Marianne Doezema and Elizabeth Milroy (New Haven: Yale University Press, 1998), 12–37.

34. For biographical information, see Frank W. Bayley, *The Life and Works of John Singleton Copley,* 256.

35. The painting of Mrs. Samuel Watts was sold by Francis Watts Lee in 1928. Sotheby's website indicates the owner in 1873 as Mrs. T. J. Lee, FWL's mother. In a 1928 letter to his wife Marion, FWL indicates he is opening a savings account "and into this I propose to deposit the net proceeds from the sale of the Copley which I think is on the edge of being effected" (FWL to MLL, 28 August 1928, FWL-LC). This date coincides with Sotheby's documentation that the portrait was in the hands of Mr. Frederick S. Moseley of Boston in 1928.

36. *Loan Collection of Portraits of Women, for the Benefit of The Boston Children's Aid Society, and The Sunnyside Day Nursery,* Copley Hall, Clarendon Street, 11–31 March 1895 (Boston: The Society, 1895), exhibition catalog in Boston Public Library collection, electronic edition available at https://archive.org/details/loancollectionofoobost; *Boston Evening Transcript,* 12 March 1895, 5. Also mentioned in Trevor J. Fairbrother, *John Singer Sargent and America* (New York: Garland, 1986), 188–89, and by Erica E. Hirshler, "'A Prince in a Royal Line of Painters': Sargent's Portraits and Posterity," in Gallati, *Great Expectations,* 165 n. 35, 178. Sargent's entries in this exhibition included a portrait of Miss Katherine Pratt, the sister of Frederick Haven Pratt. This portrait is currently in the collection of the Worcester Art Museum along with a portrait of Sargent by Frederick Haven Pratt.

37. Harlan Lane, *A Deaf Artist in Early America: The Worlds of John Brewster Jr.* (Boston: Beacon Press, 2004). The portrait of Watts is the cover image of this biography.

38. Gleeson White, "The Nude in Photography," *Photographic Times* 29 (May 1897): 209–20.

39. F. Holland Day, "Photography Applied to the Undraped Figure," in *The American Annual of Photography and Photographic Times Almanac for 1898* (New York: Scovill & Adams, 1897): 190.

40. Adams, *In Nature's Image,* 63.

41. Ibid., 63–64.

42. F. Holland Day, "Is Photography an Art?,", 20-page typescript, n.d. [c. 1900], 9–10, FHD-LC.

43. White, "The Nude in Photography," 215; Adams, *In Nature's Image,* 67.

44. White, The Nude in Photography," 218.

45. Anne Higonnet, *Pictures of Innocence: The History and Crisis of Ideal Childhood* (London: Thames and Hudson, 1998), 129–30.

46. Peter C. Bunnell, *Clarence H. White: The Reverence for Beauty* (Athens: Ohio University Gallery of Fine Art, 1986), 14.

47. Osborne Yellott, "The Third Philadelphia Salon," *Photo Era* 5, no. 6 (December 1900): 170.

48. I thank Cashman Kerr Prince for the translation of this phrase as "The child, who now already could be loved, the Nymph called Narcissus."

49. I thank Cashman Kerr Prince for the translation of this phrase as "You practice pastoral poetry [playing] on a slender reed." Re: Charles Kingsley's *The Water Babies*, see particularly the illustrations by Jessie Willcox Smith in the 1916 edition. Yellott, "The Third Philadelphia Salon," 170.

50. LIG to FHD, 15 May 1898, LIG-LC; Joseph T. Keiley, "The Salon, Its Purposes, Character, and Lesson," *Camera Notes* 3, no. 3 (January 1900): 163.

51. "Pictures at the Exhibitions. The Photographic Harvest," *Photography*, 28 September 1899, 660.

52. Charles H. Caffin, "The Philadelphia Photographic Salon, 1901," *Camera Notes* 5, no. 3 (January 1902): 209; Herbert W. Taylor, "Fourth Philadelphia Photographic Salon," *Photo Era* 7, no. 6 (December 1901): 210.

53. Caffin, "The Philadelphia Photographic Salon, 1901," 209.

54. W. F. L., "The Photographic Salon, Pennsylvania Academy of Fine Arts," *Photographic Times* 32, no. 11 (November 1900): 516.

55. Joseph T. Keiley, "The Salon," *Camera Notes* 4, no. 3 (January 1901): 212.

## 6. THE HERITAGE OF MOTHERHOOD

1. Joseph T. Keiley, "Eva Watson-Schütze," *Camera Work*, no. 9 (January 1905): 23. Keiley likely saw the image in mid-August 1904 when he visited Käsebier, according to Barbara Michaels, e-mail correspondence with the author, 22 January 2014. Keiley also apparently changed his mind about the image, see Barbara L. Michaels, *Gertrude Käsebier: The Photographer and Her Photographs* (New York: Harry N. Abrams, 1992), 136.

2. Giles Edgerton [Mary Fanton Roberts], "Photography as an Emotional Art: A Study of the Work of Gertrude Käsebier," *The Craftsman* 12 (1907): 92.

3. Ibid., 90.

4. "I want to see": Edgerton, "Emotional Art," 90; "three days": Lillian Sabine, "The Women's Page!," *Abel's Photographic Weekly*, 19 September 1931, 351.

5. Citing family sources, Michaels writes, "Mr. Lee came to believe that the disaster [Peggy's death and Alice's deafness] was a curse visited upon him for not having become a clergyman" (*Gertrude Käsebier*, 51, 170 n. 10). This view has since been disproved. Alice was not deafened by the same illness that took Peggy's life; further, Lee later remarried.

6. Harriet Sarnoff Schiff, *The Bereaved Parent* (New York: Crown, 1977), 57. Reiko Schwab, "A Child's Death and Divorce: Dispelling the Myth," *Death Studies*, 22 (1998): 445–68, notes the lack of evidence for this belief, as do A. Lang and L. Gottlieb, "Parental Grief Reactions and Marital Intimacy following Infant Death," *Death Studies* 17 (1993): 233–55.

7. "normal divorce rate": studies compiled by Therese A. Rando, "The Unique Issues and Impact of the Death of a Child," in *Parental Loss of a Child*, ed. Therese A. Rando (Champaign,

IL: Research Press, 1986), 29–31; "no one else knew the child": Paul C. Rosenblatt, *Help Your Marriage Survive the Death of a Child* (Philadelphia: Temple University Press, 2000), 13.

8. LIG to FHD, 8 May 1903, LIG-LC.

9. LIG to FHD, 31 August 1892, LIG-LC.

10. LIG to FHD, 8 May 1903, LIG-LC.

11. Agnes Lee to FHD, 26 May 1902, FHD-LC. Susan L. Taylor, in "The Heritage of Motherhood and the Agony of Agnes Lee," *Bulletin of the Detroit Institute of Arts* 75, no. 2 (2001): 14–25, incorrectly quotes the letter as "my heart still aches" rather than "my head still aches."

12. FWL to LIG, 19 April 1903, Louise Imogen Guiney Papers, College of the Holy Cross, Worcester, MA (hereafter Holy Cross); Martha A. Lee v. Francis W. Lee, case no. 6235, 1910 (vol. 2), 831–36, Suffolk County Superior Court, Commonwealth of Massachusetts.

13. "The Second Chicago Photographic Salon," *Camera Notes* 5, no. 3 (January 1902): 206.

14. Charles H. Caffin, "The Philadelphia Photographic Salon, 1901," *Camera Notes* 5, no. 3 (January 1902): 209.

15. Patricia J. Fanning, *Through an Uncommon Lens: The Life and Photography of F. Holland Day* (Amherst: University of Massachusetts Press, 2008), 136, 232 n. 2; FWL to Alfred Stieglitz, 15 December 1901, Series I. Correspondence, box 30, folder 706, Alfred Stieglitz / Georgia O'Keeffe Archive, Yale Collection of American Literature, Beinecke Rare Book & Manuscript Library, Yale University.

16. A. C. R. Carter, "The Two Great Exhibitions. The Photographic Salon," *Photograms of the Year 1902* (London: Dawbarn & Ward, 1902), 144. There is no known extant image of *Anacreon: Ode XL*. I thank Cashman Kerr Prince for the translation of *Beata mea Domina* as "My Blessed Lady."

17. FWL to LIG, 19 April 1903, Holy Cross.

18. LIG to FHD, 8 May 1903, LIG-LC. Lee was quite aware of LIG's connections to others at the BPL. Letters to LIG from Edward B. Hunt indicate Lee sending his love via Hunt's correspondence [Hunt to LIG, 24 February 1904, Holy Cross].

19. FWL to LIG, 19 April 1903, Holy Cross.

20. E. B. Hunt to LIG, 24 February 1904, Holy Cross. My thanks to Gale Eaton for calling this letter to my attention.

21. LIG to FHD, 8 May 1903, LIG-LC; LIG to FHD, 27 July 1904, LIG-LC.

22. Guiney's father, Patrick Robert Guiney (1835–1887), grew up in Gorham's Corner, a colorful section of Portland dominated by Irish immigrants. See *They Change Their Sky: The Irish in Maine*, ed. Michael C. Connolly (Orono: University of Maine Press, 2004), 171–73; LIG to van Allen, 29 September 1897; LIG to Clement Shorter, 4 July 1898; LIG to Herbert Clarke, 12 October 1897, all in *Letters of LIG*, 1:202–3, 207.

23. LIG to FHD, 15 October 1908; LIG to FHD, 25 June 1898; LIG to FHD, 27 December 1912, all LIG-LC.

24. LIG to FHD, 25 June 1898; 27 July 1904, LIG-LC.

25. Kahlil Gibran to FHD, 20 August 1903, private collection, quoted in Jean Gibran and Kahlil Gibran, *Kahlil Gibran: His Life and World* (Boston: New York Graphic Society, 1974), 118.

26. William Innes Homer, *A Pictorial Heritage: The Photographs of Gertrude Käsebier* (Wilmington: Delaware Art Museum, 1979), 23.

27. Michaels, *Gertrude Käsebier,* 148. Käsebier took a third photograph in Day's chalet in 1913 of the Clarence H. White family, which she titled *Sunshine in the House.*

28. "finger play": Michaels, *Gertrude Käsebier,* 149–50; "benediction": Homer, *Pictorial Heritage,* 24. Additionally, the gesture is reminiscent of sign language for the deaf, linking the image to Alice Lee as well.

29. Michaels, *Gertrude Käsebier,* 150.

30. "confident idealism": Homer, *Pictorial Heritage,* 24; Michaels, *Gertrude Käsebier,* 148.

31. Taylor, "Agony of Agnes Lee," 16. The series is also discussed in Edgerton, "Emotional Art," and Michaels, *Gertrude Käsebier.*

32. Homer, *Pictorial Heritage,* 23.

33. On Käsebier's plans, see Arthur Davies to FHD, 21 July 1904, FHD-LC; LIG to FHD, 27 July 1904, LIG-LC.

34. On FHD's Maine home, see Fanning, *Through an Uncommon Lens,* 165–74. On Agnes Lee's surprise at the photo's being taken, see Agnes Rand Freer to William Stanley Braithwaite, 1 January and 10 February 1914, William Stanley Braithwaite Papers, 1897–1930, (MS Am1444) (634) Lee, Agnes (Rand)—39 letters to WSB, 1910–1928, Houghton Library, Harvard University. Apparently one of the images taken this day in Maine was Alice Stephana Lee's favorite photograph of her mother. In response to Braithwaite's request for a photograph, Agnes wrote, "Now this picture is my daughter's, and the very apple of her eye, and she is making a great concession in letting me have it. . . . So, Mr. Braithwaite, if you do use this, please promise me, *promise me* not to take it unless you are absolutely sure that you can return it safely to me after its usefulness is over" (1 January 1914).

35. Edgerton, "Emotional Art," 92. The photo is discussed in Homer, *Pictorial Heritage,* 24; Stephen Petersen, "The Complexity of Light and Shade: Gertrude Käsebier and the Field of Modern Photography," *Gertrude Käsebier: The Complexity of Light and Shade,* ed. Stephen Petersen and Janis A. Tomlinson (Newark: University of Delaware Museum, 2014), 17.

36. Petersen, "Complexity of Light and Shade," 18. The glass-plate negative of the image is in the Library of Congress, Prints and Photographs Division.

37. See Joanne Hardy, "Appendix A: Seeley's Printing Techniques," in George and Joanne Hardy Dimock, *Intimations and Imaginings: The Photographs of George H. Seeley* (Pittsfield, MA: Berkshire Museum, 1986), 58.

38. Alice Boughton, "Photography, A Medium of Expression" (1905), in *Camera Fiends and Kodak Girls: Fifty Selections by and about Women in Photography, 1840–1930,* ed. and intro. Peter E. Palmquist (New York: Midmarch Arts Press, 1989), 142–43.

39. Petersen, "Complexity of Light and Shade," 18.

40. "monumental dignity": Homer, *Pictorial Heritage,* 23; "brushing away": Sarah E. Kelly, "'A New and Living Spirit': Pictorialist Principles and the Arts and Crafts Movement," in *Apostles of Beauty: Arts and Crafts from Britain to Chicago,* ed. Judith A. Barter (New Haven: Yale University Press, 2009; dist. for Art Institute of Chicago), 141–42.

41. Taylor, "Agony of Agnes Lee," 20.

42. Michaels, *Gertrude Käsebier,* 52.

43. Ibid., 171 n. 12, 52.

44. Petersen, "Complexity of Light and Shade," 18.

45. Roderick Phillips, *Putting Asunder: A History of Divorce in Western Society* (New York: Cambridge University Press, 1988), 462–63.

46. Glenda Riley, *Divorce: An American Tradition* (New York: Oxford University Press, 1991), 121–22.

47. On civil divorce laws, see Phillips, *Putting Asunder,* 465–67; on Episcopal Church rulings, see William L. O'Neill, *Divorce in the Progressive Era* (New Haven: Yale University Press, 1967), 37–40.

48. Martha A. Lee v. Francis W. Lee, case no. 6235, 1910 (vol. 2), 831–836, Suffolk County Superior Court, Commonwealth of Massachusetts.

49. Record of Marriage, Town of Rye, New York, No. 718, Otto Tiger Freer to Martha Agnes Lee, 18 May 1911; Record of Marriage, Town of South Kingstown, Rhode Island, Francis Watts Lee to Marion Lincoln Chamberlain, 1 July 1911. That Agnes was married at her brother's home in Rye is stated in letter from Agnes Lee Freer to William Stanley Braithwaite, 25 February 1912, William Stanley Braithwaite Papers, 1897–1930, (MS Am1444) (634) Lee, Agnes (Rand)—39 letters to WSB, 1910–1928, Houghton Library, Harvard University.

## 7. ALICE STEPHANA LEE

1. LIG to W. H. van Allen, 7 February 1898, *Letters of LIG,* 1:217–18.

2. Agnes Lee, "Stephana," *Border of the Lake* (Boston: Sherman, French, 1910), 14.

3. For Gallaudet biography, see Douglas C. Baynton, *Forbidden Signs: American Culture and the Campaign against Sign Language* (Chicago: University of Chicago Press, 1996).

4. Margret Winzer, "The Ladies Take Charge: Women Teachers in the Education of Deaf Students," in *Women and Deafness: Double Visions,* ed. Brenda Jo Brueggemann and Susan Burch (Washington, DC: Gallaudet University Press, 2002), 111; Baynton, *Forbidden Signs,* 26–27.

5. Winzer, "The Ladies Take Charge," 114.

6. Ibid. According to Baynton, "By the turn of the twentieth century, nearly 40 percent of deaf students in America were no longer taught sign language in their classrooms; within twenty years the number had reached 80 percent" (*Forbidden Signs,* 25).

7. "Deaf Tots in School," *Chicago Daily Tribune,* 3 October 1897, p. 50.

8. Ibid., 50. Alice's attendance at McCowen Primary in Chicago, Sarah Fuller Home, and Clarke are all noted in the Clarke Alumni Register (1867–1967), Clarke School for the Deaf Records, Special Collections & University Archives, University of Massachusetts Amherst Libraries.

9. Alice Lee to Frederick Haven Pratt, 3 May 1906, photocopy in Pratt file, FHD-LC.

10. Ibid.

11. Fanning, *Through an Uncommon Lens,* 174; Jane White, "A Photographer's Holiday," typescript carbon, 1938–1939, p. 43, Clarence H. White Collection, Princeton University Art Museum, Princeton, NJ.

12. Agnes Lee to FHD, 11 September, 1908, FHD-LC.

13. Alice Lee to FHD, 11 September 1908, FHD-LC; Agnes Lee to FHD, 11 September 1908, FHD-LC; LIG to FHD, 8 May 1903, LIG-LC.

14. For Clarke School history, see Baynton, *Forbidden Signs*, 57, and Susan Burch, *Signs of Resistance: American Deaf Cultural History, 1900–World War II* (New York: New York University Press, 2002).

15. Winzer, "The Ladies Take Charge," 110–27; Baynton, *Forbidden Signs*, 56–66.

16. Winzer, "The Ladies Take Charge," 121–22; Baynton, *Forbidden Signs*, 66.

17. Baynton, *Forbidden Signs*, 59–60.

18. *Annual Report of the Clarke School for the Deaf*, year ending August 31, 1900 (Northampton, MA: Press of Gazette Printing Company, 1900). At Clarke, "every one of the teachers . . . from its founding in 1868 through 1904, were women" (Baynton, *Forbidden Signs*, 57). Clarke also became a training school, as its principal, Caroline Yale, recruited females, especially from nearby Smith College, to fill the ranks of instructors both there and at oralist schools across the country (Winzer, "The Ladies Take Charge," 121–23). One of Clarke's teachers during Alice's tenure was Grace Goodhue, who taught there from 1902 until 1905, when she left to marry Calvin Coolidge, future president of the United States (*Clarke School and Its Graduates: A Memorial Volume Issued to Commemorate the Fiftieth Anniversary of the Founding of the School, 1867–1917* [Northampton, MA: Alumni, 1918], 80.) For Alice's award: *Annual Report of the Clarke School for the Deaf*, year ending August 21, 1912 (Northampton, MA: Press of the Gazette Printing Company, 1912), 19. "was her *bent*": Agnes Lee to FHD, 9 January 1917, FHD-LC.

19. According to *Clarke School and Its Graduates*, although Alice attended the school from 1899 until 1912, she did not officially graduate. Page 119 of this volume indicates her attendance at the University School for Girls and the Chicago Art Institute, and the Clarke Alumni Register includes her attendance at Miss Church's Art School as well. Alice's transcript from the School of the Art Institute of Chicago confirms her class work at that institution. For Alice's study of wood carving in Boston, see Agnes Lee to FHD, 9 January 1917, FHD-LC.

20. Edward S. Cooke Jr., "The Aesthetics of Craftsmanship and the Prestige of the Past: Boston Furniture-Making and Wood-Carving," in *Inspiring Reform: Boston's Arts and Crafts Movement* (Wellesley, MA: Davis Museum and Cultural Center, 1997), 48.

21. Ibid., 53.

22. Ibid., 53, and e-mail confirmation to the author, 23 February 2014.

23. Alice Stephana Lee, "Wood-Carving," *The Bulletin* 10, no. 10 (October 1929): 6.

24. William A. Coles, "Hermann Dudley Murphy, An Introduction," in *Hermann Dudley Murphy (1867–1945): Realism Married to Idealism Most Exquisitely* (New York: Graham Gallery, 1982), 10–11. For Sydney Sargent, see Verna Posever Curtis and Patricia J. Fanning, "F. Holland Day: Beauty Is Youth," in *Priceless Children: American Photographs 1890–1925* (Greensboro, NC: Weatherspoon Art Museum, 2001), 36–37. Sydney Sargent was the model for F. Holland Day's *The Marble Faun*. Sargent had apprenticed with Murphy beginning in 1905, became a member of the Society of Arts and Crafts, Boston, in 1910, and was granted Master Craftsman status in 1916.

25. A. J. Philpott, "Talent Shown by Two Boston Women," *Boston Daily Globe*, 12 December 1912, p. 16. FWL's friendship with Emily and Charlotte Hallowell is mentioned in Catherine Nicholson (for Zoltan Haraszti) to Barbara L. Michaels, 29 October 1974. I thank Barbara Michaels for sending me a copy of this letter.

26. Lee, "Wood-Carving," 6.

27. Karen Evans Ulehla, ed., *The Society of Arts and Crafts, Boston: Exhibition Record 1897–1927* (Boston: Boston Public Library, 1981); Art Institute of Chicago, *Catalogue of the Twentieth Annual Exhibition of Applied Arts, 22 September to 23 October, 1921* (my thanks to Nathaniel Parks, assistant archivist, Ryerson & Burnham Libraries, Art Institute of Chicago, for locating this catalog); Lee, "Wood-Carving," 6.

28. Charles Prendergast, "Revival of Wood-Carving," *House Beautiful* 26, no. 3 (August 1909): 70; Lee, "Wood-Carving," 6.

29. Lee, "Wood-Carving," 6.

30. Agnes Lee to FHD, 16 December 1918, FHD-LC.

31. Ulehla, *Society of Arts and Crafts Exhibition Record;* Art Institute of Chicago, *Catalogue;* Agnes Lee Freer to FHD, 9 January 1919, FHD-LC.

32. Alice Stephana Lee, "My Trip Abroad" (part 2), *The Bulletin* 10, no. 1 (January 1928): 5–6, and "My Trip Abroad" (part 1), *The Bulletin* 8, no. 12 (December 1927): 5.

33. Lee, "My Trip Abroad" (part 1), 3–4.

34. Lee, "Wood-Carving," 6.

35. Item following "St. Francis," a letter to the newsletter by Louise B. Graves, *The Bulletin* 9, no. 9 (September 1928): 4–5. For the Woman's World's Fair, see TJ Boisseau, "The Woman's World's Fairs (or the Dream of Women Who Work), Chicago 1925–1928," ed. *Gendering the Fair: Histories of Women and Gender at World's Fairs,* ed. TJ Boisseau and Abigail M. Markwyn (Chicago: University of Chicago Press, 2010), 131–48; Maureen A. Flanagan, *Seeing with Their Hearts: Chicago Women and the Vision of the Good City, 1871–1933* (Princeton, NJ: Princeton University Press, 2002), 201. "Proceeds from the 1927 Fair . . . were earmarked for the Immigrant's Protective League and the Chicago Public School Art Society" (Flanagan, 201).

36. "Clarke School News," *Clarke School Bulletin,* no. 33 (July 1926): 4; *Clarke School Alumni Register; The Bulletin* 9, no. 9 (September 1928): 4–5; "Art Exhibit," *The Bulletin* 10, no. 10 (October 1929): 2. *Lucem Demonstrat Umbra* can be translated as "The shadow shows the light." This sundial was cast by the Gorham Manufacturing Company (Archives of American Art, Gorham Mfg. Co., microfilm reel 3680, Casting records of statuary and small bronzes owned by sculptors, p. 233). A second example of Lee's Peacock sundial is situated at Belle Isle Park in Detroit, Michigan. I thank Lori Feret of the Belle Isle Conservancy's Historical Committee for her confirmation of this sundial.

37. "Art Exhibit," *The Bulletin* 10, no. 10 (October 1929): 1–2. The League gave particular notice to the photography of Beatrice Tonnesen. A favorite portrait photographer of Chicago society families, the hearing-impaired Tonnesen was born in Wisconsin and trained in photography at the Oshkosh Normal School. She moved to Chicago in 1895, where, with her sister, she took over the existing studio of a prominent photographer. In addition to portraits, Tonnesen pioneered the use of live models for print advertisements. In 1900, the Chicago philanthropist and reformer Bertha Palmer promoted her participation in the International Congress of Photography held in Paris as part of the Universal Exposition of Photography, where among the other outstanding American photographs on display was Käsebier's *Blessed Art Thou among Women.* Verna Posever Curtis, "Frances Benjamin Johnston in 1900 Staking the Sisterhood's Claim in American Photography," in *Ambassadors of Progress, American Women Photographers in Paris 1900–1901,* ed. Bronwyn A. E. Griffith (Giverny, France:

Musée d'Art Américain Giverny in association with Library of Congress, Washington, DC, 2001; dist. by University Press of New England, Hanover, NH), 27.

38. "Alice Lee" (obituary), Chicago Hearing Society, Inc., *News*, June/July/August 1957, 2; Prashant Chittiboina, David E. Connor Jr., and Anil Nanda, "Dr. Otto 'Tiger' Freer: Inventor and Innovator," *Neurosurg Focus* 33, no. 2 (August 2012): 1–5; "Dr. Otto T. Freer, Widely Known Surgeon, Is Dead," *Chicago Tribune*, 22 April 1932, p. 34.

39. Agnes Lee Freer to William Braithwaite, 25 February 1912, William Stanley Braithwaite Papers, 1897–1930, (MS Am1444) (634) Lee, Agnes (Rand)—39 letters to WSB, 1910–1928, Houghton Library, Harvard University (WSBP)

40. LIG to FHD, 12 December 1912, LIG-LC.

41. On the Freer family, see Margaret Bullock, "Frederick Warren Freer (1849–1908)," *Illinois Historical Art Project*, www.illinoisart.org; Frederick W. Morton, "Frederick W. Freer, Painter," *Brush and Pencil*, 8, no. 6 (September 1901): 289–300. Agnes Lee Freer to William Braithwaite, 1 January 1914, WSBP; Agnes Lee Freer to William Braithwaite, 17 July 1928, WSBP; "Martha A. Freer, Poet and Widow of Surgeon, Dies," *Chicago Tribune*, 24 July 1939, p. 16.

42. Agnes Lee Freer to William Braithwaite, 17 July 1928, WSBP; Agnes Lee Freer to FHD, 9 January 1917, FHD-LC.

## 8. MARION LEWIS CHAMBERLAIN LEE

1. Marion Mahony Griffin, *The Magic of America: Electronic Edition* (Chicago: Art Institute of Chicago, 2007), sec. III, 72–73, www.artic.edu/magicofamerica/index.html.

2. For history of MIT architectural school, see Margaret Henderson Floyd, *Architectural Education and Boston* (Boston: Boston Architectural Center, 1989), 2.

3. Floyd, *Architectural Education*, 1–2. For MIT history, also see Douglass Shand-Tucci, "American Aristocracy: The Gods of Copley Square—Cornerstone," *Open Letters Monthly*, July 2012, www.openlettersmonthly.com, secs. 1–10.

4. "Sophia Gregoria Hayden." in *Notable American Women: The Modern Period*, ed. Barbara Sicherman and Carol Hurd Green (Cambridge: Belknap Press of Harvard University Press, 1980), 322–24.

5. Alice T. Friedman, "Girl Talk: Feminism and Domestic Architecture at Frank Lloyd Wright's Oak Park Studio," in *Marion Mahony Reconsidered*, ed. David Van Zanten (Chicago: University of Chicago Press, 2011), 24; Griffin, *Magic of America*, sec. IV, 175. Mahony worked with Wright until he fled to Europe with his mistress, Mamah Cheney. She married fellow architect Walter Burley Griffin in 1911, and the two shared a successful collaborative partnership and career. My thanks to Barbara J. Rand for her observations on Marion's dress.

6. "beautiful, brilliant, and charming": Griffin, *Magic of America*, sec. III, 72–73, sec. IV, 175; for Herbert Chamberlain biography: "Chamberlain, Herbert William," in *A Forty-five Year History of the Class of 1896, MIT* (Cambridge: MIT, 1942), 101, and "Herbert W. Chamberlain," Death Notice, Cleveland Necrology File, reel #014, Cleveland Public Library.

7. Walter Muir Whitehill, *Boston Public Library, A Centennial History* (Cambridge: Harvard University Press, 1956), 142; Ralph Adams Cram, *My Life in Architecture* (Boston: Little, Brown, 1936), 35.

8. Dee Garrison, *Apostles of Culture: The Public Librarian and American Society, 1876–1920* (New York: Free Press, 1979), 22.

9. Ibid., 39, 38, 13–14, 40, 178.

10. Ibid., 173.

11. For a discussion of women as librarians at this time, see Garrison, *Apostles of Culture*, 175; on women employed by the BPL, see Sarah Deutsch, *Women and the City: Gender, Space, and Power in Boston, 1870–1940* (New York: Oxford University Press, 2000), 75–76, and Molly Matson, ed., *An Independent Woman: The Autobiography of Edith Guerrier* (Amherst: University of Massachusetts Press, 1992), xi–xii.

12. "Special Libraries," *Boston Public Library Annual Report of 1896* (Boston: BPL, 1897), 46; Matson, *An Independent Woman*, xxvii.

13. On salaries at the BPL, see Deutsch, *Women and the City*, 110; "New Woman": Jean V. Matthews, *The Rise of the New Woman: The Women's Movement in America, 1875–1930* (Chicago: Ivan R. Dee, 2003), 13, 15.

14. Matthews, *Rise of the New Woman*, 15, 17; see also Theodora Penny Martin, *The Sound of Our Own Voices: Women's Study Clubs, 1860–1910* (Boston: Beacon Press, 1987). These clubs were often not religious, charitable, or particularly political.

15. Marion L. Lewis, "A Women's Club House," thesis (seven-page handwritten manuscript), 1896, B.S., Non-circulating Collection 3, Thesis Archives and Special Collections, Institute Archives, MIT.

16. "Special Libraries," *Boston Public Library Annual Report of 1899* (Boston: BPL, 1900), 86.

17. FWL to LIG, 19 April 1903, Holy Cross.

18. Marion Lewis Chamberlain to LIG, undated [1903], Holy Cross.

19. For Marion Chamberlain's salary, see BPL, *Boston Public Library, Annual Report of Departments 1899–1900* (Boston: BPL, 1900), 40.

20. Alice T. Friedman, "Girl Talk," 26.

21. James Weirick, "Marion Mahony at M.I.T.," *Transition* (Winter 1988): 52.

22. Nancy K. Morris Smith, ed., "Letters, 1903–1906, by Charles E. White, Jr. from the Studio of Frank Lloyd Wright," *Journal of Architectural Education* 25, no. 4 (Fall 1971): 104–9. According to a family story, Marion Chamberlain strongly disliked Wright, calling him "a womanizer" (Cristine Bridges Piane, conversation with the author, 2010). Irrespective of Chamberlain's opinion, Wright met Mamah Cheney and began a very public affair with her during the time Chamberlain was working at his studio.

23. "Lee, Mrs. F. W. (Marion Lincoln Lewis)," in *A Forty-five Year History of the Class of 1896, MIT*, 152. Named for Henry Ogden Avery, the first professor of architecture at Columbia, the Avery Architectural and Fine Arts Library built its holdings around Avery's own drawings and personal book collection, which ranged from architecture to archaeology and the decorative arts. For more history, see Avery Architectural & Fine Arts Library History and Collections at www.library.columbia.edu/locations/avery/about.html. In 1905, Marion was the only architectural graduate (out of 266) engaged in library work (*Bulletin of M.I.T., Register of Graduates* 40, no. 3 [March 1905]: 67).

24. "Lee, Mrs. F. W. (Marion Lincoln Lewis)," 152; for history of the New York Society Library, see www.nysoclib.org/history.html. The New York Society Library was the oldest library in the city and had served as the nation's first Library of Congress.

25. GK to FHD, 17 April 1906, FHD-LC: "Saw Mr. Lee the other day and had quite a visit with him." Further evidence of Francis and Marion's renewing their friendship at this time is provided by a prayer book [G. H. S. Walpole, *The Eucharistic Offering* (New York: R. W. Crothers, 1906)] embossed on the inside front cover with the words "Marion, May 24, 1906, Ora Pro Me [Pray for Me]" and blind-stamped "FWL," FWL-LC.

26. "Lee, Mrs. F. W. (Marion Lincoln Lewis)," 152; Sarina Wyant, Special Collections, University of Rhode Island, e-mail to the author, 13 August 2009. Chartered in 1888 as the state's agricultural school, the institution became the Rhode Island College of Agriculture and Mechanic Arts in 1892. It functioned as such until 1909, when Home Economics was added as a course of study for women and the school was renamed. With this addition to the curriculum, the first on-campus dormitory for women opened, with Marion Chamberlain as its dean. For a history of Rhode Island College, see www.uri.edu/home/about/history.html.

27. FWL to MLL, 26 August 1928, FWL-LC.

28. FWL to MLL, 20 August 1928, written on stationery with heading "Halfway Farm, Robbins Road, Walpole, Massachusetts." Lucy Lee was born in 1912, Francis Lincoln Lee in 1915.

29. On childhood in this era, see David I. Macleod, *The Age of the Child, Children in America 1890–1920* (New York: Twayne Publishers, 1998).

30. Liz Knox, Parish Administrator, Epiphany Parish, Walpole, e-mail to the author, 17 July 2013; Agnes Lee Freer to FHD, 9 January 1917, FHD-LC.

31. FWL to MLL, 28 August 1928, FWL-LC.

32. "quite unofficially": Agnes Lee Freer to FHD, 18 November 1921, FHD-LC; "emotional tension": FWL to MLL, 26 August 1928, FWL-LC; "verbal lash" and "physical violence": FWL to MLL, 11 January 1935, FWL-LC.

33. Biographical information on Christine Lewis and Lucy Lee's leaving home to live with her from interview of Cristine Bridges Piane by the author, 2010; FWL to MLL, 26 August 1928, FWL-LC, was written from Springfield, and Lee mentions "two week-ends with Lucy and Christine."

34. FWL to MLL, 11 January 1935, FWL-LC; biographical information on Francis Lincoln Lee from interview of William Watts Lee by the author, 2010.

35. Griffin, *Magic of America*, sec. III, 72–73; FWL to LIG, 19 April 1903, Holy Cross.

36. Marion also apparently miscarried a child in 1914. She later recorded "lost tiny one" on 5 February 1914 in the calendar pages of the *Eucharistic Offering* prayer book given to her by FWL in 1906, FWL-LC; FWL to MLL, 11 January 1935, FWL-LC; C. Macfie Campbell, MD, affiliation, from stationery of letter to MLL, 19 July 1937, FWL-LC; see also George E. Gifford Jr., ed., *Psychoanalysis, Psychotherapy, and the New England Medical Scene, 1894–1944* (New York: Science History Publications, 1978).

37. Obituary of Charles Macfie Campbell, M.D., *Journal of Nervous and Mental Disease* 98 (5) (1943): 561–63.

38. "responsible for" and "exhaustively probed": Gifford, *Psychoanalysis*, 301, 372. See also Nathan G. Hale Jr., *Freud and the Americans: The Beginnings of Psychoanalysis in the United States, 1876–1917* (New York: Oxford University Press, 1971), 440–41.

39. A series of letters from FWL to MLL in the FWL-LC detail this trip. For Gardner Lewis's response, FWL to MLL, 12 August 1928; for Christine Lewis's response, FWL to MLL, 26 August 1928.

40. Marion Lewis Lee, "The Lure of the Question Mark," three-page typescript, FWL-LC.

41. Ibid.

42. Agnes Lee Freer to FHD, 20 April 1931, FHD-LC.

43. "Lee, Mrs. F. W. (Marion Lincoln Lewis)," 152. My thanks to Barbara J. Rand for her analysis of the dress. Several letters from Lucy Lee in FWL-LC collection document the ongoing struggle between Marion and her family. Lucy shared her beliefs with her daughter, who wrote, "Marion was a most difficult and imperious woman" (Cristine Piane, e-mail to the author, 8 February 2009).

44. FWL to Lewis Perry, 2 April 1936, FWL-LC.

## 9. FRANCIS WATTS LEE

1. Patricia J. Fanning, *Through an Uncommon Lens: The Life and Photography of F. Holland Day* (Amherst: University of Massachusetts Press, 2008), 45; Susan Otis Thompson, *American Book Design and William Morris* (New York: R. R. Bowker, 1977).

2. T. J. Jackson Lears, *No Place of Grace: Antimodernism and the Transformation of American Culture, 1880–1920* (Chicago: University of Chicago Press, 1981), 9.

3. Stephen Maxfield Parrish, *Currents of the Nineties in Boston and London* (New York: Garland, 1987), 75; Ralph Adams Cram, *My Life in Architecture* (Boston: Little, Brown, 1936), 6.

4. LIG to van Allen, 7 February 1898, *Letters of LIG*, 1:218.

5. LIG to Herbert Clarke, 21 April 1892, *Letters of LIG*, 1:30–31; "The Quest," *Knight Errant* 1, no. 1 (April 1892): 1.

6. Cram, *My Life*, 85.

7. Maynard quoted in Nancy Finlay, *Artists of the Book in Boston, 1890–1910* (Cambridge: Department of Printing and Graphic Arts, Houghton Library, Harvard College Library, 1985), x; *Boston Transcript*, 2 April 1892, clippings, FHD-LC; Walter Crane: Thompson, *American Book Design*, 41; *Critic* 25 (29 September 1894): 211.

8. "Book Talk & Tattle," *American Bookmaker* 14, no. 5 (May 1892): 171.

9. FWL to FHD, 26 September 1892, FHD-LC.

10. *Knight Errant* 1, no. 1 (April 1892): frontispiece.

11. "an enthusiastic notice" and "a book, sober in content": Thompson, *American Book Design*, 78; "to secure copies of it": Francis Watts Lee, "Regarding Recent Books and Bookmaking," *Knight Errant* 1, no. 1 (April 1892): 32. The full title of the privately printed book is *On the Dedications of American Churches: An Enquiry into the Naming of Churches in the United States, Some Account of English Dedications, and Suggestions for Future Dedications in the American Church. Compiled by Two Laymen of the Diocese of Rhode Island.*

12. Francis Watts Lee, "Regarding Recent Books and Bookmaking," *Knight Errant* 1, no. 1 (April 1892): 32.

13. Francis Watts Lee, "Some Thoughts Upon Beauty in Typography Suggested by the Work of Mr. William Morris at the Kelmscott Press," *Knight Errant* 1, no. 2 (July 1892): 63.

14. FWL to FHD, 26 September 1892, FHD-LC.

15. FWL to FHD, 26 September 1892; FWL to FHD 7 November 1892, FHD-LC.

16. Cram, *My Life*, 88; Parrish, *Currents*, 89 n. 25.

17. Parrish, *Currents*, 94–95.

18. On the Depression of 1893, see http://projects.vassar.edu/1896/depression.html.

19. Carl Smith, *Urban Disorder and the Shape of Belief: The Great Chicago Fire, the Haymarket Bomb, and the Model Town of Pullman* (Chicago: University of Chicago Press, 1995).

20. *Bibliographia Pullmanensis* compiled by Francis Watts Lee, cut from *The Dawn*, October 1894. Someone else made handwritten bibliographic additions to the BPL copy for writings published after FWL's compilation. To indicate the significance of the Pullman strike, when Finley Peter Dunne (who, according to Ralph Adams Cram, had joined the Visionists on occasion [Cram, *My Life*, 17]) submitted a "Mr. Dooley" column depicting George Pullman ordering champagne and cranberry pie after hearing of the hardships endured by working-men's families, Dunne biographer Elmer Ellis describes the reaction at the *Chicago Evening Post*: "When the typesetter ran off his proof of this piece he passed it about the composing room, and later when Dunne stepped into the room for a moment, the typesetters started to drum their sticks on their cases, and then broke into the more customary applause of handclapping. It was painfully embarrassing because it was so unusual and yet so natural, and Dunne remembered it as one of the great thrills of his life." Elmer Ellis, *Mr. Dooley's America: A Life of Finley Peter Dunne* (New York: Alfred A. Knopf, 1941), 86, quoted in Charles Fanning, *Finley Peter Dunne and Mr. Dooley, The Chicago Years* (Lexington: University of Kentucky Press, 1978), 270 n.27. Francis Watts Lee would have surely joined in the applause.

21. FWL to FHD, 31 May 1892, FHD-LC.

22. Walter Muir Whitehill, *Boston Public Library, A Centennial History* (Cambridge: Harvard University Press, 1956), 174.

23. "Printing Department," *Boston Public Library, Annual Report of Departments 1895–1896* (Boston: BPL, 1896), 16–17.

24. It is interesting to note that in the obituary of William H. Rand, FWL's father-in-law, Rand is given credit for helping to develop the linotype machine: "In 1885 he . . . organized the syndicate which brought to perfection the type, or matrix setting machine, known as the Mergenthaler Linotype, and it was Mr. Rand who suggested the expressive name of that wonderful machine" ("William H. Rand," *Boston Transcript*, 22 June 1915, on Harvard College Library Clipping Sheet, Harvard University Archives [HUG300 box 819], Harvard University).

25. "Printing Department," *Boston Public Library, Annual Report of Departments 1900–1901* (Boston: BPL, 1901), 88–90.

26. "Printing Department," *Boston Public Library, Annual Report of Departments 1895–1896*, 16–17.

27. Ibid. Lee notes the three presses were "a Quarter Medium Gordon, a No. 3 Stop Cylinder, and a modern self-inking proof press."

28. Francis Watts Lee, *Boston Public Library, Memoranda concerning the Printing Department, 1897*, 18–19. FWL-LC. This thirty-page pamphlet included a detailed account of the department's work, the 1896–1897 Annual Report, and several examples of printing possibilities.

29. Edwin H. Anderson, "Linotype Work at the Carnegie Library of Pittsburgh," *Library Journal* (1898).

30. LIG to van Allen, 8 May 1899, *Letters of LIG*, 1:257.

31. "Printing," 6 December 1900, memo by Chief of Printing Department, carbon copy, FWL-LC. Opening states, "Replying to the circular request for information . . ."

32. FWL to FHD, 31 October 1899; FWL to FHD, 3 August 1899, FHD-LC.

33. LIG to van Allen, 8 May 1899, *Letters of LIG*, 1:257.

34. "Printing Department," *Boston Public Library, Annual Report of Departments 1901–1902* (Boston: BPL, 1902), 99–102; "Printing Department," *Boston Public Library, Annual Report of Departments 1902–1903* (Boston: BPL, 1903), 101–3.

35. LIG to van Allen, 7 February 1898, *Letters of LIG*, 1:218; FWL to FHD, 26 September 1892, FHD-LC.

36. Frank W. Birchall (hereafter FWB) to FHD, 25 May 1905, FHD-LC.

37. FWL to FWB, quoted in FWB to FHD, 11 November 1908, FHD-LC.

38. FWL to FHD, 26 September 1892, FHD-LC; FWB to Lindsay Swift, 17 January 1909, Lindsay Swift Collection, MS Am 783, Letters to Lindsay Swift from Frank W. Birchall (238), 1 folder, Houghton Library, Harvard University.

39. FWB to Lindsay Swift, 17 January 1909, ibid. Swift died in 1921 while still employed at the BPL.

40. FWL to FWB, quoted in FWB to FHD, 11 November 1908, FHD-LC. Lee was always among the better-paid workers at the BPL. In 1909, when the average yearly compensation of employees was about $720 (Whitehill, *Boston Public Library*, 191), Lee was earning over $2,000 (Henry F. Scannell, Curator, Microtext Department, BPL, e-mail to the author, 25 March 2009), an income that would be difficult to duplicate as a novice farmer.

41. FWL as a difficult man: Michaels, "Portraits" 31, 76 n. 29; FWL to FHD, 10 March 1921, FHD-LC.

42. Whitehill, *Boston Public Library*, 219–20. Zoltan Haraszti replaced Lindsay Swift upon Swift's death in 1921 after more than forty-three years at the BPL (Whitehill, 220).

43. This information was in a series of letters from FWL to MLL while she was on her ocean voyage. FWL to MLL, 22 August 1928, 24 August 1928, 26 August 1928, FWL-LC. The suit FWL wears for the later portrait is probably the one he wore to a party for son Francis in 1934. In a letter to Marion about the event, FWL remarks that his son "did drive out to Walpole and got my glad rags and it seemed to amuse him to see me in them." Lee likely did not have more than one good suit. FWL to MLL, 6 January 1934, FWL-LC.

44. FWL to MLL, 6 January 1934, FWL-LC. The return address is 22 Blagden Street, Boston. "Printing Department," *Boston Public Library, Annual Report of Departments 1933–1934* (Boston: BPL, 1934), 99.

45. "Printing Department," *Boston Public Library, Annual Report of Departments 1935–1936* (Boston: BPL, 1936), 101.

46. "Trustees Minutes," *Public Library of Boston*, 17 January 1936, BPL Archives; FWL to Lewis Perry, 2 April 1936, FWL-LC.

47. "Trustees Minutes," *Public Library of Boston*, 7 May 1937, BPL Archives; "Certificate of Merit Awarded by the City of Boston," FWL-LC; "Trustees Minutes," *Public Library of Boston*, 21 May 1937, BPL Archives.

48. Carl Purington Rollins to Zoltan Haraszti, 5 September 1949, BPL Rare Books Department. In 1974, Zoltan Haraszti noted that he had "only learned of Lee's aesthetic

interests indirectly." Catherine Nicholson, Assistant to the Keeper of Prints, BPL, to Barbara L. Michaels, 29 October 1974. I thank Barbara Michaels for sharing this letter with me.

49. "Lee, Francis Watts," *Boston Herald,* death notice, 17 October 1945, 19. The notice simply reads: "Lee, Francis Watts. Funeral at Story Chapel, Mount Auburn, Thursday, October 18 at 3 pm. Please omit flowers." On 2 March 1939, FWL requested of Mount Auburn "to have two graves, to the left of Harriet Templeton Lee, . . . reserved for the burial of Francis W. and Marion Lincoln Lee" (Request from Proprietor, Mount Auburn Cemetery, 2 March 1939, signed by FWL among Lot 3277 burial documents and ancillary materials, Mount Auburn Cemetery, Cambridge, enclosed with letter to the author from Caroline Loughlin, 19 June 2008).

## EPILOGUE AND ACKNOWLEDGMENTS

1. "Model of Housing Displayed at Fair," *New York Times,* 5 May 1939, 44. Parkchester was built by the Metropolitan Life Insurance Company. A scale model of this unique complex was displayed at the New York World's Fair in 1939.

2. In 1941, the Chicago League for the Hard of Hearing changed its name to the Chicago Society for the Hard of Hearing. In 1947, the name was changed to the Chicago Hearing Society. A letter from Lucy Lee Bridges to her mother, dated 11 May 1943, mentions Marion's "not wanting to go back to Parkchester," FWL-LC.

3. Lucy Lee Bridges to MLL, 19 June 1943, FWL-LC. Several letters exchanged between Lucy and Marion chronicle FWL's visit to California in 1943. Lucy and her mother had a difficult relationship with many disagreements, miscommunications, and misunderstandings. In these same letters, Lucy reveals her pregnancy and the birth of her second child, a daughter, she named Martha. She tells her mother that she had refused to allow her father to tell Marion of the pregnancy: "As to the baby: I forbade mention of it to you . . . because I got fed up with your advice and interference last time" (11 May 1943). Lucy also challenged Marion's belief that she had named her daughter Martha for Martha Rand, Francis's first wife. She explained that her husband, Charles, had selected the name "because it was a pretty name, not odd and yet not too common . . . and was the name of a friend he respected. Only after the whole matter was decided did Father remark that it had been his first wife's name and might cause repercussions" (19 June 1943).

4. FWL to MLL, Western Union telegram from Chicago, 23 June 1943, FWL-LC.

5. According to Mount Auburn Cemetery records, Francis Watts Lee died on 14 October 1945 of chronic kidney failure; Marion Lincoln Lewis Lee died on 18 July 1947 in Oklahoma City, Oklahoma, of hypertensive heart disease. Her cremated remains were interred at Mount Auburn alongside her husband. According to Graceland Cemetery, Chicago, records, Martha Agnes Freer died on 23 July 1939; Otto Freer died on 21 April 1932; Alice Stephana Lee died on 4 June 1957. A separate stone was placed on Alice's grave in April 1958 by Helen Chappell Hanks, the daughter of Mary Robinson Rand Chappell, Agnes's sister.

6. Vassar College alumni records; "shrewd and opinionated observer": Bill Aldrich, Norwich, Vermont Historical Society, e-mails to the author, 30 January and 31 January, 2009; other biographical data: Cristine Bridges Piane, e-mail to the author, 11 March 2009. Lucy Lee Bridges died in 1990.

7. Notes about FLL's education, Lewis Perry, Principal of Phillips Exeter, to FWL, 10 April 1936; FLL to George M. Amerige, attorney, 6 December 1942, all in FWL-LC. In the letter to Amerige, Francis Lincoln Lee informs the lawyer of his "active military service" and asks that any income which he is owed from the Lee estate (set up by his grandmother, Alice Haskell Lee) be used to provide "whatever aide possible in restoring my Father's health" and "to help defray the expenses of his sickness." Francis Lincoln Lee died in 1985.

8. "very oriented to art": Cristine Piane, e-mail to the author, 14 February 2009; "civil legal aid and access to justice": Lee Bridges webpage, University of Warwick, School of Law, www2.warwick.ac.uk/fac/soc/law/staff/academic/bridges/; "ink in his blood": William Watts Lee, interview by the author, 18 July 2010.

# INDEX

*Page numbers in italics refer to illustrations; pl. refers to plates*